Faithful to Each Other Forever

A CATHOLIC HANDBOOK OF PASTORAL HELP FOR MARRIAGE PREPARATION

Committee for Pastoral Research and Practices
National Conference of Catholic Bishops

United States Catholic Conference • Washington, D.C.

In its 1987 planning document, as approved by the general membership of the National Conference of Catholic Bishops in November 1986, the Bishops' Committee for Pastoral Research and Practices was authorized to continue the preparation of a publication that would address the Church's call to those involved with marriage preparation. This present document, *Faithful to Each Other Forever: A Catholic Handbook of Pastoral Help for Marriage Preparation* is the fruit of a multidraft process. The final text was reviewed by the members of the Committee for Pastoral Research and Practices, approved by the NCCB Administrative Committee in September 1988, and is authorized for publication as a document of the Committee for Pastoral Research and Practices by the undersigned.

Monsignor Daniel F. Hoye
General Secretary
NCCB/USCC

Design and Illustrations: Al Porter Graphics, Inc., Washington, D.C.; C. Lowry, illustrator.

Excerpts from the English translation of *Rite of Baptism for Children* © 1969, International Committee on English in the Liturgy, Inc. (ICEL); excerpts from the English translation of *Rite of Marriage* © 1969, ICEL. All rights reserved.

Excerpts taken from DEAR ABBY column by Abigail Van Buren, copyright © 1987 by Universal Press Syndicate. Reprinted with permission. All rights reserved.

Excerpts from the *New American Bible*, copyright © 1970 (including the Revised New Testament © 1986), used with permission of the copyright holder, the Confraternity of Christian Doctrine, Washington, D.C. All rights reserved.

ISBN 1-55586-252-7

First Printing, May 1989
Fourth Printing, April 2000

Table of Contents

Section II: Proximate Preparation

Section III: Immediate Preparation

Section IV: Pastoral Care after Marriage

Appendices

Introduction

Dan: "I was very apprehensive about our pre-Cana before we started. I was sure the couples were going to test me on 'how Catholic' I was! To my surprise and delight, we shared hours of friendly conversation on the ins and outs of marriage, along with a few beers."

Vicky: "Our hosts were so warm and open with us! I feel my fiance and I really learned some important things about ourselves and our relationship. I thoroughly enjoyed sharing funny stories of the trials and tribulations of beginning a life together.

"We knew our wedding would turn out great when we had the first meeting with Father Gene. He gave us the freedom to plan a wedding that would be special to us. Our priest even allowed us to include the "Irish Blessing," something which was very difficult for him to do, especially with an Italian last name!"

(Ohio)

This handbook of pastoral help for marriage preparation is our response to the call of the Church and to the concerns of contemporary couples.

That call of the Church has been manifested to us in our day through the words of the Second Vatican Council, the Apostolic Exhortation *On the Family*, issued by Pope John Paul II, and the revised *Code of Canon Law*.

Call of the Church

The bishops assembled in Rome for the Second Vatican Council spoke about fostering the nobility of marriage and the family.[1] They taught that our Creator established the intimate partnership of married life and love. As its very author, God has surrounded matrimony with definite purposes, divine laws, and distinct benefits.

According to the eternal plan, a man and a woman by a marriage covenant of conjugal love become one and give mutual help and service to each other through this intimate union of their persons and actions. That oneness, which is to grow daily more perfect, by its very nature has been destined for the procreation and education of children, who are the ultimate crown of the spouses' union.

This mutual gift of two persons to one another in such an intimate union, as well as the good of the children springing forth from that bond, requires total fidelity from the spouses and argues for an unbreakable oneness between them.

To strengthen husbands and wives, and in this fashion help spouses to fulfill these conjugal and family obligations, Jesus, Savior of the world and Spouse of the Church, comes into the lives of married Christians through the sacrament of matrimony. He abides with them thereafter so that, penetrated by the spirit of Christ, they may love each other with perpetual fidelity through mutual self-bestowal and

---

1. "Pastoral Constitution on the Church in the Modern World," *Vatican Council II: The Conciliar and Post Conciliar Documents*, Austin Flannery, OP, gen. ed. (Northport, N.Y.: Costello Publishing Company, 1975), art. 47-52.

receive a kind of consecration in the duties and dignity of their state. By filling their whole lives with faith, hope, and charity, that spirit enables them to advance in perfection, sanctify one another, and thus contribute jointly to the glory of God.

The spouses, forming with their children a truly Christian family, can thereby manifest to all people the Savior's living presence in the world and the genuine nature of the Church.

Nevertheless, the bishops, while presenting in a clearer light the natural dignity and superlative value of the married state, acknowledged the serious difficulties which the institution of marriage and the family face in our modern world. They urged, therefore, those both in the sacred and secular sectors, members of the Church and leaders in the state, to promote the welfare of marriage and the family.

Pope John Paul II, in his rich document *On the Family*, issued in 1981, built upon that teaching of the Second Vatican Council.[2] He developed more fully our understanding of God's plan for marriage and the family. The Holy Father, however, while sketching some bright spots for the married state today, also pointed out some dark shadows that cloud the horizon and threaten matrimony in this modern world. Consequently, observing that preparation of young people for marriage and family life is "more than ever necessary in our times," he declares that "not only the family but also society and the church should be involved in the effort of properly preparing young people for their future responsibilities."[3]

Pope John Paul II goes on, in explicit terms, to say:

> The church must therefore promote better and more intensive programs of marriage preparation in order to eliminate as far as possible the difficulties that many married couples find themselves in, and even more in order to favor positively the establishing and maturing of successful marriages.[4]

Finally, he likewise speaks to us as bishops of an episcopal conference, hoping that just as we

> are concerned with appropriate initiatives to help engaged couples to be more aware of the seriousness of their choice and also to help pastors of souls to make sure of the couples' proper dispositions, [so we] will also take steps to see that there is issued a directory for the pastoral care of the family.[5]

The revised *Code of Canon Law*, promulgated in 1983, translates some of these theological and pastoral proclamations of the Church about Christian marriage into a legal framework.[6] Several canons deal specifically with the spiritual care of those about to marry and give explicit directions concerning the steps that need completion before the celebration of matrimony.

These regulations charge pastors of souls with the task of seeing to it that their own church community provides couples with assistance in preparing well for and living out properly a Christian marriage. This responsibility includes preaching and teaching about the sacrament of matrimony; personally preparing the engaged for marriage; planning and executing a grace-filled wedding liturgy; and providing aftercare to those already married.[7]

Another canon names the local bishop as the one who must assume the duty of overseeing this marriage preparation and enrichment effort to ensure that it is properly organized and, if it seems appropriate, to consult men and women of proven experience and skill.[8]

Finally, still a third directive calls upon us as the conference of bishops to issue norms and offer aid for the effective carrying out of the necessary steps prior to marriage.[9]

This rather substantial handbook, therefore, is a response on our part to that serious and expressed call of the Church.

Concerns of Contemporary Couples

We are also, however, responding to the concerns of contemporary couples, those about to marry or those already married, and all persons who genuinely care about them. People such as Dan and Vicky, the couple whose comments appeared at the start of this Introduction, come to the Church filled with joyful enthusiasm, anticipation, and hopes. They dream of a satisfying marriage and of being faithful to each other forever.[10] Priests, such as their friend Father Gene of Ohio, deacons, and the many, many persons involved today in the matrimonial preparation ministry share similar aspirations with these young and perhaps not so young lovers.

Nevertheless, both the engaged couple and all those who assist them recognize simultaneously the

---

2. *On the Family* (*Familiaris Consortio*), Apostolic Exhortation of John Paul II, issued December 15, 1981 (Washington, D.C.: USCC Office of Publishing and Promotion Services, 1982).
3. Ibid., no. 66.
4. Ibid.
5. Ibid.
6. The revised *Code of Canon Law*, promulgated by John Paul II on January 25, 1983 (Washington, D.C.: Canon Law Society of America, 1983).
7. Ibid., c. 1063.
8. Ibid., c. 1064.
9. Ibid., c. 1067.
10. *On the Family*, no. 20.

sober realities of modern society—seemingly countless obstacles to successful marriages and the huge number of marital disruptions. Despite their vibrant love, which appears strong enough to overcome any challenge, the couple about to marry may still experience moments of hesitation and worry brought on by the sometimes dismal picture of matrimony surrounding them. They seek reassurance and help from our Church.

This handbook supplies the clergy and all others committed to marriage preparation efforts with extensive and invaluable resources. Aided by them, they should, in fact, be able to give the engaged such reassurance and help.

Purpose and Nature of This Handbook

The handbook has been designed for a specific audience—those directly and indirectly involved in marriage preparation work. It is written in a readable style, with abundant illustrations and stories, to facilitate practical use in religion classes and pre-Cana conferences as well as in personal counseling and couple interviews. It tries to present the official teaching and values of the Church on marriage-related issues with clarity and succinctness. At the same time, it attempts to acknowledge the often contrary climate of today's culture and to suggest ways of dealing with those challenges. It is not a book to be read through, but a resource volume to which we frequently refer—the detailed table of contents in the beginning and index of topics at the end should aid in locating the desired material. It has been published in bound form for stability, but punched for easy insertion in a suitable binder, thus facilitating the addition of current and future diocesan or regional directives and adaptations.

The style of writing in this handbook varies from the technical to the practical and from the theological to the anecdotal, according to the nature of the topic under consideration. For example, the legal technicalities of interreligious marriages require a different treatment than does the suggested format for an initial interview, and the theology/spirituality of marriage demands an approach quite distinct from the testimonies of people on behalf of Natural Family Planning.

We have sought to weave the actual lives of people into the fabric of this manual. The letters introducing each section illustrate one attempt to achieve that goal. We thank the Family Life Directors from the regions encompassing Ohio, Idaho, Florida, California, and Mississippi for securing those testimon-

ies. They represent, in order, a newly wedded couple who had just finished a formal marriage preparation program; a couple married over thirty years; a woman concerned about her brother's troubled marital situation; a priest who regularly prepares couples for marriage; and a religious sister involved in a pre- and post-marriage ministry.

In the text itself, and especially in the footnotes, we have cited certain available publications or programs. Inclusion within this handbook does not imply that such items are necessarily the best or only materials on a particular topic in existence today. We have incorporated the information or resources merely for the convenience of those working in this ministry. We understand fully that in such an enormous field of endeavor there are or could be other praiseworthy materials and there will be new ones ever developing for the future. In fact, as will be noted in several places, we repeatedly encourage creative authors and publishers to prepare fresh items, incorporating concepts contained in this handbook, that will help serve those in the marriage preparation ministry.

Ethnic and Regional Adaptations

The handbook has been produced for the Catholic Church on a national level. It, therefore, does not and cannot respond to all the needs of the Asian, black or native-American faith communities or to specialized ethnic or regional circumstances. We hope that marriage and family life specialists in those sectors will develop appropriate perspectives on this handbook that can be added to the end of the text. The Secretariat for Black Catholics has already committed itself to that task. The few comments about Asian marriage customs, noted under the section on "Liturgical Celebration," are meant to illustrate how important and helpful those type of additions would be for *Faithful to Each Other Forever*.

The Hispanic community among us, however, represents at once a unique blessing and a distinct challenge both for the Church in general and for this handbook in particular.[11]

While exact current statistics about the Hispanic population lack the desired coverage, reasonable estimates place the total U.S. Hispanic population at about 20 million.[12] Furthermore, Hispanics are increasing at a rate five to six times faster than the regular population, and the median age among Hispanic people is twenty-five.[13] Moreover, Hispanic Catholics can be found in every state of the Union and nearly every diocese.[14] Finally, sociologists estimate that Hispanics currently make up as much as 40 percent of the Catholic Church in the United States, with this percentage constantly rising. Soon, almost half of the Roman Catholics in this country will be Hispanic.

Those numbers alone would justify giving special attention to the Hispanic community in this handbook. But, as we mentioned in 1983, they also exemplify and cherish values central to the well-being of our Church and society. Among them are the following:

- profound respect for the dignity of each *person*;
- deep and reverential love for *family life*;
- a marvelous sense of *community*;
- loving appreciation for God's gift of *life*; and
- authentic and consistent devotion to *Mary*, the Mother of God.[15]

In our *National Pastoral Plan for Hispanic Ministry*, a document that resulted from years of work by thousands of people who participated in the *III Encuentro Nacional Hispano de Pastoral*, we proposed an ambitious plan to serve that massive number of Catholics and to draw upon the profound riches of those values cherished by Hispanics in our country.[16]

This plan seeks to assist Hispanic people in their efforts to achieve integration and participation in the life of the Catholic Church and in the building of the kingdom of God.[17] To foster that integration, and thus avoid creating a parallel image of the Church, our plan employs the methodology of a *pastoral de conjunto*, where all the elements of pastoral ministry, all the structures and all of the activities of pastoral agents, both Hispanic and non-Hispanic, are coordinated with a common objective in view. To integrate this plan into the planning process of church organization, departments and agencies at all levels (national, regional, diocesan, parish) will require local adaptation so that all elements of pastoral ministry are operating in unison.[18]

We have tried to make this handbook an example of such a coresponsible, collaborative ministry in several ways: by consultation with appropriate Hispanic leaders; by incorporating the Hispanic presence

---

11. *The Hispanic Presence: Challenge and Commitment*, Pastoral Letter of the National Conference of Catholic Bishops on Hispanic Ministry, issued December 12, 1983 (Washington, D.C.: USCC Office of Publishing and Promotion Services, 1984). English and Spanish editions.
12. Ibid., no. 6 with its first two footnotes.
13. *National Pastoral Plan for Hispanic Ministry*, National Conference of Catholic Bishops, November 18, 1987 (Washington, D.C.: USCC Office of Publishing and Promotion Services, 1988). Bilingual edition.
14. *The Hispanic Presence*, no. 6.
15. Ibid., no. 3.
16. *National Pastoral Plan for Hispanic Ministry*.
17. Ibid.
18. Ibid.

within the text through pertinent observations, suggestions, and illustrations; and by making the publication available in Spanish translation at some future date.[19]

Nevertheless, Hispanic marriage and family life specialists will very likely wish to develop further local and regional perspectives that can be appended to *Faithful to Each Other Forever,* which should greatly enhance its usefulness for particular Hispanic communities.

Outline of Topics

Pope John Paul II indicates that marriage preparation must be seen and put into practice as a gradual and prolonged process. That process includes three main stages—remote, proximate, and immediate—together with aftercare efforts to sustain and nurture the marital bond. The Holy Father, through this teaching, has expanded our vision considerably, leading us to view those programs, which we have commonly termed marriage preparation, as only a part of the process and possibly not even the most important ingredient in preparing people for matrimony.[20]

This handbook follows those stages, first explaining each particular stage and then covering elements that fall rather naturally into that category. While the stages are chronological in nature, the topics discussed within them frequently overlap into some or all of the other stages. Those who direct marriage preparation or family life efforts may wish, therefore, to examine the entire text and judge through that study how various elements may be beneficial to them.

Resource People

We are extremely grateful to scholars in the behavioral science field who have shared their professional research with us and to the many lay persons whose personal lived experiences of marriage and family form such an essential part of this manual. We also acknowledge our indebtedness to the numerous advisors who so freely offered their insights at the beginning and who have made valuable comments during the consultation process. The text would not have become a reality without their original suggestions and is better because of their criticisms at the end. In the section on "Process and Acknowledgments," we have described the procedure followed in the development of this handbook and also sought wherever possible to credit those whose input has been a significant contribution.

Hope for the Future

The *Code of Canon Law* expresses the hope that married couples, by being faithful to their nuptial covenant, may "day by day come to lead holier and fuller lives in their families."[21] In doing so, they will also be recognizing and freely accepting their vocation to follow Christ and to serve the kingdom of God in the married state.[22]

Better marriages of this type mean better families in our society today; better families, in turn, mean better communities, a better Church, and ultimately a better world. We pray that our handbook will help build those kinds of better marriages and better families in the United States during the years ahead.

With Pope John Paul II, we invoke the protection of the Holy Family of Nazareth upon all couples about to marry or already married, as well as upon those who are involved in any way with the marriage preparation ministry. May Jesus, Mary, and Joseph enable all "to be faithful to their day-to-day duties, to bear the cares and tribulations of life, to be open and generous to the needs of others, and to fulfill with joy the plan of God in their regard."[23]

---

19. Ibid.
20. *On the Family,* no. 66.
21. *Code of Canon Law,* c. 1063.
22. *On the Family,* no. 51.
23. Ibid., no. 86.

Section I: Remote Preparation

"Here are a few thoughts on what has helped our marriage last these more than thirty years.

"We had a commitment made before marriage. When we decided to marry, we made the decision that it would be for life! We married in the church; one a cradle Catholic, the other a convert at marriage. We knew we were committed, and the sacrament really served to strengthen our promise to each other. We also agreed never to go to bed angry at each other nor to sleep in separate beds when we both were at home.

"There are certain words that are just not in our vocabulary, such as *divorce, leaving, separation, lost love.*

"Our marriage has had its ups and downs, and they could be charted on parallel graphs with our relationship to Christ and our involvement in the church. We can look back and see that when we turned inward and decided our partner wasn't looking out for us instead of turning toward Christ and trying to discern his will, then we had problems.

"Things have improved through the years, and we judge that a marriage encounter gave us a new beginning in communication.

"We have acknowledged that we are different.

"When we were less than ten years married, I read a book that inspired me to try a new approach. Instead of blaming all my problems on my mother or husband or his mother, I would take responsibility for myself. I decided to try treating him as if he were all that I ever dreamed of in a husband, instead of the source of all my troubles. It worked.

"We have realized that there are various stages in personal and family life and tried to prepare for them. We deliberately spent time alone together before the children left home so that we were not strangers. We have found that the transition from parenting to becoming friends has been relatively easy and very rewarding."

(Idaho)

Definition of Remote Preparation

This remote preparation begins in early childhood and includes all those family as well as other environmental factors that influence and prepare the person in positive and negative ways for marriage. Every individual is constantly being prepared, for better or for worse, for a possible future married life from the first moment of her or his existence in this world.

Some of the *positive* influences and effects during this period are the following:

- A wise family training that leads children to discover themselves as being endowed with a rich and complex psychology, together with a particular personality having its own strengths and weaknesses.[1]

- A gradual formation of the young person's character that, among other goals, instills esteem for all authentic human values, enhances skills in interpersonal and social relationships, develops an understanding and correct use of one's inclinations, and promotes a proper regard for and ability to mix with the opposite sex.[2]

- Solid spiritual and catechetical training that pictures marriage and parenting as a true vocation and mission, without in any way minimizing the vocation and mission to the priestly or religious life.[3]

Some of the *negative* influences and effects can arise from the family background, from the situations in which people live, and from the general climate of our contemporary culture. A number of these potentially harmful factors will be touched upon in the material that follows.

Elements of Remote Marriage Preparation

 A Concerned Church and the Behavioral Sciences: Partners in a Common Cause

Pope John Paul II has called for a collaborative effort on the subject of marriage in our day between all church members and experts in the various behavioral sciences.[4]

He urges not only pastors but also lay persons in the Church to discern the wisdom of the Holy Spirit through their faith-filled and prayerful reflections upon married and family life.[5]

He acknowledges that lay specialists (e.g., doctors, lawyers, psychologists, social workers, consultants), either as individuals or as members of organizations and projects, can offer enlightenment, advice, orientation, and support.[6]

He values sociological and statistical research that can prove helpful to our understanding of the present situation and to the development of constructive actions that will strengthen marriages.[7]

He sees science, with its technical applications, as offering immense possibilities for fostering a new and healthy humanism.[8]

At the same time, the pope cautions that the research, statistics, and theories of these behavioral sciences are not in themselves expressions of the sense of faith. Their data and recommendations need to be interpreted according to the truth of Christ and the teachings of the Church.[9]

This handbook will seek in its approach to observe that collaborative course.

 Hard Facts and Ever-Present Hopes

We can only conjecture what is the fundamental intention of those who enter into marriage in our day. Even though the couple speak promises of love and honor all the days of their lives until "death do them part," are they in reality committed to such a lifelong relationship, regardless of what happens? Or do they consciously or unconsciously accept a condition that if matters go badly between them, separation and eventual divorce is a permissible possibility?

The hard facts summarized below clearly indicate that not all marriages turned out as well as did the union of the couple from Idaho. Do those statistics mean that many—nearly a majority—of today's married couples either did not mean the marital commitment to be lifelong or else later changed those views about the permanence of the marriage bond when their life together became more difficult than anticipated? Thus:

- The rate of divorce for the general population in the United States increased only gradually, although steadily, from 1860

---

1. *On the Family,* no. 66.
2. Ibid.
3. Ibid.
4. Ibid., nos. 5, 8, 75.
5. Ibid., no. 5.
6. Ibid., no. 75.
7. Ibid., no. 5.
8. Ibid., no. 8.
9. Ibid., no. 5.

through the early 1960s. Then, the pace of divorces more than doubled over the next two decades. For example, almost half of the 1973 marriages will end in divorce if the current rates continue, as opposed to 5% of the marriages in 1860.[10] This means that for white females, the probability of a divorce increased from 14.0% during the period 1940 to 1945, to 45.2% during the period 1975 to 1980; for black females, the rate grew from 17.6% to 47.1%.[11] To illustrate what those percentages mean, we could cite the fact that in 1976, there were 2,133,000 marriages and 1,077,000 divorces.[12]

- Several factors, including the continuous and extensive flow of immigration and emigration, make it difficult to secure accurate figures about marriage, divorce, and remarriage among Hispanics. However, as we noted in our recent *National Pastoral Plan for Hispanic Ministry* (Section II), certain current social realities indicate that Hispanic Catholics likewise suffer from the deterioration of marriage and family life in the United States.

  For example: only 8% of Hispanics graduate at the college level; 25% of families live below the poverty level; 28% are single-parent families; lack of education and professional training have led to high unemployment among Hispanics; 88% are not active in their parish churches; frequent mobility, poor education, a limited economic life, and racial prejudice have resulted in low participation among Hispanics in political activities.

- The U.S. National Center for Health Statistics showed a decline in the 1982 and 1983 total number of divorces by four and one percent respectively. Still, the mere massive amount of divorces (1,170,000 in 1982; 1,158,000 in 1983) reflects an alarming deterioration in the stability of married life. Moreover, provisional studies by the independent Population Reference Bureau pointed to a renewed increase in divorces for 1984 and 1985.[13]

- The rates of separation and divorce among U.S. Catholics and other Americans have become nearly equal.[14]

- Most divorced people remarry and generally do so soon after divorce. About half of all women who divorce while still relatively young remarry within three years and from 60% to 70% remarry within five years. Men are even more likely than

women to remarry eventually after divorce.[15]

- There are two other statistics that have some connection with the issue of current marital stability and rising divorce rates: the growing number of young unmarrieds and the burgeoning total of couples cohabiting without matrimony.

  In 1960, for example, 64% of women between twenty and twenty-four were married and living with their husbands; in 1982, that figure had dropped to 39%.

  Between 1970 and 1977, the number of unmarried American adults sharing a household with an unrelated person of the opposite sex tripled and nearly doubled again from 1977 to 1982. By 1983, there were 1.9 million couples living together without the benefit of marriage, up almost 1 million from 1970.[16]

The many implications and explanations related to these statistics about the unmarried and those cohabiting without matrimony will be discussed later in this volume. At this point, we simply cite them as a further contribution to the picture of radical shifts in the contemporary marital and family structure throughout the United States.

Another important insight that can aid one's understanding of contemporary marriage and family life is found in our document *A Family Perspective in Church and Society*.[17] In addition to evidence from demographic studies, this document presents a sociological analysis that reveals that many functions that were traditionally within the domain of families are now largely performed by institutions. Among these are recreation, employment, health care, education, etc. Today, the two primary functions that remain within the family are its role as the primary source of intimacy and identity, and its role

10. "The Changing American Family," by Thornton and Freedman, in *Population Reference Bureau Bulletin* (October 1983): 7-8.
11. "Marriage Trends in America: Estimates, Implications and Causes," by Thomas J. Espenshade, in *Population and Development Review* II:2 (June 1985): 205.
12. "Premarital Counseling: Appraisal and Status," by Dennis A. Bagarozzi and Paul Rauen, in *The American Journal of Family Therapy* 9:3 (Fall 1981): 13.
13. "Fewer Divorces Are Not a Trend," by Jerry Filteau, in *Long Island Catholic* (January 16, 1986).
14. "Lag by Catholics in Marriage Found," by Kenneth A. Briggs, in *New York Times* (March 10, 1985); "Study of American Catholics Is Misleading," by Rev. Andrew M. Greeley, in *New York Times* (March 21, 1985); "Canonical Bases for Deferral or Refusal of Marriage," by Most Rev. Anthony J. Bevilacqua, presentation to the Canon Law Society of America.
15. "The Changing American Family," p. 10.
16. Ibid., p. 11.
17. *A Family Perspective in Church and Society: A Manual for All Pastoral Leaders*, Ad Hoc Committee on Marriage and Family Life, National Conference of Catholic Bishops (Washington, D.C.: USCC Office of Publishing and Promotion Services, 1988).

as the cradle of reproduction. While this erosion of the role of families has tended to make the family more fragile, it has also brought into clearer focus the central role of marriage and family life, which has been described by Pope Paul the VI in *Humanae Vitae*, as contained in the twofold meaning of conjugal love (i.e., unitive and procreative). Perhaps, this sociological, cultural development can help clarify and complement what has been the Church's teaching about the very essence of marriage. At the same time, this cultural change has contributed, at least during the present time of transition, to the destabilization of family life.

Despite all of these generally well-known, but alarming facts about marriage and divorce, we believe that nearly every couple pronouncing nuptial vows both within and outside the Church do so filled with hope. They sincerely anticipate, in our judgment, that their marriage will succeed, that their future is bright, and that they will never end up in the divorce court.

Those hopes and anticipations may be more romantic than realistic. However, we continue to presume, despite the hard statistics cited above, that couples preparing for matrimony are filled with good will and noble intentions for the future. They want their marriage to work.

Everything in this handbook is based upon that presumption. We offer the pastoral helps in the present volume as an aid to such couples and to those in

marriage preparation. We pray that its many suggestions will help transform, perhaps, even those sometimes too romantic hopes into realistic expectations and assist a man and a woman to enter a marriage that will fulfill their dreams and last for life.

Our Holy Father has noted how experience teaches us that young people who have been well prepared for family life generally succeed better than others. In view of that, we wish to make Pope John Paul's words our own:

> The Church must therefore promote better and more intensive programs of marriage preparation in order to eliminate as far as possible the difficulties that many married couples find themselves in, and even more in order to favor positively the establishing and maturing of successful marriages.[18]

Where We Come from and Who We Are Now

When a man and a woman call upon the parish priest or another representative of the parish seeking marriage in the Church, they obviously bring with them the influences of their own personal family backgrounds. Some of those influences, of course, have a very beneficial impact upon their attitudes about their future union. These might include a model of successful marriage in the family, a careful religious upbringing, and a strong spirit of commitment to responsibilities. But some of those influences may also exert a detrimental effect upon their approach to matrimony.

The hard facts about divorce and remarriage in our society noted above clearly mean that many potential brides and grooms today will carry with them to the parish representative the experience of marital disruption in their own backgrounds. Relatively current estimates indicate that almost half of today's children will spend some time in a single-parent family and, for those whose mothers remarry, about half will experience yet another family disruption as a child.[19]

While the effects of such disruptions upon children are still largely unknown, there are indications that even very young boys and girls tend to blame themselves both for the discord between parents and also for the eventual separation and divorce. This conscious or unconscious assuming of responsibility for the marital disruption, irrational as that appropriation may be, will naturally have a long-term harmful impact upon a child's self-image. This can cause later and continual complications in that person's life. Moreover, many such young persons came

18. *On the Family*, no. 66.
19. "Children and Marital Disruption: A Replication and Update," by Larry L. Bumpass, in *Demography* 21:1 (Fall 1984): 71.

to the point of marriage filled with fear of making an exclusive, permanent commitment because they have witnessed their own parents' failure in matrimony.

However, in addition to those prospective brides and grooms who bring a backgound of parental separation or divorce to the parish representative, the couple may have experienced other familial situations, which Pope John Paul II terms "objectively difficult." Among those difficult circumstances that he has listed are the following:

- Families of migrant workers; of those obliged to be away for long periods, such as members of the armed forces, sailors, and all kinds of itinerant people; of those in prison; of refugees and exiles.

- Families in big cities living, practically speaking, as outcasts, with no homes; with disabled children or children addicted to drugs; with alcoholics.

- Families uprooted from their cultural and social environment or in danger of losing it; discriminated against for political or other reasons; ideologically divided; unable to make ready contact with the parish.

- Families experiencing violence or unjust treatment because of their faith; of teenage married couples; of the elderly who are often obliged to live alone with inadequate means of subsistence.[20]

Church representatives—clergy or otherwise—need to be sensitive to the complexity of the backgrounds of the couples who come to them, aware that those factors do exert a significant influence upon their approach and attitude toward marriage.

Moreover, church representatives would do well to reflect upon and pray over their own family backgrounds. They, too, carry to these encounters in the pastoral ministry of marriage preparation individual family circumstances and situations that impact the way they think, feel, and speak about matrimony. It could be helpful in this regard for them to discuss those matters with people who possess expertise in psychology, or even to undergo personal counseling as a way of understanding better the fact that where we come from does significantly influence who we are now.

4. Several Negative Contemporary Developments

There are in our modern environment within the United States some elements that directly or indirectly attack or undermine the marriage and family values that the Catholic Church upholds. These would include the following:

AN EXCESSIVE INDIVIDUALISM AND PREOCCUPATION WITH SELF-FULFILLMENT

Some analysts of today's society in the United States maintain from their research that Americans have for the most part abandoned an older self-denial ethic in favor of a contemporary self-fulfillment norm.[21] In earlier years, family members, particularly spouses and parents, tended to postpone immediate pleasures for long-term goals. Those distant objectives were usually economic growth and family stability. Thus, for example, parents sometimes might delay a second car, a summer home, or a long vacation so they could set aside funds for their children's future college education. Husbands and wives, likewise, sometimes persevered in a struggling marital relationship supposedly for the sake of the children.

Termed by one observer a "giving-getting" type of compact or ethical philosophy, a spouse or parent following that code of living might say: "I give hard work, loyalty, and steadfastness. I swallow my frustrations and suppress my impulse to do what I would enjoy and do what is expected of me instead. I do not put myself first; I put the needs of others ahead of my own. I give a lot, but what I get in return is worth it. I receive an ever-growing standard of living and a family life with a devoted spouse and decent kids. Our children will take care of us in our old age if we really need it, which thank goodness we will not. I have a nice home, a good job, the respect of my friends and neighbors; and a sense of accomplishment at having made something of my life."

However, by the 1970s, surveys indicated that the majority of Americans were increasingly preoccupied with self, and the intense drive for self-fulfillment had spread to virtually the entire population of this country. The self-denial ethic was no longer seen as valid and deferment of desires were not a virtue.

In the old self-denial ethic, these were typical questions: "Will I be able to make a good living?" "Will I raise happy, healthy, successful children?"

In the self-fulfillment philosophy, these are the common inquiries: "How can I find self-fulfillment?" "What is worth sacrificing for?" "How can I grow?" "How can I best realize the commitment I have to develop myself?"

An appropriate self-fulfillment attitude can be constructive, and an inappropriate self-denying approach toward life can be destructive for individuals and for relationships. Nevertheless, an excessive concern for self-fulfillment and the total absence of a self-sacrificing spirit will obviously wreak havoc upon marriage and family life and, subsequently, upon

20. *On the Family,* no. 77.
21. *New Rules: Searching for Self-Fulfillment in a World Turned Upside Down,* by Daniel Yankelovich (New York: Random House, 1981), for the comments on self-fulfillment, see esp. pp. 4-5, 8-9, 76-78.

society and the Church. Moreover, it runs contrary to the Christian concept of the cross and the Paschal Mystery with its parodoxical death and resurrection, its dying and yet fulfilling motif. Indeed "self-fulfill-ment" not rooted in a generous sacrificial disposition of self-denial is but a counterfeit of that "life to the full" Jesus came to give.

Connected with the question of self-fulfillment is the issue of an unrestrained individualism in American life and the impact that attitude of mind or heart has upon commitments of every kind. Some contemporary sociologists have grown concerned, through their own research, that our praiseworthy and productive American individualism may have become cancerous, destroying the very social structures that moderate the harmful tendencies of an absolute individualism.[22]

While nearly all Americans continue to hold the ideal of two people sharing a life and home together, a majority do not expect couples currently getting married to remain married for the rest of their lives.[23] Perfect love and lifelong commitments appear for people in the United States today to be desirable, but not easy.[24]

Americans, according to these social scientists, are thus "torn between love as an expression of spontaneous inner freedom, a deeply personal, but necessarily somewhat arbitrary, choice, and the image of love as a firmly planted, permanent commitment, embodying obligations that transcend the immediate feelings or wishes of the partners in a love relationship."[25]

OUR CURRENT CONSUMERISM AND DISPOSABLE CULTURE

An excessive individualism and preoccupation with self-fulfillment can erode the type of permanent commitment required for a stable and satisfying marriage and family life. The consumerism of our age, with its attendant practice of built-in obsolesence and disposable goods, has similar—even if more subtle—negative effects.

We are accustomed now to casting aside and throwing away items that have grown worn, outdated, or tiresome. America is the land of instant, but fleeting popularity of temporary fads. We, with great frequency, discard cars and clothes, change jobs and homes, flip from one television or radio station to another. The notion of being committed to one person in good times and in bad for life, and the struggle to keep that pledge, run contrary to the way we practically live each day. Moreover, that pledge and struggle contradict the manner in which the media, especially through advertising, generally urge us to live.

Moreover, the surrounding culture in this fashion often emphasizes values and desires for us that are selfish, wasteful, and opposed to the Scriptures.

It tends to transform all our personal wants into critical needs. This, too, can erode the qualities necessary for steady, successful marriages.

The questions we posed in *Economic Justice for All*, our pastoral letter on the U.S. economy, are pertinent here. Are we becoming ever more wasteful in a "throw-away" society? Are we able to distinguish between our true needs and those thrust on us by advertising and a society that values consumption more than savings? Are we not called to adopt a simpler lifestyle in the face of the excessive accumulation of goods characteristic of an affluent society? Are husbands and wives not called to weigh their needs carefully and establish proper priorities of values as they discuss the issues of both parents working outside the home and the responsibilities of raising children with proper care and attention?[26]

A DISREGARD OF TRADITIONAL SEXUAL ETHICS

The basic traditional Judeo-Christian code of sexual ethics was expressed in the 1975 *Declaration on Certain Questions concerning Sexual Ethics*: "Every genital act must be within the framework of marriage. . . . Sexual union therefore is only legitimate if a definitive community of life has been established between the man and the woman."[27]

Within the past two decades, there has been a widespread theoretical rejection of that moral norm and an equally common practical disregard of it, even among Roman Catholics.

Some surveys taken in the 1980s, for example, indicate that almost half the Catholic adult population thinks that premarital sex is not wrong at all.[28] A similar or higher figure would hold true for those who are not Roman Catholic.

That theoretical rejection of this code has understandably impacted the practical order. A 1971 survey among leading high school students, to illustrate, revealed that 60% of them had engaged in premarital sexual intercourse.[29] Since we have come to recognize that there is not a significant difference in the behavioral pattern of Roman Catholics and others in

22. *Habits of the Heart: Individualism and Commitment in American Life*, by Robert Bellah (Berkeley/Los Angeles: University of California Press, 1985), p. viii. Of particular note: ch. 1 and 4.
23. Ibid., p. 90.
24. Ibid.
25. Ibid., p. 93.
26. *Economic Justice for All: Pastoral Letter on Catholic Social Teaching and the U.S. Economy*, National Conference of Catholic Bishops (Washington, D.C.: USCC Office of Publishing and Promotion Services, 1986), nos. 334-335.
27. *Declaration on Certain Questions concerning Sexual Ethics*, Sacred Congregation for the Doctrine of the Faith (Washington, D.C.: USCC Office of Publishing and Promotion Services, 1975), p. 7, no. 7.
28. *American Catholics since the Council: An Unauthorized Report*, by Rev. Andrew M. Greeley (Chicago: The Thomas More Press, 1985), p. 85.
29. "The Revolution Is Over," *Time* (April 9, 1984): 74-76.

this country, that figure, therefore, probably would be verified in our youth as well.

While this rejection and disregard contain many disturbing features within them, a central concern is the elimination of personal commitment from sexual activity. Empty, noncommitted, nonrelational, impersonal sex can be extremely destructive in various ways; a long-term, involved, committed, total relationship is required for the type of sexual relations that will sustain and deepen a joyful intimacy between partners.[30] The harmful effect of such non-commitment upon marriage and marriage preparation should be evident.

However, we have an encouraging bit of news in this otherwise bleak cultural picture. There are those who set the years of our sexual revolt at roughly 1965 to 1975, and see patterns today of a shift toward traditional norms in sexual matters. More and more people, according to these observers, find desirable the traditional values of fidelity, obligation, and marriage. Words such as *commitment* and *intimacy* frequently surface in contemporary literature and everyday conversation. One psychiatrist comments, "People are looking for more lasting relationships, and they want babies."[31] A 1986 survey of University of Notre Dame freshmen might confirm those words. It found that most oppose legal abortion, want to raise families, and believe that couples should not live together before marriage.[32]

Those alleged attitudinal changes would presumably be reflected and confirmed in modified behavioral patterns. A survey of Yale students in a class on sexuality could be cited as one example of this modification. It revealed that in 1976, only 25% had never experienced sexual intercourse; in 1983, the percentage of virgins in the class had risen to 33%.[33]

If, in fact, there is a higher regard for traditional sexual ethics on both the theoretical and practical level, that ultimately should help foster better marriages in the future.

MISTRUST OR RESENTMENT OF AUTHORITY

There are those who maintain that our society has consciously sought to replace the effective role of parents in the process of socializing children with childrearing experts. Thus, the functions of nurturing and disciplining, once combined in the same parent or parents, have often either been taken from the parents or separated. In former times, children frequently came to terms with their own sexual and aggressive instincts through the symbolic process of learning to live with their parents. Today, because of the removal from the parents of these tasks of nurturing and disciplining or because of their separation, boys and girls as they grow up may not have the opportunity to socialize those instincts in a way that is personally strengthening.[34]

If this analysis is true, the consequent mistrust

of structures, rituals, and authority or even a certain resentment toward them will have an obvious impact upon all those involved in marriage preparation efforts. A simple awareness of such a culturally mistrusting or resentful attitude could assist the clergy and others as they work with couples about to marry. Conscious that this questioning or hostility is neither directed to them personally nor emanating from deeply personal ill will, but more an effect of our surrounding environment, these church representatives might realize the increased importance of gentleness, patience, and friendliness in their dealings with those preparing to marry.

 ## Several Positive Contemporary Developments

Throughout the Church's history, positive forces always have emerged under grace and in God's plan to counter negative influences during a particularly challenging period of time. Great saints surface when sinners seem to abound; distinct religious communities spring up to fill special needs of the moment; ecumenical councils convene to clarify teachings, restore order, or promote renewal.

We have several of these positive forces in our contemporary society and Church that help counter some of those negative influences sketched above.

FAMILY SYSTEMS THEORY AND THERAPY

The family systems theory currently taught and practiced by so many instructors and counselors describes the family as a well-regulated, relatively stable unit, unique in the way it organizes to meet the needs of its members and in the overt or covert rules by which it lives. It is a small boundary-maintaining natural group, in which the behavior of any one member affects the behavior of all other members.

When a member of the family is experiencing some type of dysfunction—physical, mental, emotional, or relational—this theory views that as a symptomatic problem not isolated within the one person, but as also including interacting patterns of behavior and communication among other persons in the family and with society at large. The goal of therapy in such a circumstance is away from concentration solely on effecting some healing change within the troubled individual alone, to establishing healthier, less destructive relationships between that disturbed person and all the members of the family.

30. *How to Save the Catholic Church*, by Rev. Andrew M. Greeley and Mary Greeley Durkin (New York: Elizabeth Sifton Books/Viking, 1984), ch. 7 and 9.
31. "The Revolution Is Over," pp. 74-76.
32. "In Sight: Notre Dame Frosh Surveyed," *America* (April 4, 1987): 268.
33. "The Revolution Is Over," p. 76.
34. *A Process Called Conversion*, by David K. O'Rourke (Garden City, N.Y.: Doubleday and Company, 1985), pp. 158-159.

If properly understood and implemented, family systems theory, therapy, or ministry respects the individual's ultimate responsibility over her or his life and, yet, considers the important constructive or destructive impact that other family members may exert upon the troubled person's continued illness or improved health. Moreover, it takes into account those aspects in the social environment that can either help or hinder the functioning level of the family and the person with the presenting problem.

This theory thus helps us to understand and to cope with the many contemporary forces or situations detrimental to family life as outlined by Pope John Paul II, which we noted earlier. It also assists other members to see how they have a role in promoting harmony or discord within the family. It likewise focuses on learning new skills rather than being bogged down trying to change basic personality structures that are often rigid and inflexible. Furthermore, while it alters and betters the family's way of relating, it also causes individual improvement as well. Finally, this theory and therapeutic approach offer a flexibility and creativity in understanding all of the forces that impact upon our lives and in adjusting to them in a fashion that promotes growth for everyone.[35]

We look forward to the special contributions that the Hispanic extended family, with its communitarian and personalistic values, can make to the nuclear family and to the healing of these familial dysfunctions. Even more so, we believe that contribution will strengthen the sacramental dimension of the family.

THE FAMILY OF ORIGIN

During the past few decades, there has been an ever-increasing and praiseworthy use of married couples to prepare engaged couples for the sacrament of matrimony and for their future marital life. This movement toward a "like-to-like" ministry finds explicit support in the directives of the Second Vatican Council, which listed among the various works of the family apostolate the task of "assisting engaged couples to make a better preparation for marriage."[36]

In a subsequent section, we will outline specifically some of the current programs for marital preparation and how they involve married couples in that process. Generally speaking, the couples preparing for marriage are assigned or select married couples other than their own parents or members of their immediate family. There is, of course, a certain prudential wisdom to this overall pattern because prophets, as Jesus reminded us, are "never without honor except in their native places, indeed in their own houses."[37]

Nevertheless, in view of the family system theory sketched above, in light of the Church's official statements on the value of the family in the education of children, and in the contemporary recognition of the primary significance of the family of origin in a person's development, creative efforts should be made whenever possible to involve the entire family, particularly the parents and also grandparents, with the remote, proximate, and immediate marriage preparation efforts.[38] We can learn from the traditional wisdom handed down from generation to generation in the Hispanic extended family, where this is a natural process and actually occurs.

To do so, however, will require the availability of some practical instruments or procedures that can help overcome the recognized reluctance of many parents and children to discuss such personal issues. We hope that educators and publishers will produce these kinds of imaginative tools, which will facilitate the desired communication between a family of origin and those preparing for marriage. This sort of sharing need not be restricted to the daughters and sons who have attained marriageable ages, but ideally would begin, with obvious adjustments, at the earliest years. If the instruments or tools we envision being created are designed from that multiple-level usage, then dialogue on these sensitive areas would seem merely to be the natural outgrowth of exchanges that have been going on throughout the growing up period of a young man's or a young woman's life.

COMMUNICATION SKILL BUILDING

Within the past decade, all elements of our society have come to recognize the essential importance of good communication skills for healthy and satisfying relationships between people. Industry and government, educational institutions and church bodies regularly sponsor or encourage training programs in this area for employees and members. Moreover, nearly every individual counseling or therapy session today touches upon some dimension of the communication process.

Those general courses and individualized meetings, together with the ever-growing body of published materials on the subject, treat matters such as active or reflective listening; passive, aggressive, and

35. For a treatment of both the theory and practical application of the family systems concept, see *Family Communication*, by Kathleen M. Galvin and Bernard J. Brommel (Glenview, Ill.: Scott, Foresman and Company, 1986).

36. "Decree on the Apostolate of Lay People," in *Vatican Council II: The Conciliar and Post Conciliar Documents*, Austin Flannery, OP, gen. ed. (Northport, N.Y.: Costello Publishing Company, 1975), art. 11 and 13.

37. Mt 13:57.

38. For official statements on the family as prime educators, see *Vatican Council II*, esp. "Decree on the Apostolate of Lay People," art. 11-14; and "Pastoral Constitution on the Church in the Modern World," part II, ch. I. See also *On the Family*, which radiates that concept throughout, esp. nos. 36-41 that deal expressly with the family and education.

assertive behavior; problem solving; and conflict management.[39]

Building communication skills is an extremely important, ongoing, never ending process. We can always grow in this area of our lives. Most people understand that fact and welcome practical assistance that enhances their abilities to communicate in an effective manner.

While a section on communication skills is or should be an essential element of every formal marriage preparation program, we propose that certain aspects of this skill-building process be integrated into nearly all of our educational formation events. For example, parish sessions for parents preparing their children for the sacraments naturally cover the theological and pastoral elements of baptism, penance, confirmation, and Eucharist. We call these opportunities teachable moments for the parents and seek to capitalize on the openness of those participants by using the occasions to deepen their comprehension and appreciation of the faith. However, weaving into those meetings a relatively brief instruction, demonstration, and actual practice of some communication skill might be very positively received by the parents and certainly a help to them in their daily lives. A similar integration of communication skill building into the religious education courses for our young children seems to us equally desirable.

For the Hispanic community, building communication skills is happily a matter of using the existing teachable occasions and capitalizing on the openness of the moment, such as baptism, penance, marriage, *Quinceañera*, first communion, and various family fiestas. The Hispanic is eagerly awaiting to hear the Word of God during these deeply religious moments.

Pastoral leaders would need help in developing and implementing this ideal of an inclusive, long-range approach to communication skill building on the parish and school levels. We hope that a collaborative effort among those in the communication field, in family ministry, and in the religious education area could produce both the programs and the publications required to see this dream realized.

In our fractured, alienated, and intense society, good communication skills seem even more crucial than perhaps in previous eras. The Church can be of great service here by providing instruction and training in that area, not only for the couple about to marry but also for its members before and after marriage.

THE DEVELOPMENT OF FAITH

We understand faith as a precious gift from God, but one that requires constant care if it is to grow or even be retained. Contemporary psychologists and theologians have helped us grasp better this dynamic, as opposed to static, nature of faith, a comprehension

that has significant practical consequences for pastoral ministry.

First of all, it is clear from reflection on pastoral experience that adults come to faith in unique, gradual, and unpredictable ways. These processes involve time, change, and growth. They are more complex than a single event or a moment in life. They include duration, continuity, and not only an event or a number of isolated events but a series of related events extending over a period of time.[40] The *Rite of Christian Initiation of Adults* recognizes this phenomenon and provides a flexible approach adaptable to those varying situations of adult catechumens or candidates seeking to enter the Church.[41]

Second, scholars from both the psychological and theological fields have deepened our appreciation of the developmental process of faith in a person. The kinds of faith usually found in a two-year-old, an elementary school child, an adolescent, a young adult, a middle-age person, and a retired individual are different. As every person passes through the life experiences in each period, inner changes occur, normally growth shifts within the individual resulting in a deeper, stronger, and more secure faith.[42]

Third, as John Paul II points out, the family is the "domestic church," and the family members' level of faith and religious practice, especially the parents, will profoundly affect the child's development.

Finally, we can draw from the highly regarded and widely used research into the stages of dying and grieving some parallels about the stages of faith development.[43] Those who are dying, those who care for those who are near death, and those who experience any deep personal loss tend to experience certain common feelings or move through particular attitudinal periods. Denial, anger, bargaining, depression or sadness, and acceptance are the more notable among them.

However, these steps or stages are neither chronological nor static, nor always present. People do not necessarily move from the first stage through each subsequent stage to the last as if they were going to school and would graduate with a diploma when and if they reach acceptance. They may, likewise, go back and forth, in and out of different stages, even experiencing all the five feelings or attitudes within, for example, a given hour. Finally, some may skip

39. A good sample of the technical literature on this topic is *Communication Skills in Ministry*, by John Lawyer and Neil Katz (Dubuque: Kendall Hunt Publishing Company, 1985). Second edition.
40. *A Process Called Conversion*, p. 33.
41. *The Rites of the Catholic Church: Rite of Christian Initiation of Adults* (New York: Pueblo Publishing Company, 1976), pp. 13-182.
42. For a summary treatment of theories on psychological and faith development, see *Becoming Adult, Becoming Christian*, by Jones W. Fowler (San Francisco: Harper & Row, Publishers, 1984).
43. *On Death and Dying*, by Elizabeth Kübler-Ross (New York: McMillian, 1969).

one step or another or not ever reach the final stage of acceptance.

The stage or level of faith within a Catholic Christian follows a somewhat similar pattern. Movement from an early to a later state of faith is neither automatic nor static nor strictly chronological. Moreover, while the adult stages of faith are deeper, stronger, and more secure—thus, highly desirable and to be encouraged—many persons for various reasons never seem to attain those levels. Nevertheless, they are still good persons, possess the essential faith needed for membership in the Church, and have a right to receive the sacraments.

These four points about faith development should exert considerable impact upon our pastoral practices. Obviously, they support efforts within the parish and in other settings to provide ongoing education and formation in the faith from the beginning until the final days of people's lives. From lighting a special candle at dinner on the anniversary of a child's baptism to whispering biblical words of hope into a dying person's ear, the Church, through its members, wishes to sustain and strengthen the faith of every person called Catholic. Moreover, they also provide reasons for an understanding patience in dealing with couples who are preparing to marry, whose levels of faith and religious behavior are less than ideal. We will treat that current and delicate issue later on in this manual.

 The Sacrament of Matrimony

Over the many centuries before the Word of God became flesh and lived among us, men and women

were constantly matching up with each other, through diverse procedures, and entering into marriage. Christ did not establish the married state.

But Jesus did grace a wedding with his presence; he spoke words of wisdom about marriage and elevated matrimony to a lofty status. He performed his first miracle during the nuptial celebration at Cana in Galilee, indicating—according to the judgment of many—by that action his unique interest in and blessing upon marriage.[44] He made specific comments about the ideal of oneness between husband and wife, stressed the unbreakability of the marital bond, and sharply challenged the prevailing view in his time about the permissibility of divorce.[45] He raised marriage to the dignity of a sacrament so that it might more clearly recall and more easily reflect his own unbreakable union with his Church. In that fashion, Christ helped and helps spouses to assist one another in attaining holiness within their married life.[46]

Nevertheless, it required a millenium before the Church was able to articulate a more complete understanding about the sacramental nature of marriage. Throughout most of the first thousand years of Christianity, the state handled most details of marriage and divorce. Only with the breakdown of civil society, during the last part of that initial millenium, did the Church begin to take a more active role in the marriage arrangements.

Such a growing involvement in both the legal and ceremonial dimensions of marriage caused the Church to reflect upon and ultimately clarify several issues: the sacramental nature of marriage, its indissolubility, and the legal and ritual requirements for a valid sacramental marriage.

Within the twelfth and thirteenth centuries, church leaders began to view marriage as one of the seven official sacraments. The Second Council of Lyons (1274) listed marriage among the seven sacraments of the Church. The Council of Florence (1439) and the Council of Trent (1563) further developed the Church's teaching on the sacramentality of Christian marriage. That teaching, as we have already noted, was reiterated in more recent times by the Second Vatican Council.[47]

In the other sacraments, generally, clergy minister the sacrament and do so with words, gestures, and material elements such as the water at baptism or the bread and wine for the Eucharist. However, in

44. Jn 2:1-11.
45. Lk 16:18; Mk 10:2-12; Mt 5:31-32.19:3-9.
46. "Dogmatic Constitution on the Church," in *Vatican Council II,* art. 11. See also, *Rite of Marriage,* Introduction, no. 2.
47. More extensive consideration of the history of marriage may be found in *Marriage—Human Reality and Saving Mystery,* by E. Schillebeeckx (New York: Sheed and Ward, 1965); *Doors to the Sacred,* by J. Martos (Garden City, N.Y.: Doubleday and Company, 1981); and *What Is Marriage?* by T. Mackin, SJ (New York: Paulist Press, 1982).

matrimony, the bride and groom minister the sacrament to one another; the clergy simply serve as the Church's witness.

Moreover, the essential element is not the pouring of water with accompanying words or the proclamation of a formula over bread and wine, but the matrimonial consent between baptized persons. By that exchange of promises, a man and a woman, through an irrevocable consent, give and accept each other in a partnership for the whole of life—a relationship designed both for the good of the spouses through their close, special unity and for the procreation and education of offspring.[48]

The sacrament, then, is the mutual and irreversible commitment and the living out of that commitment for life. This means that Christ becomes present, through grace, in a new and deeper way at the moment of the exchange itself. It also implies that Jesus will continue to be present in a unique and ever-deepening manner whenever husband and wife carry out those mutual marital promises. It is often in the ordinary, daily events of work, conversation, recreation, and prayer that a couple, out of good will and loving care, strengthen their bond of commitment or fidelity and become more fully one. In so doing, they live out what might be called their matrimonial "spiritual exercises." Finally, the sacramental nature of matrimony likewise suggests that the couple can count on particular actual graces from time to time that will assist them in fulfilling their responsibilities "in good times and in bad, in sickness, and in health."[49]

In our own time, the Church is being blessed with a vital awareness of the married state as a specially graced fulfillment of the Christian's baptismal vocation. Both the teaching of the Church and the experience of married Catholics are shedding a new light of faith on the fundamental community of life and love, which is the heart of marriage. Our appreciation of the sacramental and spiritual dimensions of marriage has been enlarged and enriched. Subsequent portions of this handbook will draw out some of the implications of our renewed understanding of this sacrament.

The Church: Rich Symbol and Powerful Resource for Marriage

For years prior to the Second Vatican Council, bride, groom, and guests at a nuptial Mass always heard as the first scriptural reading the words of Ephesians, chapter 5, on the relationship of Christian wives and husbands. That text is still included among the biblical texts provided in the order of marriage published as a result of the liturgical reforms. While some couples may pass over this passage in favor of another New Testament excerpt because of its Pauline teaching about submission of wife to husband, others select those verses (22-32) precisely because of the instruction connecting Christ, the Church, and marriage. " 'For this reason a man shall leave [his] father and [his] mother and be joined to his wife, and the two shall become one flesh' This is a great mystery, but I speak in reference to Christ and the church."[50]

There is, therefore, a symbolic interplay between marriage, the Church, and Jesus Christ. The relationship between Christ and the Church symbolizes the kind of relationship that does or should exist between wife and husband. Conversely, the relationship between wife and husband symbolizes the relationship that exists between Jesus and his Church.

A married couple, therefore, by examining in prayerful reflection the relationship between Christ and the Church, can discover how they should relate to one another. In essence, this means they ought to love, care, respect, serve, and be in union with each other as Jesus did and does, was and is for the Church.

God's love for us reached its ultimate fullness when the Word of God abandoned heavenly status and became united with humanity, assuming our human nature. That love, however, was further manifested in the sacrifice that Jesus made of himself on the cross for his bride, the Church. Finally, this love continues today with the outpouring of Christ's Spirit upon us, giving those open to it new hearts and making it possible, among other things, for a man and a woman to love one another as Jesus has loved us.[51]

In Paul's words, ". . .Christ loved the Church and handed himself over for her to sanctify her, cleansing her by the bath of water with the word, that he might present to himself the church in splendor, without spot or wrinkle or any such thing, that she might be holy and without blemish."[52]

On the other hand, a married couple can move from the experience of their own loving relationship and those similar relationships within their family to a better awareness of God and Christ's love for us, God's people, the Church. Thus, every time they love and care for one another, respect and serve each other, enter into a union or communion with one another, the husband and wife as well as family members are mirroring in a visible, even if limited, way, the manner in which God relates to us. Their heads tell them God and Jesus love and care for them in a total, unconditional, everlasting fashion; but their hearts and whole being probably best grasp this truth by experiencing profound love and care from their spouses or children and realizing that such love and care is but a reflection of God and Christ's far greater and more perfect love and care for us.

---

48. *Code of Canon Law*, cc. 1055-1057.
49. *Rite of Marriage*, nos. 3, 25.
50. Eph 5:31-32.
51. *On the Family*, no. 13.
52. Eph 5:25-27.

Those mutual, interacting symbols of Christ, the Church, and marriage are the root reasons why contemporary official church documents term the family "the domestic church"; "the small-scale church"; the "church in miniature"; or the "church of the home."[53]

The Church, however, is not only a rich symbol of what marriage and family life should be, but also a powerful resource offering wisdom and strength, guidance and power for husband, wife, and children.

In our time, when great confusion exists even among people of sincere intention about many marital matters, the Church serves as a clarifying *teacher*, as the one authentic guide for the people of God.[54] Obedient to the truth that is Christ, whose image is reflected in the nature and dignity of the human person, the Church interprets, with clear authority, moral norms and proposes them to all people of good will without concealing their radical demands and their call to perfection.[55] She offers wisdom and guidance to persons struggling often with darkness and doubts.

The Church also serves as a *mother*, close to married couples in all their difficulties and aiding them as they strive for Christian holiness in marriage.[56] She does so by:

- Proclaiming the Word of God in such a way as to reveal to the Christian family its true identity, what it is and should be according to the Lord's plan;

- Celebrating the sacraments so that the Christian family is enriched and strengthened with the grace of Christ for its sanctification to the glory of the Father;

- Repeating continually the new commandment of love so that the Christian family may imitate and relive the same self-giving and sacrificial love that the Lord Jesus has for the entire human race;

- Supporting, counseling, suffering with, and rejoicing over the couples as they struggle to live the ideals of that self-giving love;

- Recalling over and over again the truth that through the sacrament of matrimony Christian married couples and parents have their own special gift among the people of God.[57]

In 1978, we offered a *Plan of Pastoral Action for Family Ministry: A Vision and Strategy*, which attempted to implement in parishes, dioceses, and interrelated institutions practical efforts that would carry out those roles of the Church as teacher and mother. These included Ministries for Pre-Marrieds and Singles, Married Couples, Parents, "Developing" Families, "Hurting" Families, and Leadership Couples or Families.[58]

Since then, many creative programs and publications have been developed to achieve that end. For example, aware that the parish community can exert a positive influence in shaping the attitudes and values of the families within its membership, the marriage handbook of one archdiocese suggests these practical steps:

- Homilies that relate the Scriptures to everyday family experience assist parents in assessing their relationship and improving the quality of the faith life in their home.

- A reverence for the sacrament of matrimony in the parish will call the family to become what it is, a domestic church, wherein the drama of redemptive love is lived out in each day's events. Couples, for example, might be asked to serve together on parish committees, when appropriate, and to join with their families in liturgical ministries such as hospitality.

- Workshops in parenting skills, aids for family communication, and prayer not only support family life but also lay foundations for the marital success of the next generation.[59]

Our own United States Catholic Conference has produced *Catholic Household Blessings and Prayers*, which provides a variety of religious rituals and traditions for use in the home. These should help us recognize the sacredness of both extraordinary and ordinary family life events such as birth, death, and reconciliation. Moreover, they could promote as well the development and implementation of appropriate religious celebrations for those moments.

These few practical examples indicate what kinds of steps the clergy, teachers, parents, relatives, and the parish or diocesan community can take today to foster the remote preparation of our young people for their marriages of tomorrow.

53. *On the Family*, nos. 21, 48, 49, 52.
54. Ibid., no. 31.
55. Ibid., no. 33.
56. Ibid.
57. Ibid., no. 49.
58. *The Plan of Pastoral Action for Family Ministry: A Vision and Strategy*, National Conference of Catholic Bishops/United States Catholic Conference (Washington, D.C.: USCC Office of Publishing and Promotion Services, 1978).
59. *Marriage in the Church: A Common Policy for Ministry to the Engaged—A Handbook for Ministers*, Archdiocese of Louisville (Louisville: 1986), p. 9.

Section II: Proximate Preparation

"My brother has always been considered the 'wanderer' of our family. Though married twice before, he has always enjoyed the wild, carefree life. Even the previous two marriages did not occur because of a conscious commitment but rather were the result of being 'pressured' into marriage by unplanned pregnancies.

"Though infatuated at the time, no true love relationship existed. Because the pregnancies were the sole reasons for the marriages, predictably, the marriages did not survive.

"Now Bob was getting married again. Considerably older than Wendy, they had lived together for five years. Because of a vasectomy before he and Wendy met, Bob no longer worried about 'unplanned pregnancies.' He could have all of the fun without any of the responsibility.

"Bob and Wendy lived in a city farther south, so, until they moved back home, they did not have the worry of disapproving family nearby. Approval from the family, especially from Mom, was always very important to Bob. I believe this need for Mom's approval led to Bob's announcement that he and Wendy were getting married. He wanted, in Mom's eyes, to somehow do the right thing—to be Mom's 'good boy.'

"He went through all the proper channels—talking to the parish priest, seeking an annulment from his first marriage. Wendy even converted to the Catholic faith.

"My husband and I were very concerned. Though Bob had stayed with Wendy longer than he had stayed with anyone before, we felt that they did not have a healthy relationship. Bob was the boss, with Wendy being more like a subservient child rather than an equal partner. Bob cared about Wendy, but his caring seemed limited. Wendy, on the other hand, almost worshiped Bob, but in a very fearful way—much like a child afraid of getting into trouble with her father. Bob was her first love and his word was her command.

"Both Bob and Wendy had the attitude of marriage not being any different than living together, not realizing they were lacking a permanent, loving commitment to one another.

"We were concerned because both Bob and Wendy were very immature. We felt that they did not appreciate or comprehend the serious commitment of marriage. They saw the wedding ceremony as just a formality rather than the beginning of ministering a sacrament to one another."

(Florida)

Definition of Proximate Preparation

The proximate preparation for marriage is based upon, flows out of, and deepens the earlier remote preparation. Beginning at a suitable age, usually around the time of puberty, it involves through appropriate catechesis a more specific preparation for and rediscovery of the sacraments. There should be an integration here of the religious formation of young people with their preparation for life as a couple.[1]

During this period, marriage should be presented as an interpersonal relationship between a woman and a man, which is in need of continual development. Those involved will need to study the nature of conjugal sexuality and responsible parenthood, including the essential medical and biological knowledge connected with it.[2]

Moreover, the proximate preparation must cover the basic requisites for a well-ordered family life such as stable work, sufficient financial resources, sensible administration, and proper housekeeping.[3]

Throughout this stage, the young persons must also be given a vision of both their serious responsibility to reach out toward others and also of the rich resources available to them in the church and community to sustain a strong family life.[4]

The challenge of this integrated approach is great. Pope John Paul II, in his *On the Family* (*Familiaris Consortio*), speaks of a gradual process of conversion and preparation for marriage.[5] The time of proximate preparation is a critical period in the life of young Christians. The developmental and formational agenda is long and varied; how the issues posed by adolescence and young adulthood are faced has lasting effects on the human person. Fortunately, two other approaches to sacramental preparation, which have developed or been restored since the Second Vatican Council, provide models for the integrated view of marriage preparation in its proximate stage.

The first of these is the *Rite of Christian Initiation of Adults* (RCIA). This rite sees Christian initiation as occurring in four stages: precatechumenate, catechumenate, period of enlightenment, and mystagogia. Proximate preparation for marriage most resembles the catechumenate. Catechumens go through a process that includes instruction in the faith of the Church as it is expressed in her dogmas and precepts. From this knowledge flows the praxis of Christian living. In and through instruction and praxis, the catechumen experiences a conversion of morals, the development of a prayer life, and the appropriation and integration of a Christian outlook on the meaning of human existence. The RCIA aptly describes this stage as a journey made in company of the clergy, the godparents, and the entire Christian community. Each has a crucial role to play in the formation of the catechumen as a full member of the Body of Christ.[6]

The second may be found in the *Program of Priestly Formation*, which embodies the principles and requirements of formation of candidates for the ministerial priesthood. Here, too, the critical elements of process and integration are found. The candidate for priesthood is engaged in a gradual process of human and Christian development, which supports his vocation to priesthood. The integration of the intellectual, spiritual, and ministerial dimensions of the person provides the foundation of the future priest's ability to make and to fulfill the commitments that the sacrament of Holy Orders entails. This process of integration is accompanied by the efforts and resources of countless others: spiritual directors, professors, counselors, the seminary community itself, family, friends, and not least, the Christian communities that call forth from the candidate his faith and pastoral love as a future minister of the Gospel.

Process and *integration*, then, are the key words to keep in mind in considering proximate preparation for marriage. It, too, is a journey with its own particular challenges and experiences. Parents, teachers, chaplains, and counselors all journey with the young Christian, who is undergoing critical years of human development and Christian maturation. The example they give and the efforts they expend will bear fruit in the Christian marriage and family life of the next generation.

The points discussed in our treatment of remote preparation will continue to have significance during this period of proximate preparation for marriage. We sketch below some additional critical areas in need of coverage. It is not an all-encompassing list, but rather a few significant matters particularly pertinent for young people as they move through adolescence on to adulthood and the marital state. The troubled relationship just noted between the Floridians, Bob and Wendy, illustrates from a negative point of view just how essential for a successful marriage are the understanding, acceptance, and implementation of values such as love, intimacy, commitment, and chastity covered in this section.

---

1. *On the Family,* no. 66.
2. Ibid.
3. Ibid.
4. Ibid.
5. Ibid., nos. 9, 66.
6. *Rite of Christian Initiation of Adults,* no. 19.

Elements of Proximate Marriage Preparation

Quality Textbooks

Throughout the proximate period of preparation, there will be an obvious need for quality textbooks that cover the sacrament of matrimony in particular, as well as the other sacraments and related topics. Those published works should combine a clear and forceful presentation of Catholic ideals, with an accurate and helpful treatment of the various contemporary experiences related to marriage, both positive and negative, that young people face in our times. We should remember that quality textbooks should also cover the pertinent and necessary cultural adaptations, not only in reference to the Hispanic family but also as they apply to Asian, black and native-American situations.

There are numerous texts on the market today. Diocesan or regional religious education resource centers and offices generally have samples of such current volumes. Parish leaders would do well to examine these publications and decide which is best suited for their local needs. We also urge writers, educators, and publishers to continue their efforts of creating new and ever-improving textbooks for this purpose. In that context, furthermore, we urge those same persons and companies to direct their creative energies toward the needs of the Hispanic community, especially by producing works in Spanish and including appropriate cultural additions and adaptions.

Appropriate Sex Education

An eighth-grade girl and boy, both troubled and confused, recently made, through written notes, urgent pleas to a visiting lecturer for information and assistance on some sexual issues.

The young woman, in typical teenage style, used a third person, hypothetical, and semianonymous approach. The misspelled words and incorrect grammar merely dramatize her pathetic concern:

> If you were pregnant and you were only 13 and 3 months along, would you tell your mother, even though your mother has warned you that if you ever got pragnet she would kill you, or something threating? . . . PLEASE HELP ME!

The young man, in similar fashion, posed a less dramatic question, but one equally painful for him:

> What if you really don't like sex, but it's the only way you can make friends. There's this

girl wants to do it with me, but I can't turn her down because she will tell everyone I am immature.[7]

Those two youngsters are, in fact, asking for that education in conjugal sexuality and responsible parenthood that Pope John Paul II urged in his letter on the family, which we noted above. They, likewise, seek the kind of guidance and formation that the bishops at the Second Vatican Council recommended: "As they grow older, they should receive a positive and prudent education in matters relating to sex."[8]

If today's youth in America are crying out for education in sexual issues, their parents just as strongly wish to see some type of sex education for children in school. A 1987 poll of the general public revealed these figures: 86% of the parents surveyed approved of sex-education courses in school; 79% wanted students taught that sex at too early an age is harmful; 67% desired that children be urged not to have sexual intercourse.[9]

While there may be an emerging consensus about the important need for sex education, there are sharp divisions over the content of such courses or the approach to contemporary issues such as the sex-related health problem of AIDS or the question of teenage pregnancies.

Some believe that mere explanation of biological facts, thorough information about contraceptives, and free distribution of condoms will resolve these issues. For example, one New York City official in charge of a massive $218,000 free condom distribution project maintains:

> Education is our only weapon. Only sustained exposure to information will reduce the risks, and the greater exposure people have to AIDS information and literature and condoms, the greater the possibility they'll use them.[10]

We recognize the plight of both those suffering from AIDS and of those, particularly teenagers, struggling with a pregnancy outside of marriage. Furthermore, we here pledge our continued and increased efforts to provide support and care for persons in such trying circumstances. But we reject value-absent sex education and distribution of artificial contraceptives as not only morally wrong, but practically ineffective. Our November 18, 1987 *Statement on School-based Clinics* deals with this issue in detail.

7. "Teen Age Sex," by Linda Matchan, in *The Boston Globe* (March 13, 1987): 21-22.
8. "Declaration on Christian Education," *Vatican Council II*, art. 1.
9. "Sex and Schools," *Time* (November 24, 1986): 54-63.
10. "Care Packages for Single Bars," by Marcia Kramer and Charles W. Bell, in New York *Daily News* (May 31, 1987): 5, 9.

In the past few decades, over $1 billion in public and private monies have been expended upon this type of sex education, contraceptive dispensing, and abortion referrals.[11] During 1985, for example, 70% of all high school seniors had taken sex education courses, up from 60% in 1976. Yet, statistics about the sexual behavior of our American students raise the question whether that type of teaching and guidance does any good at all. Consider these figures:

- More than one-half of America's young people have had sexual intercourse by the time they are 17.

- More than 1 million teenage girls in the United States become pregnant each year. Of those who give birth, nearly half are not yet 18.

- Teen pregnancy rates are at or near an all-time high. A 25% decline in the birthrate between 1970 and 1984 is due to a doubling of the abortion rate during that period. More than 400,000 teenage girls now have abortions each year.

- Unwed teenage births rose 200% between 1960 and 1980.[12]

A Stanford University professor has thus reached this conclusion: "Decade after decade . . . statistics have demonstrated the ineffectiveness of such courses in reducing sexual activity and teenage pregnancy."[13]

Nevertheless, the push continues for active promotion of contraceptive education and materials in schools. Supporters of this movement cite two recent major studies which, they claim, prove that such efforts do not increase promiscuity among adolescents and actually lower abortion rates. However, other sociologists who have examined this research in detail judge that the data do not warrant such conclusions.[14]

There are significant educational leaders in the United States who disagree with the value-absent sex education concept noted above. We applaud and make our own these remarks of our former national Secretary of Education, William J. Bennett:

Sex education courses should teach children sexual restraint as a standard to uphold and follow.

Sex is not simply a physical or mechanical act.

Sex education courses should speak up for the institution of the family. To the extent possible, when they speak of sexual activity, courses should speak of it in the context of the institution of marriage. We should speak of the fidelity, commitment, and maturity of successful marriages as something for which our students should strive. . . . Teachers . . .

must not be afraid to use words like *modesty* and *chastity*.

Sex education courses should welcome parents and other adults as allies.

It is crucial that sex education teachers offer examples of good character by the way they act and by the ideals and convictions they must be willing to articulate to students.[15]

In addition, we would like to express our approval and encouragement of the following remarks from a joint statement by former Secretary Bennett and Surgeon General C. Everett Koop, M.D., which said:

And as with sex education courses in general, it is especially important in a sensitive area like this one that school officials consult widely with parents, local public health officials, and community members to determine when and how to introduce such material into the classroom.

Young people must be told the truth—that the best way to avoid AIDS is to refrain from sexual activity until as adults they are ready to establish a mutually faithful monogamous relationship. Since sex education courses should in any case teach children why they should refrain from engaging in sexual intercourse, AIDS education should confirm the message that should already be there in the sex education curriculum. AIDS education (as part of sex education in general) should uphold monogamy in marriage as a desirable and worthy thing.

AIDS education guided by these principles can help protect our children from this terrible disease. But an AIDS education that accepts children's sexual activity as inevitable and focuses only on "safe sex" will be at best ineffectual, at worst itself a cause of serious harm. Young people should be taught that the best precaution is abstinence until it is possible to establish a mutually faithful monogamous relationship.[16]

11. Cf. research by Sr. Miriam Paul Klause, M.D., director of National Family Planning Center of Washington, 8514 Bradmoor Drive, Bethesda, MD 20817.
12. "Sex and the Education of Our Children," address by William J. Bennett, U.S. Secretary of Education, to National School Boards Association (January 22, 1987), Washington, D.C. as printed in *America* (February 14, 1987): 120-125.
13. Ibid., p. 121.
14. "Numbers Versus Principles: Moral Realism and Teen-Age Pregnancies," by James R. Kelly, in *America* (February 14, 1987): 130-136.
15. "Sex and the Education of Our Children," pp. 124-125.
16. "Statement on AIDS Education," by William J. Bennett, U.S. Secretary of Education, and C. Everett Koop, M.D., U.S. Surgeon General (Washington, D.C.: U.S. Department of Education, Office of the Secretary, January 30, 1987).

There are across the country a number of educational programs produced by secular agencies that offer, in a creative and convincing manner, information for adolescents that fosters the goals sketched by Mr. Bennett and Dr. Koop.

One, for example—a Washington state-based, nonsectarian, nonprofit organization—even provides a public high school curriculum that includes the value of each individual before and after birth and dating information that stresses the healthful advantages of abstinence prior to marriage, the qualities needed in a successful relationship, fidelity in marriage, the importance of a strong family, and the serious, but joyful, experience of parenting. Their approach is "based upon a tradition of moral and value principles. It strongly supports the family and teaches that the deepest meaning of the sexual act derives from the marriage commitment."[17]

A catchy flier for teens and adults, published by that organization, bluntly states that "the only real safe sex is having sex only with your marriage partner who is having sex only with you." After listing the advantages of abstinence, it quotes Dr. Koop: "When you have sex with someone, you are having sex with everyone they have had sex with for the last ten years." The leaflet describing "Secondary Virginity" declares that "after having been sexually active, it is possible to regain the advantages of abstinence," and then recommends steps to achieve them. In a section directed to adults, this flier warns that "responsible religious leaders can no longer believe that sex education is being adequately handled in school. The home, church, and school must care enough to enable young people to build strong relationships not based on sexual activity."[18]

As another example, one teen-services hospital program developed a somewhat similar approach following its study of girls who had come for assistance. In 1980, the hospital surveyed over 1,000 young women under 16 and discovered that 87% wanted to learn how to say "no" without hurting anyone's feelings. The resulting program focused on decision making, assertiveness, and the ability to articulate values and feelings as ways of helping them postpone sexual involvement.[19]

An educator and psychologist teaching character development at a State University of New York campus, in his book *Raising Good Children*, suggests some negative and some positive core ideas for parents to help kids develop responsible attitudes toward sex.[20]

One of the negative cautions he mentions is the following:

Don't send mixed messages. The mother who says to her 16-year-old daughter, "I don't think you should have sex, but just in case, I'm going to get you a prescription for the pill," is sending two messages: "Don't," and "I

expect you to." The literature on adolescent sex is full of stories of young girls, outfitted with birth control by "enlightened" mothers, who look back with regret. "I wish I had waited until I met someone I really cared for," says Martha, who went on the pill and lost her virginity at 14.[21]

Among the positive concepts he stresses:

No matter what your religious beliefs, the decision to have sexual relations is a serious moral decision. Whatever you say and whatever kids decide about "waiting," they should understand that the decision to be sexually intimate with someone may have profound consequences, for themselves and their partner. That makes it a moral decision. . . . There's another risk that requires the perspective of maturity to realize: premature sexual involvement can hinder a youngster's development as a person.

Sex can be emotional dynamite. For teenagers, who tend to be intensely emotional anyway, a sexual relationship can easily become obsessive, filling their lives.[22]

These kinds of programs and publications could prove helpful to Catholic educators-parents, clergy, teachers, and others involved with the formation of our youth as they seek to provide sound sex education for them. There can be no real conflict between the teachings of reason and faith correctly understood. Such courses or materials, in a certain sense, articulate the reasonable bases of divinely revealed sexual ethics as taught authentically by the Church. We, therefore, welcome them as useful tools in our own educational efforts, providing, of course, that they are founded upon and reflect sound moral norms and principles.[23] They should aid all of us—parents and teachers —to teach young people about sex prudently and in a manner suited to their age, thereby leading them to a proper psychological, emotional, and moral maturity.[24]

Nevertheless, such secular printed materials, visual aids, and education courses, as well as the instructors who employ them, suffer necessary and understandable limitations. Designed for pluralistic audiences responsible to pluralistic governing boards, supervisors, or parents and growing out of a pluralistic culture, they must avoid all religious support

17. For information on this program, contact Teen-Aid, Inc. West 22 Mission, Spokane, WA 99201-2320; phone: (509) 466-8679.
18. Ibid., *Is There Real, "Safe Sex"? For Teens and Adults.*
19. "Sex and Schools," *Time* (November 24, 1986): 63.
20. *Raising Good Children*, by Dr. Thomas Lickona (New York: Bantam Books, 1985).
21. Ibid., p. 372.
22. Ibid., pp. 376, 378.
23. *On the Family*, no. 37.
24. *Declaration on Sexual Ethics*, no. 13.

for their message of premarital chastity, except in the most general and vague manner. We naturally are not hindered by those restrictions.

To all those valuable human insights, we add a powerful divine dimension and to their natural reasons for appropriate behavior, we add a supernatural motivation. Fundamentally, we build upon their secular foundation with our sacred approach in three ways:

By clear teaching. The Church's official teaching on sexual ethics is unambiguous, authoritative, and specific, even if controversial or rejected by many in today's world.

It upholds an objective code of morality that simply, but clearly, states that "relationships of sexual intimacy are reserved to marriage, because only then is the inseparable connection secured—which God wants—between the unitive and procreative meaning of such matters, which are ordained to maintain, confirm, and express a definitive communion of life. . . . Therefore, sexual relations outside the context of marriage constitute a grave disorder, because they are reserved to a reality that does not yet exist. . . ."[25] It applies those general statements quite specifically to particular issues such as premarital genital intimacies, autoeroticism or masturbation, and homosexual activity.[26]

As we mentioned in an earlier context, there is at the present moment in the United States a desire among many to return to traditional values of chastity, commitment, and fidelity. These people seek a clarity of teaching on sexual concerns, definite and practical rules to follow, as well as an objective moral code or ideal of conduct toward which they can strive. Our Church offers precisely that type of guidance.

Those clear norms can help the wavering adolescent, subject to the pressure of peers or besieged by the contemporary culture that holds a different view. A college sophomore recalls her struggles in that regard:

> I started going steady when I was a junior in high school. My friends kept hounding me, "What's wrong with you? Didn't you lose your virginity yet?" I just wasn't ready to have sex with my boyfriend—to me, it was a big thing. But finally I lied and said, "Yes, I did." It was the only way to get them to leave me alone.[27]

Even with a definite code to follow, young people and not so young persons may stumble, slip, and sin, making bad choices out of weakness or confusion.

A Virginia high school student made these comments about some of her close colleagues: "I get upset when I see friends losing their virginity to some guy they've just met. Later, after the guy's dumped them, they come to me and say, 'I wish I hadn't done it.'"[28]

Here, too, the clear teaching of the Church is valuable and helpful. It proclaims over and over in multiple ways the wonderful mercy of God. It preaches the ever-available compassion of Jesus, as well as the Holy Spirit's forgiveness, which brings peace. It urges us to learn from past mistakes, leave them behind, and move forward to a better future. This, indeed, is good news for troubled teenagers who can't seem to let go of poor choices of the past and get on with their lives.

By providing religious motivation. The secular programs noted have assembled an impressive array of natural arguments for postponing genital activity until marriage. Nevertheless, as one of these publications notes, a reason frequently given by teens for postponing sexual involvement is that such activity goes against religious beliefs. Those projects must necessarily tread lightly in this area.

On the other hand, we can and should speak openly about the religious dimension of sexuality in our Catholic schools, our religious education classes for youth, our ministry efforts for the young, and our adult enrichment courses.

Naturally, this religious aspect of sexuality must also permeate the formation of our children in the home, where sex education should begin. It is here that boys and girls learn about themselves, as females and males, from the different ways they are treated by their parents and significant others. They also absorb attitudes and information. As they grow older, children need further data and increasing guidance. Unfortunately, many parents feel uncomfortable speaking about sex, leaving this to others, especially their children's adolescent friends and the media. The Church needs, by encouragement and educational efforts, to assist parents to assume in an effective way their role as primary educators of their children.

There are many fundamental Catholic beliefs and principles that both directly and indirectly relate to sexuality. They include, to mention a few, the Maker's creation of a good world; God's unconditional love for each human being; the existence of sin and disorder around and within us; Jesus' saving actions and rich compassion; the indwelling of the Trinity; the body as the temple of the Holy Spirit; the sufficiency of grace; the biblical norms for sexual behavior; and the Church's application of those principles to contemporary situations.[29]

25. *Educational Guidance in Human Love: Outlines for Sex Education*, Sacred Congregation for Catholic Education (Washington, D.C.: USCC Office of Publishing and Promotion Services, 1983), no. 95, p. 30.
26. Ibid., nos. 96-103, pp. 30-33.
27. *Raising Good Children*, p. 366.
28. "Sex and the Education of Our Children," p. 124.
29. For further ideas on this approach, see *Educational Guidance in Human Love*. Also, *Education in Human Sexuality for Christians*, prepared by USCC National Committee for Human Sexuality Education (Washington, D.C.: USCC Office of Publishing and Promotion Services, 1981).

Grace does not take away, but presupposes or builds upon nature. We are doing precisely that by adding further religious motivation to those already powerful natural reasons, urging a positive, integrated, and chaste style of sexual behavior for our youth. We will expand upon that point in a subsequent part of this section, "The Case for Chastity."

By offering sources for spiritual strength. As we have seen, statistics indicate that secular sex education devoid of values has not significantly changed the sexual behavior of adolescents. But for that matter, merely knowing what is the proper course of action does not ensure our adherence to it. And even with sound secular and sacred motivation, we still occasionally—even often—make poor choices, fail to postpone gratification, and yield to our unruly impulses.

It has always been so. At the moment of need in Gethsemani, Jesus said to the nodding Peter, "Be on guard, and pray that you may not undergo the test. The spirit is willing but nature is weak."[30]

The Church offers to young people, struggling to understand and integrate their sexuality, great resources of spiritual strength to help them rise above and overcome human weaknesses. Prayer, the sacred Scriptures, the Eucharist, the sacraments of penance and confirmation, retreats, renewal weekends, and support groups are but some of divine fountains from which our youth can drink of God's grace, a grace that is sufficient for them and for us.[31]

There are a number of current commercially produced or church-sponsored programs for sex education. Diocesan religious education, family life, and Catholic school offices should be able to suggest what is available locally and to give an evaluation of each course.

But this is a dynamic issue and, therefore, we encourage ongoing efforts to develop effective materials for appropriate sex education that will blend within them the best of contemporary secular and sacred wisdom.

Formation in a Christian Understanding of Intimate Loving Relationships

The mere use of the words *intimate* or *intimacy* can create serious misunderstandings and stir up defensive reactions in any discussion of relationships. The terms seem, at least for many, to signify only or mainly activities of a physically genital nature between two persons. While this may be a common perception, the fact is that a dictionary definition lists "closeness" as the primary or first meaning of the word.[32]

Contemporary writers speak about intimacy in similar fashion. Two, for example, acknowledge that the word has connotations of sexual closeness, but really is much broader and more basically has an element of "being with" others. Those others include a spouse in marriage, friends or relatives, and people with whom we work or come in contact with on more than a casual basis. Such intimate encounters involve an intense closeness that "invites me to risk myself, to expose part of myself to another." That exposure or risk connected with drawing "up close" to others or to another creates double possibilities: of being hurt or healed; of being laughed at or loved; of being embraced or rejected; of experiencing joyous exhilaration or sad disappointment. Closeness or oneness can bring joy; separation or distance does tend to cause sadness.[33]

Part of today's confusion among the young and the not so young stems from the God-given power of genital sex, especially when carried to consummation, to create temporarily that eagerly sought sense of closeness, with its attendant joy, comfort, and reassurance. Sex seems to produce rather easily an instant intimacy, a close relationship, almost desperately needed by some in our deeply fragmented world. For many, sex appears to work.

However, the ephemeral nature of such an intimacy and the complications of genital relationships outside of a permanent commitment eventually do surface. It is at this point that the troubled person may begin to grasp better how sex and intimacy are connected, but distinct, and how personal closeness is possible without genital involvement.

A teenage girl in Connecticut reflected both that confusion over sex and this quest for intimacy in a letter to "Dear Abby." The young woman wanted to know if she had to have sex in order to make a relationship last. "Howie on Long Island" responded to her question:

> I'm a 20-year-old male university student who is not a virgin, although I am celibate now.
>
> I'd like to tell "Hurting in Hartford": You are not weird for wanting a relationship with a guy without having sex.
>
> There are plenty of attractive, available guys who don't really care about scoring.
>
> Trust me. I know. I'm one of them. I've been going steady for two years, and she's the only girl I've ever dated with whom I haven't slept. It's possible to be in love without sleeping together.
>
> I agree with Abby: "All relationships do not include sex—many longstanding rela-

30. Mt 26:40-41.
31. 2 Cor 12:7-10.
32. *Webster's Third New International Dictionary* (Springfield, Mass.: G. and C. Merriam Company, 1976), p. 1182.
33. *Marrying Well: Stages on the Journey of Christian Marriage*, by Evelyn Eaton Whitehead and James D. Whitehead (Garden City, N.Y.: Image Books/Doubleday and Company, 1983), ch. 13, esp. pp. 221-229.

tionships are based on friendship and mutual interest."

Today, the risks of sex far outweigh the pleasures.[34]

The meaning of *love* or *loving* is, perhaps, equally ambiguous for contemporary persons. We often use the word to describe our fondness for a person or a place, for an object or an activity. "I love John, Mary, Dad, Mom, or you" may be spoken a few minutes after saying, "I love New York." "I love chocolate chip cookies" and "I love football" could well be part of a long list of "loves."

We also frequently identify or associate love with positive feelings and warm emotions. "Loving you makes me feel so good." Love linked solely to a fondness or like for someone or something surrounds the term with a certain self-centeredness or selfishness. Love limited to good feelings rules out both its stability as well as its persistence in tough times.

However, the love required for a close, committed, long-term relationship, for the type of intimacy essential in a satisfying friendship or a successful marriage must, on the other hand, be self-giving or unselfish, as well as steady and sometimes even courageous. Several contemporary authors describe that kind of love in the following ways:

- Love is "primarily giving, not receiving. In the very act of giving, we experience our strength, wealth, and power; we experience ourselves as overflowing, spending, alive, and hence joyous."[35] It should be observed, nevertheless, that a very high form of giving can be the act or attitude of allowing others to love or give to us.

- Love is "the will to extend one's self for the purpose of nurturing one's own or another's spiritual growth." This definition includes self-love as well as love for the other, implies that love demands effort, and indicates that love is an act of the will, which entails choosing, making a choice.[36]

- Love is a "personal decision characterized by commitment, self-sacrifice, and perseverence. It isn't an emotion, and it certainly isn't sexual activity."[37]

Those notions of love as giving, extending one's self, and self-sacrificing find a basis in the Scriptures. "God is love," we read, and that love is manifested or revealed to us by God's giving his only Son to us that we might have life through him, and by sending the Son as offering for our sins.[38] Jesus emptied himself, took the form of a slave, was born in our likeness, humbled himself and obediently gave himself for us through death on the cross. The Savior also said explicitly, "There is no greater love than this: to lay down one's life for one's friends."[39]

St. Paul, whose classical passage on the excellence of love ("Love is patient, love is kind . . .") appears to be the most popular choice for wedding liturgies, likewise, tells us that there is more happiness in giving than receiving.[40]

Pope John Paul II reiterates this message and teaches that love of such a self-giving type is the fundamental and innate vocation of every human being; we cannot live without it; our lives are senseless unless we encounter this love, experience it, make it our own, and participate intimately in such love.[41]

That love may, indeed, overflow into our feelings—but not necessarily. The self-sacrificing love between friends or spouses may demand occasional heroic effort and perseverence in most difficult circumstances. Yet, even at those moments, there is a deep joy, peace, and contentment in the act of loving and giving.

How does one find or pick a partner with whom we can enter into such a loving, intimate, and committed relationship?

Even prior to resolving that critical matter, however, we need to face the more fundamental issue of discerning our vocation in life. Questions such as the following need to be pondered and prayed over, perhaps at a retreat or during a confirmation preparation program or at one of those teachable and touchable moments described later in this text: Do I have the essential qualities needed for a successful marriage? Is Christ inviting me to the religious life as a brother, priest, or sister? Am I being summoned by the Creator to live as a single person and to build a better world and Church in this fashion? Those who judge that they are called to the married state or at least seem to possess the necessary qualities for a viable marriage, then can move on to the task of picking or, better, discovering one's lifelong partner.

In primitive societies, marriage may have been almost totally a physical mating process; even in certain contemporary cultures, nuptial matches may be arranged in complicated or simple ways by the two families; in our country, on the other hand, a man and a woman, in most instances, enter the marital state supposedly because they love one another.

Parents and friends in our system may suggest, advise, or even demand, but freedom-conscious Americans tend to guard jealously their rights and select partners based on love. There is much to be

34. Letter to "Dear Abby," Syracuse *Post-Standard* (April 7, 1987): D-2.
35. *The Art of Loving*, by Erich Fromm (New York: Bantam Books, 1954), pp. 8, 18-19.
36. *The Road Less Traveled*, by M. Scott Peck, M.D. (New York: Simon and Schuster, 1978), pp. 81-84.
37. *On Fire with the Spirit*, by Rev. John Bertolucci (Ann Arbor, Mich.: 1984), p. 111.
38. 1 Jn 4:8-10.
39. Phil 2:5-11; Jn 15:13.
40. 1 Cor 13; Acts 20:35.
41. *On the Family*, nos. 11-12, 18-19.

said for this custom, but the alarming divorce rate proves that "love" can be blind, or at least fallible. Consequently, the more we understand the essence of love; the conscious and unconscious factors operative in any developing relationship; the expectations that are fostered, even from early childhood; the nature of intimacy; and the true character of the other person, the better chance there is for a lasting love and a successful match.

From another cultural perspective, such as the Hispanic, the role of the family in the choice of a partner is much more positive and active. The freedom-consciousness gives way to communitarian and familial orientations. These are also valid choices operative in the Hispanic community.

Here are a few observations or insights about this partner-picking process that could prove useful for those engaged in marriage preparation efforts. They will be applied on the practical level in subsequent portions of this manual, which discuss, for example, the initial interview with the priest, the marriage preparation instruments, and the various premarital programs.

"The more mature and independent the person is, the more complex the choice of a love-partner becomes."[42]

The birth of love can rarely be explained by a single driving force. There are such a host of intertwining physical and psychological, conscious and unconscious factors that only through a course of in-depth analysis will the real explanation of the love

between two persons emerge, and even then that explication can only be tentative at best. In our society, with its emphasis on independence and freedom; its many instances of alienation, including within families; and its advertisement of immediate wants contrary to unselfish commitments, those complexities behind the choice of love partners are indeed enormous.[43]

"There are no perfect relationships."

Russian novelists of the nineteenth century may have maintained that there is only one woman in the world for any individual man and only one man for any one woman, that we must search for the partner destined for us from eternity, but such a romantic picture is a hoax and unrealistic. There is no such thing as the "one I am made for" or my "perfect other half."

Instead, we match up in love with a partner who differs from us in many ways, differences that call for constant compromises and, oftentimes, difficult adjustments. This requires patience, unselfishness, tolerance, and the type of good communication/problem solving/conflict management skills we urged earlier.

Unfortunately, couples in love are often blind to this harsh reality and only later recognize the imperfections in their relationship.

"Falling in love is always at least partly an illusion."

Falling in love or infatuation is a beautiful, overwhelming, dreamy, exhilarating, wonderful, intoxicating experience. But it is also a blind, compulsive, divorced from reality, and potentially depressing or worse, disastrous event.

Strong unconscious forces, triggered within, cause us to project an ideal image upon the other person. She is the girl of my dreams, "my ideal"; he is the man I always hoped for, "my knight in shining armor," my hero. We see only good and perfect qualities in the other.

We describe these marvelous, magical moments with such nonrational descriptions as: "I feel like I am walking on air; my head is in a whirl; I am weak in the knees." "He knocked me for a loop." "I am just crazy about her." Love songs, from golden oldies to current hits, communicate the same sentiments. "That Old Black Magic" spoke to couples years ago about how love gets under our skin and "You Are My Inspiration" expresses, for today's lovers, an idealization of the other's power in one's life.

But eventually, the bubble bursts and the dream dissolves. The real person, not the illusion stands

42. *The Psychology of Loving*, by Ignace Lepp; Bernard B. Gilligan, trans. (New York: The New American Library, 1963), pp. 50-63.
43. Ibid.

before us. That, of course, can be discouraging, even depressing. Moreover, marrying too swiftly without the time and the techniques needed to discover the real, as opposed to the dream, partner usually proves disastrous.

The falling in love or infatuation stage has a magnificent beauty and creative force to it; but it does not have lasting power and must for a satisfying marriage give way to staying in love.

"We tend to reach out in love toward our ego-complement."

Individuals in love seek and hope for their own realization in another person. Our ego-ideal, shaped from our earliest years in our psyche, is incessantly looking for its own realization throughout the ups and downs of life.[44]

Another way of saying this might be to indicate that a woman seeks to find her fulfillment and complement in her husband, and he in her. We know that opposites attract and, thus, find that often couples in love represent a mix of opposing, complementing, or blending characteristics.

For example, an excitable person may be drawn toward a tranquil partner; a shy, withdrawing individual toward a gregarious, extroverted one; a reflective, hesitant person toward a decisive, active partner.

There are positive and negative ramifications to this trend or tendency. Positively, differing partners can help each other grow out of what are probably perceived as weaknesses. For example, if I judge myself as having too swift a temper or not friendly enough or unable to make decisions, while you consider yourself as too passive when attacked unjustly or regularly failing to find time for yourself or inclined to act impetuously, then our interaction should help modify those opposite traits.

Negatively, the differences will cause friction and require compromise. The one who makes almost a fetish of orderliness and always being early will find the more laid-back and last-minute partner annoying, and vice versa.

Simple introductory interview questions, the marriage preparation instruments, and other psychological inventories can prove extremely useful in discovering these facets of the relationship.[45]

"Balancing autonomy and relatedness is an ongoing struggle in any developing relationship."

Autonomy means separateness, independence, and being "other." In their early growth, as a general rule, boys learn first and usually develop being better at the task of autonomy.

Relatedness means bonding, closeness, and being "one with." Girls, again generally, learn first and develop being better in adulthood at relatedness.

There is often, during any intimate relationship, a kind of tug-of-war involving autonomy and relatedness. "If I am close to you, will I lose myself?" "If you pull away from me, will I cease to be?"[46]

"As relationships develop, opposing life and death fears need to be acknowledged and resolved."

The death fear is the fear of being smothered, held on to too tightly, or choked by the closeness of the other.

The life fear is the fear of abandonment, of being left alone, of being unable to live without the other.

In a growing love relationship, and obviously in marriage, both independence and bonding are necessary; fears of losing either are real and natural. To understand this dynamism, to recognize and, as it were, to own the fears, to communicate in non-blaming ways with the other about them are key steps toward their resolution. Couples who do not face these issues usually resort to a type of game-playing, which is unsatisfying and can become quite destructive.

"There are signs of a healthy intimacy between two persons."

In healthy intimacy, we can note, among others, these qualities:

- *Authenticity* (they allow themselves to be known as they really are);

- *Mutuality* (there is a similar depth to self-disclosure, a balance of give and take; both bring the same amount of power to the relationship);

- *Growth* (both support and affirm, but also lovingly challenge one another);

- *Inclusivity* (they are not exclusively dedicated to each other, but relate appropriately to others as well).

"There are certain generic positive and negative qualities, characteristics, or areas which persons often use to evaluate a potential partner."

Some positive qualities would be compatibility, education and intelligence, health, disposition, desire for a home, appearance, and religion.

Some negative characteristics would be selfishness, immaturity, infidelity, irresponsibility, reli-

44. Ibid., p. 53.
45. As an example of such psychological inventories, see *Myers-Briggs Type Indicator*, Consulting Psychological Press, Inc., 577 College Ave., Palo Alto, CA 94306. Copyright © 1976, Isabel Briggs Myers.
46. *In a Different Voice*, by Carol Gilligan (Cambridge: Harvard University Press, 1982).

gious difference or indifference, and disagreement over children.

Picking a partner for a loving, intimate, long-term relationship always involves a risk. There are no guarantees. Nevertheless, the following questions might help in making a reasonable, solidly based decision in that direction:

- Could we live happily together?

- Do I have a genuine reverence for the other partner?

- Do I normally put my best foot forward in his or her presence?

- Do I tend to reveal my inner self to her or to him?

- Do I tend to be thoughtful, considerate, unselfish in his or her presence?

- Does this person help me spiritually?

4 The Case for Chastity

The official teaching of the Church on sexual activity, noted earlier, is clear, succinct, and precise: "The use of the sexual function has its true meaning and moral rectitude only in marriage; every genital act must be within the framework of marriage; sexual union is only legitimate if a definitive community of life has been established between the man and the woman."[47]

The clarity and preciseness of that teaching can be a valuable aid for developing adolescents as well as mature adults who struggle to practice the virtue of chastity. In a questioning age, it helps to have definite norms and objective standards as guides for one's conscience and behavior. Moreover, the very fact that the Church proposes, with authority, these specific rules governing sexual behavior, in itself, will be a strong motivational force for some Catholics.

Nevertheless, the pressure of peers and of the surrounding environment to follow a different, seemingly more liberated and less restrictive path can be enormous.

A young woman in her first year at Yale suffered greatly in the face of such pressure and ultimately made a tragic choice as a result of the conflict she endured. This 17-year-old visited the university's health clinic for consultation rather early on, supposedly because of acute homesickness despite the fact that academically she was doing well and had a boyfriend whom she liked a lot.

Conversation with a physician revealed the root cause of her depressed mood: the boyfriend, two years older, was pushing her to have sexual intercourse. She, on the other hand, felt reluctant about going "all the way." Her hesitation was not because of fear of pregnancy or of parental disapproval or of sex itself, but because she judged that sex would interfere with her life as a student, with her plans for herself, with her studies, her freedom. She did not want to be tied down and considered sex to be a commitment.

Her tensions were complicated by dormitory companions who, far from supporting her in this matter, became harshly scornful of her virginity.

Counseling with the physician improved the situation and enabled her to live tolerably, although unpleasantly, as the "virgin queen" of the dormitory.

However, some time later, one of her college confidants told her she had seduced the young woman's boyfriend. Crying, shaken, and incredulous, she confronted him and asked if this was true. He admitted it was so.

Liking the young man so much, she vacillated for several weeks between going to bed with him or breaking off the relationship. Finally, deciding there was no solution to her problem—at least at that time, and at Yale—she left the university and returned home.

Peers could have been supportive. Instead, they proved almost viciously unhelpful and disloyal, seeming to relish her distress and making her an outcast because of her choice for virginity.[48]

While the pressure of peers and the surrounding environment can make the struggle for chastity difficult, so, too, does the naturally strong desire for physical union within those who are deeply in love and contemplate marriage. A young collegian in Ghana, West Africa, described his painful plight this way:

I am twenty-two, a college student, due to graduate next summer. Till twenty-one, I did not know what it felt like to have a girl in an embrace. I have shunned the company of women. My father had four beside my mother. At college my mates mocked at me. Some even said I was impotent and suggested that I commit suicide. Maybe you don't know what it feels like to be told that in an African Society. You are simply useless—a toothless dog—a waste. I knew I was not. But then it is difficult.

Six months ago, I met the girl that will spell my doom or has—because we have "gone too far." Now I have realized my folly. I want to atone for this. I told her there will be no more sex till the nuptial night. But many a man have lost their mates on account of this promise. What do you say? I should call it a day? You see, I have vowed that the girl I will go to bed with should be my wife. I still pray the Lord for help. I am a Catholic, but I had

47. *Declaration on Sexual Ethics*, nos. 5, 7.
48. "What About the Right to Say 'No'?" by Richard V. Lee, M.D., in *New York Times Magazine* (September 16, 1973): pp. 90-92.

my education in Seventh Day Adventist Mission.

Natural curiosity, our weakened human condition, peer pressures, the quest for intimacy, and strong desires for a loving union make the practice of chastity a true challenge, particularly in our times. Both the young and the old thus seek compelling reasons for not going "all the way" or "too far." They look for powerful motives to help them with their struggles, beyond the mere fact that such sexual activity outside of marriage is contrary to objective moral norms. They want forceful arguments supportive of chaste behavior.

If we accept the contemporary discovery about the two hemispheres of our brain and the theory that our language is hemispheric specific—the left-brain and right-brain concepts—then our presentation of motives, reasons, and arguments for chastity will be phrased accordingly. The right-brain language is one of power and involves imaginative aphorisms, metaphors, stories; the left-brain language is one of clarity and involves rational logic, facts, and order.[49] The motivational comments below, by no means an exhaustive list or treatment, take both a left-brain and right-brain approach. The first one, for example, made up of brief, one-line arguments would be more of the right-brain style; the latter theological arguments would be more left-brain oriented.

THE ADVANTAGES OF ABSTINENCE

Some contemporary programs and publications that offer adolescents guidance about sexual behavior and motives for postponing sexual involvement follow an identical tactic: they simply list reasons, advantages, and consequences of waiting or not waiting to have sex.

The list below summarizes the advantages of abstinence from a positive-negative perspective and represents a summary of current approaches:

Good Reasons to Wait for Sex
- You don't want to;
- You're not ready physically or mentally for sexual involvement;
- You don't want to be pregnant or get someone pregnant;
- You don't want to get a sexually transmitted disease (STD);
- Your religion says it's wrong;
- You want to wait until you're in love or married;
- It would upset your parents if they found out;
- Your reputation might be hurt;
- Your boyfriend or girlfriend isn't ready;
- It could interfere with your future plans;
- You want to be free from guilt, doubt, worry;
- It could lead to the trauma of abortion or the loss of adoption;

- You might be pressured to marry early;
- You don't want certain family problems;
- You want financial stability before having a family;
- You want the freedom to become more creative in sharing feelings;
- You want the freedom to develop skills and abilities;
- You want the freedom to build greater trust in marriage;
- You want to foster a healthy self-appreciation;
- You want the freedom to become the best person you can be.

Bad Reasons to Have Sex Now
- Everyone is "doing it";
- Your boyfriend or girlfriend is pushing you;
- Your friends are pushing you;
- To be or feel grown up;
- To find out what it's like;
- To hold on to a relationship;
- To make your parents mad or get away from them or to become independent;
- To stop feeling lonely;
- To be popular;
- To hurt someone or get back at them;
- To have pleasure or fun;
- To imitate what you see on television or the movies;
- To forget problems at home.

One organization working with the young concludes by maintaining that teens can abstain, can develop self-control and that the "home, church, and school must care enough to enable young people to build strong relationships not based on sexual activity."[50]

THE POWER OF SELF-KNOWLEDGE AND SELF-DIRECTION

Dr. Hanna Klaus, an obstetrician/gynecologist who directs the Natural Family Planning Center in Washington, D.C., has discovered through scientific research that enhanced understanding of one's cyclic fertility can prove to be a significant aid in the pursuit of chastity. It fosters self-esteem, reduces the impact of peer pressure, delays sexual involvement, and underscores the power of the brain as a sex organ.

In a controlled pilot project with more than 200 adolescents, implemented after approval by parents, the women, aged 15-17, were taught fully the Billings Ovulation Method. About 50% of those who were sexually active at the beginning of the instruction ceased that type of behavior. Moreover, within three

49. *Preaching Better*, Frank J. McNulty, ed. (New York: Paulist Press, 1985), pp. 87-94.
50. *Is There Real "Safe Sex"?* Flier published by Teen-Aid, Inc.

months parents reported that the young women seemed to have moved away from the influence of peer pressure and were making their own decisions about sexual activity.

While it is often held that the height of libido occurs in the midst of a woman's fertile period, Dr. Klaus' research indicates that a good number of women reported that, within three months of starting natural family planning, this zenith of sexual desire shifted instead to the infertile phase.

Research into the male reproductive system has produced similar substantive facts that highlight the power of the brain as a sexual organ. A man feels the urge for sexual expression when his volume of semen has reached about 2.5 ml. This reservoir drains spontaneously in the course of nocturnal emission when intercourse is not available and masturbation is avoided. Moreover, the higher the level of sexual fantasy and stimulation (e.g., through daydreaming, literature, films, or television), the higher the testosterone level, which reaccumulates seminal volume. The intensity of the male sexual drive is, therefore, under greater voluntary control than we have perhaps previously judged.[51]

These clinical findings buttress our recommendation in the next portion of this section that instruction in natural family planning begin at an early age and continue throughout the educational system. It paves the way for church-approved, responsible parenthood later in marriage, but also, from the evidence here, suggests that it may support the unmarried in their challenges with chastity. As an aid to the program decision-making efforts of church leaders, further research that tests the reliability and validity of these findings of Dr. Klaus would be welcomed and encouraged.

A MATTER OF GROWTH

One single-parent mother judges from experience that delay of sexual intercourse until marriage is critical for any young person's personal growth. Adolescence, as she has discovered in her own parenting role, is a critical time for them to build self-respect, develop communication skills, and grow in freedom. Becoming active sexually, in genital fashion, retards or stunts those growth processes.

Because of limited life experiences, teenagers often find that serious talking is difficult or awkward; sexual activity can distract young persons and hinder them from the hard work involved with this task of developing good communication skills.

Adolescents have not yet attained sufficient freedom to be their true selves, to express feelings and to act on them, to change their minds wisely about behavior, or to ignore peer pressures.

Their struggle is to grow themselves and to sort out relationships among family and friends. They do not have the energy or resources also to be trying to help someone else grow and work out all her or his own relationships.

Learning how to prioritize in life—saying "no" to some things and "yes" to others—is a crucial part of the maturation process. Adolescents must learn that we cannot have everything in life. Postponing sex helps here; gratifying sexual desires, on the contrary, hinders progress in this regard.

Youthful relationships tend to be intense, short-lived, and numerous. When there is an ultimate, even if immature, gift of heart and body in such experiences, the subsequent breakup of the relationship and the rejection connected with it can terribly bruise the person's self-esteem and cause serious psychological damage. Young people are necessarily not capable of long-term commitments; to give so totally at that point in their lives is almost to guarantee that they will suffer such a bruising, corrosive abandonment, with all its negative overflow into school, family, and life.

This actual scenario below illustrates the complexity and risks of the adolescent growth struggle:

A seventh-grade girl has a crush upon an eighth-grade boy. When alone together, he flirts and treats her very nicely, leaving her elated and on a cloud. The next day, she meets the boy with his friends and greets him. To impress his buddies, he sharply responds, "Get lost, kid."

That night at dinner, stunned and broken, she breaks down and cries. The comforting mother says: "As bad as you feel now, betrayed and hurt, imagine how worse you would feel if he had asked to have sex and you had given in to him. You are not too young to be wondering how used, hurt, and deeply rejected you would feel."

The girl exclaimed, "I'd want to die!"

The mother concluded this on-the-spot, but to-be-continued lesson by saying, "Well, he's a very nice boy in most respects, but he's only 13 and boys want to impress their friends at that age. He just needs to grow up a bit. . . ."

An older, but still relatively young woman came sadly to the same conclusion about the danger of premarital genital activity retarding love and growth:

Love him, don't make love to him. It spoils everything. I know. And I regret it so much. We got caught up with each other's bodies and forgot about the minds, the ambitions, the wonders.[52]

51. "We Are in Control of Our Sexuality," by Hanna Klaus, in *Charities USA* 14:2 (March 1987): 12-13; "Natural Family Planning," *National Family Planning and Reproductive Health Association News* (February 1987): 7.
52. *Don't You Really Love Me?* by Joseph M. Champlin (Notre Dame: Ave Maria Press, 1968), p. 113.

These above comments may seem to apply mainly to young, immature adolescents. What about chastity for those who are older, involved in a serious relationship, contemplating marriage, perhaps engaged? The remarks that follow may have special meaning for them.

A QUESTION OF INTEGRITY

Those who become involved in genital activity usually discover this progression: they want sexual actions that are evermore intense, acts repeated more and more often, and a relationship that constantly seeks greater exclusivity. The trend, then, is more intense, more often, more exclusive.

That tendency toward exclusiveness, linked with sexual intercourse, is but one of the unique, complex features of genital relationships. "The act of intercourse gathers and expresses individuals in a way that few other acts do. It has a way of highlighting and bringing to consciousness all that is harmonious as well as conflictual in a relationship. That is why feelings of love and hate, fullness and emptiness, joy and sadness, anticipation and disinterestedness break in upon the act of intercourse in such astounding and unplanned ways. The act intensifies and magnifies what otherwise might be unobserved. Ecstasy or depression following the physical expression of love are but an indication of the harmony and disharmony within and between persons."[53]

To engage in such activity, therefore, on a casual basis and even on a more caring basis but without a commitment to a lasting, exclusive relationship thus violates the very nature of genital actions. These actions yearn for a unique, special, totally inclusive bond between two persons, the type of union found perfectly only in marriage. To act otherwise is to undermine the integrity and authenticity of what we are doing.

THE STRENGTHENING OF NUPTIAL VOWS

What a couple really need to practice before marriage is not sexual intercourse, but keeping promises. The essence of marriage is this: to promise, to make a solemn vow, to offer one's heart and soul and body to the beloved for life. There is a commitment made here, before God and others, to live and give in sickness and in health, for richer or for poorer, for better or for worse.

Notice that the promise is made before God and others. The ceremony of marriage, then, is not some external action that simply "makes it legal." It is, instead, the unveiling to others of an inner promise. It tells the world that this man and this woman now publicly, before their Maker and their fellow humans, vow to share each other's lives together. They embrace a common future with all of its hopes and disappointments, its pleasures and its pains, its joys and sor-

rows, its successes and its failures. Only death will cut the cord that now joins them.

The husband and wife who so seal hearts and hopes together at the altar, join their bodies together in the marriage bed. Sexual intercourse makes their lifelong promise more definitive; it deepens their commitment to each other; it physically expresses their total union.

Keeping the promises will not always be easy. Nor will the days and years ahead be ever joyful. Pain, weariness, boredom, restlessness, irritation, being taken for granted—these and how many other enemies will seek to weaken and destroy the nuptial vows.

The man and woman who have saved the joys and delights of sexual intercourse until after they have made this public promise should find the keeping and deepening of it somewhat easier. They have not experienced the total pleasure of sexual intercourse until marriage. For them, this action reinforces the nuptial commitment. It tends to be associated only with this man, my husband, or this woman, my wife. And it is seen only in a context of home, family, security, joint living together. Anticipated before marriage, these intimacies, beautiful and thrilling as they are, lose some of their uniqueness. This is probably the meaning of a popular phrase that expresses the fear that "It won't be special" after a couple are married if they sleep together before.

SUPPORT FROM SCRIPTURE

The Ten Commandments, of course, speak of adultery and entertaining wrong desires for a neighbor's wife. But such moral precepts do not seem to apply, at least on face value, to the situation we are discussing. The letters of St. Paul to Christians in various cities of the Mediterranean do, however, carry greater relevance. Several of them (1 Cor 6; Gal 5; Eph 5) contain severe warnings about fornication and fornicators, excluding them from the kingdom of God. Some background and an explanation of one actual text may make this ancient, but still living, message more meaningful.

Jesus was a Jew, as was Paul. They lived in Jewish communities and breathed the Jewish religious and ethical atmosphere. Historians indicate that, in general, Judaism did demand at the time of Christ standards of moral conduct far above anything in the surrounding pagan environment. Prostitution was strictly forbidden and an unmarried girl was supposed to be a virgin. The role, likewise, of a Jewish married woman in terms of honor and respect stood normally above that of her pagan contemporaries.

53. "Genital Relationships: A Question of Integrity," by Martin Heldorfer, in *Sexuality: A Seminar on Sexuality and Brotherhood,* Martin Heldorfer, ed. (Lockport, Ill.: Christian Brothers' National Office, 100 De La Salle Drive), pp. 57-63.

Sexual ideals apparently were a little less lofty in the Roman world and especially in Greece. One expert remarks that it would be even fairly safe to say that chastity was nowhere esteemed in the Hellenistic world except among the Jews. A man was free to do pretty much what he pleased, with impunity. The woman, not so. Unequal partner at home and insignificant outside the house, she stood as second-class citizen, even in the upper sections of society. The lack of chastity in a man, married or single, was judged a minor failing—if a fault at all. Gross sexual aberrations were not uncommon, and often the law or the consensus cast tolerant glances at them. The Roman world's view of woman and chastity rose a bit above the Greek picture but still hardly equaled the elevated Jewish notion.

Christians living in the first century at Corinth thus must have found high sexual standards difficult to follow. A commercial city with cosmopolitan status, it was notorious even in ancient times as a hotbed of every kind of vice. "To live like a Corinthian" meant complete moral collapse; "a Corinthian girl" and a "prostitute" were synonymous terms. When St. Paul wrote to the Romans (1:24-32) and sharply catalogued vices, he was at that time in Corinth and could write easily since realistic illustrations abounded around him.

We should hardly be surprised, then, to learn that early followers of Christ, hearing mention of freedom from the law and emphasis on the spirit, misinterpreted these directives. When Paul wrote words such as, "All things are lawful, but not all things are expedient," it is little wonder that Corinthian Christians (some of whom were Jews) accepted this as an approval of the common practices of the city. The idealistic Jewish chastity rules now could be forgotten, and the easier, more pleasurable procedures of paganism consecrated to the one, true God. Since legalism was out, then license must be in. Or so they thought and acted until the fiery apostle dispatched an epistle to them.

> I am writing these things not to shame you, but to admonish you as my beloved children (1 Cor 4:14).

> It is actually reported that there is lewd conduct among you. . . (1 Cor 5:1).

> Do not deceive yourselves: no fornicators, idolaters, or adulterers, no sodomites, thieves, misers or drunkards, no slanderers or robbers will inherit God's kingdom (1 Cor 6:9).

Strong words, indeed. He judges these methods of acting form serious breaches in the Christian way of life, so serious as to exclude those who practice them from active participation in the life of the Church and ultimately from the rewards of eternal life with God in the next world. A person cannot be God's friend and Christ's brother or sister and conduct himself along these lines.

In defending his position and emphasizing the malice of fornication, St. Paul manifests great understanding of sexual relations.

> Do you not know that your bodies are members of Christ? Shall I then take Christ's members and make them the members of a prostitute? Of course not! [Or] do you not know that anyone who joins himself to a prostitute becomes one body with her? For "the two," it says, "will become one flesh." But whoever is joined to the Lord becomes one spirit with him. Avoid immorality. Every other sin a person commits is outside the body, but the immoral person sins against his own body. Do you not know that your body is a temple of the Holy Spirit within you, whom you have from God, and that you are not your own? For you have been purchased at a price. Therefore glorify God in your body (1 Cor 6:15-20).

Paul, in effect, shows that sexual relations between man and woman cannot remain a merely casual affair. A oneness exists so close that it produces a practical identity of flesh. Such a union surely must flow over into the whole being of the persons involved and cannot be limited to a surface entanglement, soon to be forgotten. Modern findings of psychology confirm this.

Proceeding from that physical and psychological fact of experience, the apostle rises to a spiritual level and reminds his hearers of their noble dignity. Through faith and baptism, they become intimately united with their Lord, Savior, God, Christ Jesus.

Persons so linked to Christ, with bodies that are temples of the Holy Spirit, should never, according to St. Paul, engage in casual, noncommitted, sexual, genital activity.

ASSISTANCE FROM THE CHURCH

In addition to the clear, objective moral norms governing sexual matters, the Church also suggests and provides certain means that assist all of us in living out chaste lives.[54] These include discipline of the senses and the mind, watchfulness and prudence in avoiding occasions of sin, the observance of modesty, moderation in recreation, wholesome pursuits, assiduous prayer, as well as frequent reception of the sacraments of penance and the Eucharist.

Devotion to the Immaculate Mother of God; an awareness, veneration, and imitation of saints such as St. Maria Goretti or St. Aloysius Gonzaga, for whom chastity was a singular part of their lives; as well as the support of other believers whose examples

---

54. *Declaration on Sexual Ethics,* no. 12.

of chaste living are evident, likewise, can be most helpful in the challenging pursuit of this virtue.[55]

We conclude this part with comments from a young man from Dallas:

> I am a 20-year-old male who reinforces your advice to keep saying no until you feel you are ready.
>
> I've been dating a girl for two years. She was a virgin when we started to date, and she still is.
>
> I lost my virginity in the eighth grade, and I'd be lying if I said I never tried to talk her into going to bed with me.
>
> I even dropped her twice, but I went back because I had such strong feelings for her. I appreciated what a prize she was after I had dated the easy girls.
>
> I realized that if they'd sleep with me, they'd probably sleep with any guy who asked them.
>
> I have quit trying to wear her down. I am now willing to wait until after we're married. Sex can cheapen a relationship, not make it more valuable.[56]

Responsible Childbearing and Childrearing

Someone once said that the gift of this generation to the next generation *is* the next generation. Pope John

Paul II echoed that observation when he taught that children are the precious gift of marriage and that conjugal love bestows upon husband and wife the greatest possible gift, the gift by which they become cooperators with God in giving life to a new human person.[57] In the words of the marriage ritual, the institution of matrimony and wedded love find their ultimate crown in the procreation and education of children.[58] We are talking, then, about the miracle of bearing and rearing human life.

THE BEAUTY AND BURDEN OF CHILDBEARING AND CHILDREARING

"A Woman on Her Way to a Miracle" was just how *Life* magazine entitled its pictorial essay on the long months and unforgettable moments of a Swedish couple's experience with the birth of their first child.

The husband assisted in the delivery and recalled afterwards his thoughts at the moment their baby boy entered this world: "It was wonderful and seemed completely natural."

The wife made similar comments: "I have never felt so happy before or after. My mother had told me that I would feel unbelievably good after the baby was born, but I didn't believe it would be anything like this."

Months later, holding the infant, the new mother observed: "I never get over how beautiful he is. Every time I look at him I am surprised all over again. I've forgotten pregnancy was ever hard."

The experiential ecstatic joy of this married couple, in a sense, gives a living testimony to the abstract truths of our Catholic philosophical and theological tradition about childbearing.

We teach these truths: the birth of every child is something of a miracle; couples possess a remarkable opportunity for cooperating with God in the creation of new human life; the one conceived flows out of, manifests, and deepens the spouses' self-giving love for one another; the infant is a unique reflection of the singular and special bond between husband and wife—for no other combination of persons could have produced this particular child; parents have the awesome, but challenging possibility and duty of handing down to their offspring the very Christian faith and positive values given to them by their parents, relatives, community, and Church; a child offers the potential for repeated unique moments of tender intimacy and profound satisfaction, continuing throughout many years, that cannot be experienced in any other way.

55. For a practical application of these general suggestions and an insightful commentary on chastity, see *The Courage to Be Chaste,* by Benedict J. Groeschel, OFM cap. (Mahwah, N.J.: Paulist Press, 1985).
56. Letter to "Dear Abby," *Syracuse Post Standard.*
57. *On the Family,* no. 14.
58. *Rite of Marriage,* no. 4.

Nevertheless, the conception, gestation, and birth of a child, awesome and wonderful as that may be, also brings with it some burdens that may seem, at times, almost unbearable. The Swedish couple experienced those difficult struggles as well.

This wife commented on her pregnancy: "The first three or four months were terrible. I was tired, and I felt slightly sick to my stomach all the time."

Her husband, likewise, found the changed circumstances caused by the pregnancy unpleasant. Early on, they spent a long weekend at the beach, which proved to be disastrous. "I wanted to have a good time and go water skiing in the daylight and dancing at night. All she wanted to do was sit huddled on the beach. In the end we made a pact, one day for her and one day for me. But it wasn't much fun."

His wife added, "I cried a lot and we argued over everything, even over food."

The husband discovered that understanding her condition did not come easily. "My wife changed so abruptly that she was like a stranger. I did so much to help her around the house and we ate out so much that I couldn't believe that she was as tired as she said she was. It didn't seem possible she wanted to go to bed every night at 7:30."

He occasionally lost his temper and she seemed in the initial months to care more for the baby than for her husband.

While matters improved abruptly at the beginning of the fourth month, they still had to work through the continued uncomfortableness of pregnancy and ultimately the labor pains of birth.[59]

Those burdens of nausea and extreme fatigue, of uncomfortableness and pain directly touch the woman, but also indirectly affect the man and can cause a strain in the relationship between the spouses. Some expectant couples, likewise, suffer because of great anxiety, fear, confusion, resentment over the pregnancy, guilt over the resentment, a sense of inadequacy, and serious self-doubts brought on by their lack of enthusiasm for the child within or just born. Many of those negative attitudes or feelings may persist or reoccur occasionally after the infant's birth and throughout childrearing years. For example, the 24-hour-a-day demands of a helpless infant, the loss of freedom and privacy, even jealousy within a new father over his wife's absorption in the child can bring stress to the conjugal relationship.

That mix of joy and sorrow, of pain and pleasure, of anxiety and relief that generally accompanies childbearing and childrearing reflects the deepest pattern or rhythm of human existence. It is the paschal, passover, Easter mystery being played out in the couple's lives; it is the death and resurrection of Christ being specifically reenacted within our times; it is the crown after the cross, the gain after the pain, the victory after the struggle. Realizing the connection between their sorrow/joy experiences and the death/resurrection of Jesus can totally transform for

wife and husband, father and mother, the pregnancy-birth-parenting events and surround them with additional rich meanings.

Jesus used the very image of pregnancy and birth to illustrate his teaching on this paschal death-resurrection mystery: "You will grieve, but your grief will become joy. When a woman is in labor, she is in anguish because her hour has arrived; but when she has given birth to a child, she no longer remembers the pain because of her joy that a child has been born into the world" (Jn 16:20-21). Those observations could also apply to the parents as they watch their offspring leave home and begin their own adult lives, the fruit of years of challenging, sacrificial child-rearing.

Still, despite the sorrow, pain, and anxiety, a child's birth usually creates moments of excitement, joy, and wonder for everyone concerned. Those engaged in various aspects of marriage preparation can testify to this from both their personal experience and pastoral ministry. The comment of an older obstetrician who has monitored and participated in that process on over a thousand occasions reflects the event's marvelous dimension: "I still, after these many years, continue each time to stand in awe at the miracle of it all." Pope John XXIII noted this divine aspect of childbearing when he said that "human life is sacred," and "from its very inception it reveals the creating hand of God."[60]

The growth of a child, from first words and first steps to first church sacraments and first adult decisions, is equally wondrous, although more gradual, uneven, and perhaps less spectacular. Consequently, the childrearing process likewise manifests a divine characteristic, an assertion Pope John Paul II upheld when he stressed that "parental love is called to become for the children the visible sign of the very love of God."[61]

The Church has been emphasizing repeatedly over the recent past its belief in this divine dignity, sacredness, and value of human life. The decrees of the Second Vatican Council, several papal documents, and our own pastoral letters contain clear affirmation of that teaching.[62] The Church wishes to stand for life, promote life, and defend life.[63]

59. "A Woman on Her Way to a Miracle," by Eleanor Graves, in *Life* (July 22, 1966): 48-62B.
60. *Mater et Magistra*, AAS LIII (1961): 447, as quoted in *On the Regulation of Birth*, Pope Paul VI (Washington, D.C.: USCC Office of Publishing and Promotion Services, 1968).
61. *On the Family*, no. 14.
62. See *Pastoral Constitution on the Church*, no. 51; *Human Life in Our Day: A Collective Pastoral Letter of the American Hierarchy*, (Washington, D.C.: USCC Office of Publishing and Promotion Services, 1968); *The Challenge of Peace: God's Promise and Our Response: A Pastoral Letter on War and Peace*, National Conference of Catholic Bishops (Washington, D.C.: USCC Office of Publishing and Promotion Services, 1983), no. 285; *On the Family*, no. 30.
63. *On the Family*, no. 30.

RESPONSIBLE CONSCIENCE DECISIONS

Most Catholic couples contemplating marriage possess at least an initial appreciation for this divinely awesome aspect of childbearing and childrearing. They generally look forward to the day when they will become parents and start a family. But even while eagerly anticipating the birth of a child, the two of them normally struggle with these questions: Will we try to conceive a baby as soon as we marry? If not, when should the first child come? How many children will we have? What family planning method are we going to follow?

The Church, as "the one authentic guide for the people of God," offers some clear assistance to couples pondering those delicate and perplexing issues.[64] In essence, the Church indicates that only the husband and wife, through responsible conscience decisions, can and should answer such questions.

First of all, the Church teaches that it is the couple alone, following their morally responsible *conscience* judgments, who are to decide those many when and how issues. The bishops at the Second Vatican Council were explicit about this:

> It is the married couple themselves who must in the last analysis arrive at these judgments before God. Married people should realize that in their behavior they may not follow their own fancy but must be ruled by conscience— and conscience ought to be conformed to the law of God in the light of the teaching authority of the Church, which is the authentic interpreter of divine law.[65]

We echoed that notion several years later by assigning to the "conscience of spouses all the judgments, options, and choices which add up to the awesome decision to give, postpone or decline life."[66]

But that conscience decision must be a morally *responsible* one. We think it significant that the term "responsible" has emerged in every major church document discussing this matter throughout the last two decades. Consider, for example, these words or phrases: "the responsible transmission of life"; "responsible parenthood"; "the responsibility, under God, of the spouses who, in effect, ask the Creator to commit to their care the formation of a child"; "free and responsible cooperation in transmitting the gift of human life"; and "to live out their parenthood in a truly responsible way."[67]

A responsible conscience in this context is:

Open to life. Both scientific, statistical studies and simple everyday observation indicate clearly that today's families are smaller in size, that many contemporary couples are postponing matrimony and children until a later age, and that a growing number of spouses have voluntarily opted for a childless marriage.[68] Moreover, one can easily catch spontaneous comments from numerous adolescents who assert

that they have little or no desire to become future childbearers and childrearers. In such a negative cultural climate, which seems to ignore or reject the wondrous aspects of offspring noted above, we urge married couples to foster consciences that possess an openness to the transmission of life and that judge children as the greatest possible and precious gift of marriage.[69]

Generous and sacrificing, not selfish. Even though giving birth to and overseeing the growth of a child can be joyful and satisfying experiences, they both require constant self-giving and personal sacrifice upon the part of the parents. Husbands and wives must be aware of the selfishness and materialism of our age and of the overt and subtle ways in which they militate against any type of such self-denial.[70] In deciding to postpone the birth of a child, be it the first or an additional baby, they need to ask: Is our decision promoted merely by a desire to have more time, money, possessions, or freedom for ourselves?[71]

Trusting. Every decision in life involves a risk that launches us into the future, which we neither know nor can regulate absolutely. Bringing a child into this world, with the accompanying commitment to bring it up properly, is obviously such a risk. The fears connected with that uncertain momentous undertaking can be greatly dissipated by a strong trust in divine providence and God's grace.[72]

Wise. The married couple need to examine all the factors involved in their decision to have a child or to postpone it temporarily or indefinitely. Included are medical, economic, sociological, or psychological considerations —the health of parents and other children already born; the finances of the family; the current local, national, and worldwide situation; the mental and emotional readiness of spouses for childbearing.[73]

Humble. Conception is a joint result of cooperation between a man, a woman, and God. Spouses merely open themselves to the transmission of life; they do not totally control this process. Many couples can verify that truth by experience, through the shock of surprise unplanned pregnancies and the disappointment of sustained fruitless efforts to conceive. An awareness of these facts should make us

64. Ibid., no. 31.
65. *Pastoral Constitution on the Church*, no. 50.
66. *Human Life in Our Day*, p. 9.
67. *Pastoral Constitution on the Church*, no. 51; *On the Regulation of Birth*, no. 10; *Human Life in Our Day*, p. 9; *On the Family*, nos. 28, 35.
68. *Here to Stay: American Families in the Twentieth Century*, by Mary Jo Bane (New York: Basic Books, Inc., 1976), pp. 3-20; "Three's a Crowd," *Newsweek* (September 1, 1986): 68-76.
69. *On the Family*, no. 14.
70. "Three's a Crowd."
71. *Pastoral Constitution on the Church*, no. 50; *On the Family*, no. 30.
72. Ibid., no. 50; and no. 33.
73. *Pastoral Constitution on the Church*, no. 50; *Human Life in Our Day*, pp. 9-10.

humble before our God, who is the ultimate source of life.[74]

Mutual. Marital love, meant to be fully human, binds spouses together in such a way that they possess "one only heart and one only soul." As a total or very special form of personal friendship, it also leads husband and wife to share everything generously, without undue reservations or selfish calculations. The decision about children, therefore, must be a prayerfully talked through and mutually agreed upon judgment or choice.[75]

Church-guided. The Council bishops, while stressing the couple's conscience as the ultimate source of judgment on this issue, at the same time explained that their consciences "ought to be conformed to the law of God in the light of the teaching authority of the Church, which is the authentic interpreter of divine law."[76]

PRACTICING RESPONSIBLE PARENTHOOD

The married couple who have, through a proper conscience judgment, decided upon a course of avoiding a new birth for the time being, or even for an indeterminate period, then face the final question or issue: What family planning method are we going to follow in carrying out this decision?

The Church has offered and continues to offer clear, challenging, and prophetic—even if controversial—guidance to the husband and wife who are struggling with that sensitive and often difficult issue. It teaches that the act of sexual intercourse has two meanings, which cannot be separated: the unitive meaning, by which the love of a couple is symbolized, sustained, and strengthened; and the procreative meaning, by which the couple open themselves to the possibility of cooperating with God in the creation of a new person. Since these two meanings of the act cannot be separated without undercutting God's design of human sexuality and undermining the total, reciprocal self-giving between spouses, the Church states that "each and every marriage act must remain open to the transmission of new life." As a consequence, it approves natural family planning and rejects as immoral various forms of contraception.[77]

NATURAL FAMILY PLANNING

In natural family planning, the couple understands, accepts, and uses their God-given phases of fertility and infertility for the purpose of achieving or avoiding pregnancy. In this way, the unitive and procreative, the love and life meanings of sexual intercourse are maintained together in a responsible way.[78]

The Church considers this a "legitimate use of a natural disposition."[79] When the couple follow this procedure they "respect the inseparable connection between the unitive and procreative meanings of human sexuality, act as ministers of God's plan, and

benefit from their sexuality according to the original dynamism of total self-giving, without manipulation or alteration."[80]

Natural Family Planning (NFP) began with the discovery, in the late 1920s, that ovulation (release of the egg) preceded the onset of menstruation by a relatively constant number of days, rather than following after menstruation by any predictable or consistent number of days. The intervening decades have seen considerable development in our ability to offer couples a morally acceptable method that works, is livable, and has further side-benefits to marriage.

The history of natural methods can be briefly described by the following:

Rhythm or Calendar Rhythm (1930 on) attempted to predict fertile and infertile days for the current cycle on the basis of the variation in lengths of previous cycles. Such an approach can be effective and comfortable when cycles are quite regular in length. However, its calculations, of course, result in a method-defined fertile time considerably extended beyond what is physiologically necessary when cycles are quite irregular or when cycling is just beginning to resume or to fade away as in postpartum and premenopause, respectively.

Temperature or Temperature Rhythm (late-1930s on) allowed couples to dispense with Calendar Rhythm's "late safe days" calculation, because the sustained rise in temperature to a higher level around the time of ovulation signaled the onset of the postovulatory infertile time. The action of the hormone progesterone, associated with ovulation and the postovulatory phase, causes this rise, observable when a woman takes her "basal body temperature" ("waking temperature") daily. Couples using the Temperature Method were still using a Calendar Rhythm calculation for the preovulatory "early safe days" of the cycle.

Mucus Method (1970s on). In the late-1940s and early-1950s, several physicians on three different continents began to notice and counsel couples on the significance of a special fertile-time mucus secretion from the cervix. Infertility specialists had long told patients to watch for the development of this mucus symptom in order to identify the best time to

74. *Human Life in Our Day,* p. 6.
75. *On the Regulation of Birth,* nos. 8-9.
76. *Pastoral Constitution on the Church,* no. 51.
77. *On the Regulation of Birth,* nos. 10-12; *On the Family,* nos. 29-32.
78. *On the Family,* nos. 11, 32.
79. *On the Regulation of Birth,* no. 16. *A Positive Vision for Family Life,* USCC Commission on Marriage and Family Life (Washington, D.C.: USCC Office of Publishing and Promotion Services, 1985), pp. 11-14, with excerpts from *On the Family* and reflective questions for a dialogue, which could prove helpful to couples and those in the ministry of preparing people for marriage on this topic of responsible childbearing and childrearing.
80. *On the Family,* no. 32. For a more extensive treatment of the Church's teaching on NFP, see *A Theological Perspective on Natural Family Planning,* by J. McHugh (South Orange, N.J.: Diocesan Development Program for NFP, Seton Hall University).

conceive. But they had not thought to reverse the insight: that normally fertile couples could watch for the coming and going of this phenomenon in order to identify the beginning and end of the fertile time. The action of the hormone estrogen, associated with the preparation of the body for ovulation, causes this developing mucus symptom. This method allowed couples to do away with the Calendar Rhythm "early safe days" calculation and also to have a marker during extended preovulatory phases such as postpartum and, in some cases, in premenopause.

Sympto-Thermal Method (1950s on). As more and more became known about the mucus symptom, those who taught Temperature Rhythm began to incorporate information about mucus, and other estrogen- and progesterone-related symptoms, such as changes in the cervix itself, intermenstrual pain, and breast tenderness, into their teaching. Sympto-Thermal Method is a "multiple-index" approach in which the end of the mucus symptom and the temperature rise confirm each other in signaling the start of the postovulatory infertile time; and during the first part of the cycle, the couple may use a calendar calculation, or rely upon the start of the mucus symptom or a change at the cervix, whichever they prefer, as their marker for the start of the fertile time.

In Summary. Modern developments in NFP essentially have made Calendar Rhythm obsolete. Unfortunately, the unhappy legacy of some from the Calendar Rhythm era has prejudiced an older generation's perceptions. And even "professional" literature often enough betrays an embarrassing ignorance of current developments and distinctions. Young couples come for marriage unaware of modern NFP, often naively taking contraception for granted, and then, if they are lucky enough to hear about NFP, they find themselves ridiculed by relatives and perhaps by their physician. The Church, encouraged by new developments, and aware of the deeper values at stake, is a critical resource for the engaged and already married to help them obtain good NFP instruction in the spirit of Christ's call. As John Paul II told participants on January 15, 1981, at the First Congress for the Family of Africa and Europe, held in Rome:

> Your task will never be reduced to a question of presenting one or other biological method, much less to any watering down of the challenging call of the infinite God. Rather, your task is, in view of the situation of each couple, to see which method or combination of methods best helps them to respond as they ought to the demands of God's call.

At another meeting in Rome, July 3, 1982, the Holy Father reminded the participants:

> Since the conditions of couples are so diverse due to diverse cultures, races, personal situations, etc., it is providential that diverse methods exist, capable of better responding to such diverse situations.

We now speak in terms of "fertile" days instead of "unsafe" days and in terms of "infertile" days instead of "safe" days. We know that "natural" family planning is no longer synonymous with "Calendar Rhythm." But our culture does not. How can we help couples see the vision?

SUPPORTIVE REASONS FOR NATURAL FAMILY PLANNING

The following reasons may help pastoral leaders and ministers in their task of encouraging natural family planning and of overcoming the apparent considerable reluctance on the part of couples about to marry or already married to learn about and actually practice a natural method of birth regulation.

Natural family planning:

Is comparably effective and much healthier than artificial forms of contraception. The table below confirms both points. The effectiveness rate should reassure hesitant couples. The freedom from side effects and the naturalness of the method could be powerful motivational factors for many who share contemporary concerns about any tampering with their bodily functions or any ingestion of toxic elements. (See table on page 43.)[81]

Has an holistic sexual approach and orientation. This method recognizes that a sound sexuality and truly satisfying sexual expressions of love involve the total person. The entire body—including, and perhaps especially, the brain—and not only the specifically genital organs must be engaged for the fully human linking of a man and a woman. Natural family planning, as a result, supports and enhances the notion that we are controllable as persons, able to govern ourselves by clear reason. It helps strengthen our conviction that we can avoid a slavery that feels powerless before intense and sometimes unruly compulsions. Furthermore, this method aids in sensitizing participants to the multiple female and male components that together comprise the whole person.

Leads to a greater awareness of each other's bodies. This method requires that husband and wife develop an informed, very specific knowledge of their cyclic fertility and infertility and of all the signs that indicate these stages. The couple thus become much more conscious of their bodies' marvelous natures.

Fosters intimate communication between spouses on a vital subject and encourages the development of diverse, creative ways of expressing affection. Natural family planning methods involve both spouses, not just one partner, for effectiveness. In

---

81. This table is part of a 1987 flier/chart published by Saint Francis Hospital, 6161 So. Yale, Tulsa, OK 74136.

Artificial Methods of Contraception

Methods	Possible Side Effects	Effectiveness	
BARRIER METHODS *(act as contraceptives*)*		**METHOD**	
Condom	Condoms, diaphragms and sponges may cause allergic reactions.	Condom	97%
Diaphragm		Diaphragm (with spermicide)	97%
Sponge	Use of the sponge may contribute to Toxic Shock Syndrome	Sponge (with spermicide)	97%
VAGINAL SPERMICIDES *(act as contraceptives)*	Spermicidal agents may cause:	Spermicide	97%
Creams	1. Allergic reactions		
Jellies	2. Bladder infection		
	3. Congenital abnormalities		
Suppositories			
STERILIZATION SURGERIES *(act as contraceptives)*	Tubal ligations are associated with:	Tubal Ligation	99.96%
Tubal Ligation	1. Increased rate of hysterectomy		
Hysterectomy	2. Ectopic pregnancy		
Vasectomy	A vasectomy may cause:	Vasectomy	99.85%
	1. Impotence		
	2. Circulatory problems		
	3. Arthritis		
INTRAUTERINE DEVICE (IUD) *(act as abortifacient**)*	Use of Intrauterine Device (IUD) may cause:	Intrauterine Device	98%
IUD	1. Painful intercourse		
	2. Severe cramping with menstruation		
	3. Heavy menstrual bleeding		
	4. Irregular genital bleeding		
	5. Anemia		
	6. Pelvic inflammatory disease		
	7. Ectopic pregnancy		
	8. Perforation of the uterus		
	9. Infertility		

BIRTH CONTROL PILLS

(may act as contraceptive by suppressing ovulation or altering mucus therefore interfering with sperm penetration or may act as an abortifacient by altering lining tissue of uterus and interfering with implantation)

	Use of the birth control pills has been associated with:	Birth Control Pill	99.6%
Combination Pill *(contains both progesterone and estrogen)*	1. Breast tenderness 12. Loss of vision		
	2. Depression 13. Increased risk of some cancers		
	3. Weight gain		
	4. Inflammation of bladder 14. Liver tumor		
Mini-Pill *(contains progesterone only)*	5. Headaches 15. Congenital abnormalities (heart and limb defects)		
	6. Allergic reactions		
	7. Nausea & vomiting 16. Gallbladder disease		
	8. Decrease in glucose tolerance 17. Elevated blood pressure		
	18. Heart attack		
	9. Irregular genital bleeding 19. Stroke		
	10. Benign breast disease 20. Ectopic pregnancy		
	11. Circulatory disease 21. Infertility		

*contraception-prevents union of sperm and egg
**abortifacient-agent or device that may act to cause an abortion by interfering with or preventing implantation

The Ovulation Method, taught according to the Creighton University Model, has no medical side effects, won't harm fertility, can be used by anyone and is 99.6% effective as a method. The responsibility for using the method is shared by both the man and woman, and the 30-year cost of using the Ovulation Method is $590.

addition, the enhanced awareness and close communication resulting from the practice of this system enables husband and wife to see their love manifested in countless tender, but nongenital, expressions.

Cultivates that type of discipline that both brings joy or satisfaction and simultaneously assists spouses in coping with life's challenges. In a society that emphasizes self-fulfillment instead of self-denial, instant gratification rather than postponement of immediate pleasure for long-term goals, the discipline demanded for natural family planning may appear unappealing, unwise, or unattainable. Yet, couples who learn natural family planning methods and are reasonably motivated attest to their satisfaction with these methods and attest further that use of NFP is consistent with a satisfying marriage relationship. Moreover, Jesus teaches us the paradox of finding peace and contentment from taking up our cross and dying to ourselves. In the words of a contemporary popular author, "Discipline is the basic set of tools we require to solve life's problems. Without discipline we can solve nothing."[82]

PERSONAL TESTIMONIES

Official church teaching and abstract supportive reasons may encourage some persons to investigate and adopt natural family planning. However, the living witness of wives and husbands who follow this method and who can speak about its positive value for their married life will be the truly influential factor for most people. This represents a real ministry of like to like.[83]

Here are two such examples, which may prove useful to those engaged in marriage preparation efforts.

A wife from New York state, married at twenty-four, and her twenty-eight year-old husband decided to postpone having a child for a period of time. They practiced natural family planning for over three years, first to monitor the fertile cycle to avoid pregnancy, and then to use the fertile cycle to conceive their first child. Today, they have three children, continue to follow natural family planning, and teach the method to others. She writes:

> With all methods of contraceptives there are side effects that are generally considered to be harmful. *Natural Family Planning* is the exception to that premise. Its side effects are beneficial to the individual and to the couple. My husband and I began using the Sympto-Thermal method of NFP in the first few months of our marriage. It has become more than a totally safe, healthy, and reliable method of birth regulation to us. The essential qualities of self-restraint, self-discipline, mutual respect, and shared responsibility carry over to all facets of our marriage, making our relationship more intimate.

But as in all facets of life, including marriage, the practice of NFP has involved challenges and difficulties.

The first difficulty that my husband and I experienced as we began using NFP was the dismissal of the method by many of our friends, family members, and my gynecologists as being the same as using no method. Friends and family either recounted the story of someone who used "rhythm" and had large families or wanted to take bets on when or how soon we would have an "accidental" birth. My gynecologists seemed to have limited information about the high degree of reliability of NFP. They indicated that they would be comfortable with our decision to use the method to space our children, but really challenged us about what our commitment to NFP would be when we had all of the children we desired. We found this lack of support from so many sides quite disheartening. However, since NFP is a cooperative method of birth regulation, we had each other to bolster our commitment.

The second difficulty occurred during the time I was nursing our children. I have totally breast fed (with no supplements or pacifiers) each of our three children. This decision was made by us because it was the natural, superior nourishment for babies and is in tune with our reasons for using NFP. Because breast feeding by itself does not assure infertility, we relied on NFP during the years of nursing. The abstinence required during normal cycles (when not breast feeding) never presented a problem for us.

However, while breast feeding, the "cycle" really becomes one long "extended cycle" that can last for many months without the periodic reassurance of the temperature rise and menstrual bleeding. The danger is that one never knows when fertility will return and, when it does, what you will experience first—menstrual bleeding followed by ovulation or the reverse. The guidelines we follow, "when in doubt—abstain" and restriction of intercourse to alternate dry days, does limit the opportunity for intercourse to a greater extent. We found that to be a difficult time for us and looked forward to the resumption of normal ovulatory cycles.

---

82. *The Road Less Traveled*, p. 15. See also the summary of a nationwide study of couples using NFP, regarding their ability to understand and practice the methods, their satisfaction with NFP, and its positive implications for the marriage relationship. Available from Diocesan Development Program for NFP, Seton Hall University, South Orange, NJ 07079.

83. *On the Family*, no. 35; *On the Regulation of Birth*, no. 26.

Once again, what sustains our commitment to NFP and our desire to breast feed ecologically our children is that the two of us can talk about this as being a hardship. We know that the inconvenience is temporary and that the rewards are tremendous.

As for myself, I have learned so much about my own fertility with its physical, psychological, and emotional effect upon who I am that it has led to greater personal growth. I am not in any way harming my life-giving ability, which God has granted me.

A husband from Texas describes his experience with natural family planning in these words:

My experience of marital sexuality has been a mixture of pain and redemption. The pain comes, in part, from the natural struggle of two lovers to "tune in" to each other's needs. It also comes from my own immaturity, and some unrealistic expectations and assumptions. . . ."

My wife once told me that she might not have married me if I had insisted on a chemical form of family planning. That's tough love! She was concerned with her personal integrity and the interpersonal dynamics of our relationship. She had been charting her natural signs of fertility for over two years. For her to take full responsibility for our fertility would have been to compromise her self-gift. It took me several years to realize the meaning of this. I now view her concern as redemptive love. In other words, she taught me something important about what it means to give and accept each other in marriage.

Living a Natural Family Planning (NFP) life style has not always been easy. I am not speaking of fear of "unplanned pregnancy." I am speaking of continence, that is, refraining from intercourse during the fertile phases of our cycle when intending to postpone conception.

Some criticize abstinence or continence as unnatural and thus view NFP as too difficult. I think the difficulty lies in what continence can reveal. I discovered that I had placed more emphasis on genital intimacy than relational intimacy. Besides providing us with the possibility of invoking new life, sexual intercourse (genital intimacy) celebrates relational intimacy. In and of itself, sex does not create marital intimacy. In fact, sometimes sex isn't very intimate. I have found this to be true most often when we are not *relationally* intimate. Using a chemical or a mechanical contraceptive would represent another kind of intimacy barrier we do not need or want.

However, I do not find the periodic physical or relational tension created by continence to be the most critical aspect of NFP. Periodic genital continence reminds me that I have to attempt to gratify the relational needs of our marriage. I have to make a deliberate, reflective effort to continue to maintain the quality of our relationship regardless of when we have sex.

This experience of learning and living NFP has caused me to reflect on myself as a rather typical, twentieth-century American male. While it is natural for persons to yearn for intimacy and affection, I do not believe I was socialized to be relationally intimate. Stereotypically, men have been raised to be analytical, detached, and performance oriented. In a way, becoming relationally intimate with my wife has been "unnatural" for me. Thus, I think men have to learn to be intimate beyond the genital expression of marital love. It is *this* learning process, not continence, which I believe is unnatural, and perhaps is what can make living NFP difficult for some couples. In my own struggle, I have had to become more emotionally intimate and more vulnerable—two qualities that most women want in their relationship with their spouse.

Continence does me a favor. It provides me with a "rhythmic" opportunity to make sure it is love and intimacy, not sex, which bind me to my wife. This is why I see NFP as being nonchauvinistic, for husband and wife both mutually have to make it work. The periodic tension that sometimes comes with continence means we frequently examine our relationship, our needs, our communication, and the quality of our intimacy and affection. I am very thankful to have a spouse who loves me and herself enough to demand that I love her in a way that Christian marriage requires.

Thus, fertility acceptance (NFP) not only reminds me of our interpersonal, procreative potential but is a constant reminder that genital intimacy falls in the context of relational intimacy. As a male, that is extremely important, given my natural tendency to overemphasize the quality of the genital relationship.

Can I promise anything beneficial for persons considering or choosing NFP? Yes, depending on the quality of their relationship. NFP has helped me mature, though I have a long way to go. NFP has challenged me to question my assumptions about woman as mate and lover and begin to appreciate the "feminine" aspects of myself. It has taught me about the beauty of the female menstrual cycle. It has called me to cherish my wife rather than simply desire her. I have come to see that fertility is precious. NFP has taught me that fertility is an integral, interpersonal power to invoke new life and participate in the creativity of God. NFP has challenged me to accept and revere our fertility as we have found it and therefore accept the gift of each other in Christian marriage.[84]

TWO CONTEMPORARY CHALLENGES: COURAGE AND COMPASSION

Courage

Pope Paul VI, in his encyclical *On the Regulation of Birth* (1968), projected that "this teaching will perhaps not be easily received by all."[85] Today, two decades later, various phenomena indicate how that predication unfortunately has come true, at least in the United States.

A 1982 national survey reveals just how many Americans actually practice some form of artificial birth control. The number stood then at 19,187,000, an increase of over half a million from the time the first study was conducted in 1973. A percentage breakdown of the actual method selected follows below:

Sterilization	41.0%
Pill	19.8%
IUD	7.1%
Barrier (Diaphragm, Condom, Foam)	24.0%
Withdrawal	1.7%
Douche	0.2%
Other	1.5%

Only 4.7% of the users responded that they follow natural family planning or periodic abstinence.[86]

Moreover, that survey does not include any figures on the number of abortions performed yearly in this country, a means of birth control or family planning to which some regrettably resort.

As widespread as is the practice of methods contrary to the Church's teaching, equally commonplace is the attitude of many who simply disagree with the principles proclaimed by Pope Paul VI. Failure to observe this teaching because of human weakness in the face of difficult circumstances is one situation; mental rejection of the concepts is quite another.

This attitudinal disagreement might be expected, or at least not surprising, among those who are not members of the Church. However, there is considerable evidence that significant numbers of Roman Catholics in the United States also reject official church teaching on this matter.[87]

The fulfillment, in our day, of Pope Paul VI's projection or prediction—this practical and theoretical rejection of the Church's teaching by many—makes difficult the educational and formational task of those involved in the remote, proximate, and immediate aspects of marriage preparation. They need great courage to speak the truth with humble, but firm conviction. At the same time, they must possess a sensitive awareness of the often complex and trying conditions that make couples waver in their fidelity to the Church's teaching, or even question its validity.[88]

Compassion

If the widespread disapproval of the Church's teaching calls for much courage in persons who teach or prepare couples for marriage, it even more presupposes a deep compassion within those who counsel people about to marry or, more particularly, couples already married.

Both Pope Paul VI and Pope John Paul II acknowledged the "often very arduous" situations that leave couples "at times truly tormented by difficulties of every kind." Consequently, they counsel priests to show "patience and goodness"; to echo the "voice and the love of the Redeemer"; to encourage couples to have faith; to urge prayer and trust; and to advise couples frequently to approach the sacraments of the Eucharist and reconciliation or penance. Above all, priests must never allow the husband and wife to "be discouraged by their own weakness."[89]

From their own contact with couples, especially with those married during the 1960s and 1970s, pastoral ministers attest to often perplexing and agonizing struggles that husbands and wives went through as they sought to be faithful to the Church's teaching and yet fulfill their own human needs or responsibilities.

We hope, especially in the sacrament of reconciliation or penance, that confessors will ever manifest the gentleness and understanding of Christ, who came not to condemn but to save and was intransigent with evil, but merciful with individuals.[90] While faithfully upholding the Church's teaching on the objective evil of artificial contraception, they need constantly to recall, especially in our confused times, that circumstances may reduce moral guilt and that

---

84. *Family Planning*, by Charles Balsam (Liguori Publications, 1986), rev. ed., pp. 25-28, with modifications by the author.

85. *On the Regulation of Birth*, no. 18.

86. *National Survey of Family Growth* (1982), as quoted by Nona Aguilar, in "Family Planning," *Twin Circle* 22:16 (April 20, 1986): 11.

87. See *American Catholics since the Council*, ch. 5, pp. 80-100; 1986 Survey by Northeast Catholic Pastoral Center for Hispanics, as reported in "Hispanic Catholics: Most Disagree with Church on Birth Control," *New York Daily News* (February 8, 1986); "Rome Birth Control Ban Barren," editorial in *National Catholic Reporter* (May 9, 1986); "From the Council to the Synod," by Mary Durkin and Judi Loesch, in *Commonweal* (October 18, 1985): 560-561, 572-574; *Pastoral Life* (September 1986): 49-50; "Religion and Fertility in the United States: The Importance of Marriage Patterns and Hispanic Origin," by W. Mosher, D. Johnson and M. Horn, in *Demography* 23:3 (August 1986); and *Statement on the Twentieth Anniversary of Humanae Vitae*, NCCB Committee for Pro-Life Activities (Washington, D.C.: USCC Office of Publishing and Promotion Services, 1988).

88. *On the Regulation of Birth*, nos. 27-30; *On the Family*, no. 33.

89. Ibid.

90. *On the Regulation of Birth*, no. 29.

actions objectively wrong may be inculpable, diminished in guilt, or subjectively defensible.[91]

Confessors and spiritual guides, in the words of Pope John Paul II, should encourage married couples in the midst of any difficulties to have persistence and patience, humility and strength of mind, childlike trust in God and God's grace, as well as constant recourse to prayer. Moreover, the Holy Father urges spouses frequently to receive the sacraments of the Eucharist and reconciliation.

Thus strengthened, he teaches, "Christian husbands and wives will be able to keep alive their awareness of the unique influence that the grace of the sacrament of marriage has on every aspect of married life including, therefore, their sexuality."[92]

SOME RECOMMENDATIONS

- We praise, in a particular way, couples who are sharing their experiences of natural family planning with others preparing for or already married, and we salute those who are teaching this method of responsible parenthood. This is a unique, predominantly "like-to-like" ministry in the Church today, and persons engaged in instructing others in NFP deserve every possible support in that vital task.[93]

- We urge that in each formal premarriage program, a presentation on *Natural Family Planning* and fertility appreciation be included as an integral, not an optional, part of the schedule. This segment, after establishing the awesomeness of both female and male fertility, should contain a simple explanation of natural family planning, its comparable effectiveness, the contribution it can make to a couple's relational growth, testimony by couples practicing this method, and information about available instruction resources. A personal presentation by a couple is preferred, but if this is not possible, a film or videocassette can be employed to communicate the data and motivation.

- Indeed, given current cultural conditioning and the fact that virtually all couples begin marriage using some form of family planning, we urge that premarriage programs require a full course of instruction in natural family planning as a necessary component in the couple's effective realization of what they need and have a right to know in order to live in accord with the clear teaching of the Church. NFP instructors often note a change in perception among those required to learn NFP prior to marriage: "We would never have taken this course if it had not been required; but now we're glad we did."

- We encourage Catholic school and religious education leaders to develop a system whereby not only the methods of natural family planning but, even more fundamentally, the principles of sexuality underlying it can be taught in repeated, understandable fashion throughout our children's formative years. Such an incremental approach should build gradually within young people a greater openness to the concept so that when a couple begins actively to prepare for marriage they will be more disposed to hear the word of God and keep it.[94]

- We support strongly the efforts of scientific research to perfect ways for determining the rhythm, pattern, or phases of fertility and infertility in human reproduction. We also applaud philosophical/theological study or reflection to illustrate more clearly the biblical foundations, the ethical grounds, healthy bases, and personalist reasons behind the Church's teaching on the responsible transmission of life.[95]

- We advocate that governmental and community agencies engaged in family planning services encourage natural family planning and devote significant budget to its promotion.[96] This might serve as an initial step in reducing some of the deep differences and acrimonious frictions that have arisen between these agencies and those who object to their present philosophy or activities.

6 Teenage Marriages and Pregnancy before Marriage

The marriages of couples in their teens have a high fatality rate. Teenage marriages are twice as likely to end in divorce as marriages that occur in the twenties.[97] As might be expected, the percentage of separation and ultimate divorce for couples in their teens when a pregnancy also exists at the time of the marriage is even higher. For these reasons, many dioceses

---

91. *Human Life in Our Day*, pp. 16, 12.
92. *On the Family*, no. 33.
93. Ibid., no. 35; *On the Regulation of Birth*, no. 26.
94. *On the Family*, nos. 36-41.
95. Ibid., no. 31.
96. Detailed information about NFP resources can be secured from diocesan family life offices or the Diocesan Development Program for Natural Family Planning.
97. Cf. "Marriage Policy" (The Diocese of Cleveland, April 3, 1988), p. 15 and footnote 19.

have policies with special regulations governing teenage marriages or marriages when the bride is pregnant.[98]

Experience indicates that these are difficult pastoral situations because both parents and the couple frequently refuse to believe the hard statistical facts available or judge that their case will be the exception. A diocesan policy and process, although it should still remain flexible, can be of great assistance to pastors or pastoral ministers who must deal directly with the individuals involved.

With regard to a *teenage marriage,* besides adhering to local policies or regulations, pastors and/or parish ministers might consider these observations:

- *They should exert great care in trying to gain the confidence of the couple and to look upon their love in a positive way.* It is important not to ridicule their age, but instead, to give serious consideration to their intentions. The young couple should understand that marriage is a lifelong relationship and that the Church and her ministers do not mean to create difficulties, but rather to assure that their nuptial union will be lasting or possibly to protect them from irreparable mistakes.[99]

- *They should endeavor to establish a dialogue not only with the couple, but also with the parents in order to ascertain the strength of the commitment.* Young people frequently enter marriage as an escape from other circumstances of their lives. Efforts thus should be made to dissuade the youthful couple from marriage, at least at this time.[100]

With regard to *pregnancy before marriage,* pastors and/or parish ministers might, likewise, reflect upon these considerations:

- *Marriage is not an appropriate solution to premarital pregnancy in cases of a totally immature couple with no prospect for success in entering the sacrament.* Nor can it be considered an appropriate solution for a couple who did not intend or plan to be married. Neither is it a solution to a young couple, still dating but testing as to which person they may want to select for marriage; nor to a young couple, still dating, testing whether they are appropriate mates for marriage. Marriage is possibly an acceptable option for those who consider themselves engaged and for whom a proper marriage commitment may already have taken place.[101]

- *Use of one of the instruments or inventories designed to facilitate dialogue between*

a couple intending to marry would be especially helpful in these delicate circumstances. The three instruments commonly employed throughout the country, and described later in this handbook, should certainly prove satisfactory. Some dioceses, moreover, have developed their own local versions for such a purpose.

- *Since the cases involving pregnancies are especially difficult to handle, the couple should be advised to undertake professional counseling.* The reasons for the pregnancy should be examined, as well as the seriousness of the commitment between the individuals.[102]

- *The parents should be asked to assist in the discernment process as they will be of assistance in determining some of the background for the pregnancy, as well as the quality of the relationship between the couple.*[103]

Marriage, therefore, is not a magic solution to premarital pregnancy. Most marriages to "give the baby a name" end in divorce. Appropriate alternatives other than marriage should be considered carefully.[104]

When the pregnant person is a teenager, the potential for difficulties in the future marriage is particularly acute. But those risks also exist for individuals who are older, pregnant, and wish to marry. Pastors and pastoral ministers need to stress that there are other noble solutions to the pregnancy besides marriage, and they need to help the couple to make as free and informed a choice as possible in resolving their circumstance. If marriage is not chosen, the male partner should be reminded of his continued moral responsibility to offer support of various kinds in this matter.

 Alienation and Reconciliation

Many of the issues we have covered up to this point in the handbook indicate clearly just how often people who are preparing for marriage carry with them the burden of alienation. They may, for example, be children of divorced parents, possess a conscious or unconscious mistrust or resentment of any authority person, disagree with the Church's teachings on sex-

98. *Preparing for Marriage: A Study of Marriage Preparations in American Catholic Dioceses* (St. Meinrad, Ind.: Abbey Press, 1983), p. 30.
99. "Marriage Policy," p. 15 and footnote 20.
100. Ibid.
101. Ibid.
102. Ibid.
103. Ibid.
104. Ibid.

uality, or experience great fear and anger because of a premarital pregnancy.

Those persons who are seriously alienated in any way will have great difficulty in sustaining or deepening the marital relationship. Those, on the other hand, who have worked through such ruptures, whose wounds have been healed, even if scars may remain, who have experienced some type of reconciliation, are in a better position to sustain and deepen the marital relationship.

While the word *alienation* by itself may not suggest intense personal pain to many people, a brief description of its practical meaning or application will quickly reveal to all one of our current culture's greatest challenges.

Asking a group of people to reflect silently for a moment upon someone who, in the recent past, has exercised power over them in a presumably inappropriate manner, and then inviting these persons to share how they felt or feel about the incident will surface these typical responses: I felt "angry," "used," "powerless," "humiliated," "run over," "degraded," "distanced."

Those real experiences teach us that alienation results in a distancing between persons, which can cause or lead to pain, emptiness, sorrow, and even open hostility. *Reconciliation*, on the contrary, produces a closeness between people, which can cause or lead to pleasure, the fullness of peace, joy, and a loving concern for one another or others.

In this section, we want to identify three major alienations in contemporary society—from God, from others, from ourselves—and suggest ways that church leaders can facilitate reconciliation in all those areas.

ALIENATION FROM GOD

This type of alienation may arise from our own sinfulness or from confusion over bad things that have happened to us or to people we care about.

Sinfulness and Alienation

The Church, following the example and teaching of Christ, presents lofty and demanding ideals for its members. For example, the goals of chastity and fidelity, as well as the trust and discipline required for responsible parenting described earlier, fit into those categories. But, as Jesus warned his closest followers—and us: "Be on guard, and pray that you may not undergo the test. The spirit is willing, but the flesh is weak."[105] In that weakness, we may make a poor choice, yield to the immediate, and fail to follow our conscience. We call that choice, yielding, or failure, sin—in essence, the conscious and willing disregard of God's voice within us.

The guilt that flows from sin can be devastating. Unacknowledged and unexpiated, it can burrow deep inside, permeate the core of our being, and destroy our interior peace or serenity. In the words of one contemporary analyst, "Increasingly, it appears that the central fact in personality disorder is real guilt."[106]

The Church, however, never proposes Christian idealism without simultaneously proclaiming Christian compassion. It never tires of repeating that our God is "gracious and merciful . . . slow to anger, rich in kindness, and relenting in punishment."[107] It never stops recalling the deeds and words of Jesus, who welcomed sinners and ate with them, and who said there will be "more joy in heaven over one repentant sinner than over ninety-nine righteous people who have no need to repent."[108] It never ceases to urge and offer the virtue and sacrament of penance as a powerful instrument, giving God's peace to burdened sinners.

We wish to encourage the continuation and intensification of efforts by the clergy, pastoral staff, family life ministers, religious educators, and parents to present this message of compassion, especially in today's fractured world. Frequent preaching about God's mercy, convenient opportunities for the sacrament of penance, and positive teaching about forgiveness on various occasions (schools, religious education classes, parental preparation meetings) will help balance the high idealism of Jesus' words with the healing gentleness of his touch.

A mother expressed the joy of this sacramental reconciliation after a long absence, with these words:

> I had not been to the sacrament of penance in twelve years, the night of my wedding rehearsal. I felt as though I never "needed" it. But there I was, on that Wednesday evening, in line for confession. Afterwards, I felt as light as a feather. What a wonderful way to prepare for the season of Advent.

Disasters and Alienation

There seems to be a tendency for us immediately to raise issues or doubts about God when bad things happen to people, but not as swiftly to praise or credit God when good things occur in people's lives. However inconsistent this inclination may be, the fact remains that personal, local, national, or global tragedies frequently spur people to pose questions such as, "How could God let that happen?" or "Why did God take him?" or "If God is so good, can you explain why she has cancer?" Moreover, the anger frequently connected with death or any deep personal loss can become directed at God. The combination of unanswered questions and unresolved anger may cause, within the individual, a condition of alienation or distancing from the Lord.

105. Mt 26:41.
106. "The Decline of Private Guilt and the Need for Confession," by Donald DeMarco, in *Emmanuel* (February 1981): 99-106.
107. Jl 2:13.
108. Lk 15:1-10.

Simplistic solutions or swift answers to these profound issues generally are not very helpful. Those concerns touch upon the very ultimate mysteries of life and death, God and us—mysteries never fully to be grasped or comprehended here on earth, but only in the world yet to come.[109] Nevertheless, passages from Scripture, the teaching of the Church, and the example of suffering Christians can prove valuable in dealing with such disasters.

Perhaps, the overarching biblical text pertinent here is from Paul's letter to the Romans: "We know that all things work for good for those who love God, who are called according to his purpose."[110] God is always mysteriously, providentially watching over and directing our lives, turning tragedies, and even our own mistakes into something good for us.

Paul also tells us by his example and teaching that troubles of this sort have a value in building up the Church: "Now I rejoice in my suffering for your sake, and in my flesh I am filling up what is lacking in the afflictions of Christ on behalf of his body, which is the Church. . . ."[111]

The apostle, finally, reassures us, again by his example and words, that we will be able to endure and overcome any difficulty: "Three times I begged the Lord about this, that it might leave me, but he said to me, 'My grace is sufficient for you, for power is made perfect in weakness.' I will rather boast most gladly of weaknesses, in order that the power of Christ may dwell within me."[112]

The Church's official teaching reminds us, among other things, that our human burdens, setbacks, and hardships, united with the sufferings of Christ on the cross, are subsequently transformed and enable us to share in Jesus' work of saving the world.[113]

Suffering Christians, beginning with the Master himself, sustain us with insight and courage by their example and comments. Jesus does not explain the reasons for sufferings but simply tells us to expect them as his disciples: "If anyone wishes to come after me, he must deny himself and take up his cross daily and follow me."[114] That command to "follow me" naturally takes us to Calvary and Good Friday.

Pope John XXIII, eight decades old, afflicted with cancer, and burdened with leadership of the Church, is another Christian person who, by example and words, encourages us in our own troubles. Despite his weakened condition, that pope pushed himself to the limit one day and left the Vatican for an important ceremony that was finally to seal reconciliation between the Holy See and the Italian government. Back home, he felt drained of all strength, but recovered enough to watch television coverage of the event. He commented, then, on the contrast between the pope at the celebration and the pope confined to his rooms:

A few hours ago, I was being feted and complimented, and now I'm here alone with my pain. But that's all right. The first duty of a pope is to pray and suffer. . . . Out there the world exalts me, while here the Lord rivets me to this bed.

Several weeks later, about to be anointed with the sacrament of the sick, Pope John XXIII sat up in bed, clothed with surplice and a white stole. Even at that moment he preached and taught:

The secret of my ministry is in that crucifix you see opposite my bed. It's there so that I can see it in my first waking moment and before going to sleep. It's there, also, so that I can talk to it during the long evening hours. Look at it, see it as I see it. Those open arms have been the program of my pontificate: they say that Christ died for all, for all. No one is excluded from his love, from his forgiveness.[115]

ALIENATION FROM OTHERS

Probably, the most commonly experienced alienations are those big and little ruptures with people who have crossed our paths and form forever a small or large part of our lives. Given the wounded human condition and the imperfect world in which we dwell, none of us can ever totally escape from these distancings during a lifetime. If we reconcile, the gap closes and our hearts heal; if we do not reconcile, the chasm remains and our spirit lacks the profound, perfect peace we all crave.

These brief suggestions should help prevent some alienations and foster needed reconciliations:

Grow in sincere compassion; guard against excessive competition. Like Jesus, who, the gospels tell us, was often moved with compassion or pity, we are called as Christians to enter into solidarity with others, to rejoice with those who rejoice, to weep with those who weep.[116] Yet, in our culture, fierce competition, rather than deep compassion, dominates our lives. Our self-esteem generally depends upon negative or positive comparisons or distinctions made between ourselves and others. Are we more or less this or that depends upon those with whom we are compared or those with whom we

109. For a profound treatment of this issue, see *On the Christian Meaning of Human Suffering*, apostolic letter of John Paul II (Washington, D.C.: USCC Office of Publishing and Promotion Services, 1984). For a popular discussion of the matter, see *Healing in the Catholic Church*, by Joseph M. Champlin (Huntington, Ind.: Our Sunday Visitor Press, 1985).
110. Rom 8:28.
111. Col 1:24.
112. 2 Cor 12:8-9
113. *On the Christian Meaning of Human Suffering*, art. 26.
114. Lk 9:23.
115. *Pope John XXIII*, by Peter Hebblethwaite (Garden City, N.Y.: Doubleday and Company, Inc., 1985), pp. 494, 501.
116. See, for example, Mt 9:36; Mt 14:14; Mk 8:2; Mt 9:27; Mk 1:41; Lk 7:13.

compete. This excessively, but all pervasive, competitive spirit can block us from being sincerely compassionate.[117]

Recognize with joy others' gifts. The world can be viewed as a massive pie capable, however, of being cut into only a limited number of pieces. Consequently, if you have a piece of it, a particular gift or talent, I necessarily possess less. This can make me sad, jealous, or envious; conversely, your loss or failure may inwardly please me. More appropriately, the world can be viewed as a clear night sky brilliant with stars. Every star adds to the beauty of the night. Your gifts, in this approach, are like stars enhancing the sky, as do mine. That philosophy of gifts aids in reducing the competitive/comparative drive and in promoting a spirit of compassion.

Praise others frequently and specifically. Contemporary management or leadership manuals encourage executives to practice "positive reinforcement" and "one-minute praisings."[118] These systems of regular encouragement and thoughtful praise promote better working procedures in the business world, but they easily can and should be fostered in all our relationships. The key elements of this reinforcement and praising are doing so immediately, acting with sincerity, being very specific, and making the affirmations at unpredictable and intermittent moments.

Accept others. Probably the essential requirement for harmonious relationships—between spouses, family members, friends, colleagues—is the willingness and ability to accept people as they are, not as they should be nor as we want them to be.

Forgive and ask for forgiveness. Both Jesus on the cross and Stephen while being stoned asked God to forgive their assailants.[119] Christ was also very explicit: "If you do not forgive others, neither will your Father forgive your transgressions."[120]

All of us understand how difficult it is to forgive or to seek forgiveness. Saying, "I am sorry" or "I apologize" or, in the most profound fashion, "Please forgive me" are not attitudes and words that come easily to our hearts and lips. But without them, we never taste true peace.

The example of a Minneapolis woman may encourage those struggling to forgive others who have hurt them. A few years ago, her husband was shot and killed by three hitchhikers he had picked up.

At the funeral in the Lutheran Church, one son, a ministerial student, asked for their friends' and society's forgiveness of the three who murdered their father and husband. Later in the evening, after the burial, the wife and mother wanted to tell the three unapprehended young men that they were welcome in her home, if this was the kind of love they could understand and need. She finally wrote this "Open Letter to the Three Boys Who Murdered My Husband":

During the past three days, my grief and desolation have been eased and comforted by the love and faith of so many wonderful friends and relatives. But, in the midst of all this, and especially in the quiet moments, my thoughts keep turning to you three. You may feel that you are men, but to me you are just boys—like my own sons—and I wonder to whom you are turning for comfort and strength and reassurance.

I suppose I will never know what motivated your actions that night, but if the shots were fired out of sheer panic, my heart aches for you, and I wish there were only some way I could help you in what you must be suffering now.

If hate made you pull that trigger, I can only pray that you can come to know the love of God that fills the heart and leaves no room for hate. If you were under the influence of drugs, please, for my sake and your own, don't waste your lives, too. Get help and rid yourselves of that stuff.

Please, if you see this, find a church some place where you can be alone; then read this again. Know that God forgives you and that my family and I forgive you—then go out and make something worthwhile out of the rest of your lives.

God keep and bless you.[121]

ALIENATION FROM OURSELVES

Not caring deeply about ourselves seems to be both one of original sin's central impacts upon us and the root cause of much destructive behavior in our lives.

One of our members, in his ministry as a priest before being appointed bishop, found this to be true in his extensive work with youngsters caught up in the web of drug abuse or narcotics addiction and teenage girls pregnant out of wedlock.

These youth knew a great deal about the properties and effects of drugs, but regardless, they abused drugs as their way of coping with their own poor self-images or life's problems.

The teenage women followed a similar pattern. For example, Winnie was overweight and unhappy with herself. She desperately wanted to be loved and accepted. Any young man could hand her a line that

117. For a discussion of this point, see *Compassion*, by Donald P. McNeill, Douglas A. Morrison and Henri J. M. Nouwen (Garden City, N.Y.: Doubleday and Company, Inc., 1982), esp. pp. 16-20.
118. *In Search of Excellence*, by Thomas J. Peters and Robert H. Waterman, Jr. (New York: Warner Books, 1984), pp. 70-71; *The One-Minute Manager*, by Kenneth Blanchard, Ph.D., and Spencer Johnson, M.D. (New York: Berkley Books, 1985), pp. 36-45.
119. Lk 24:34; Acts 8:20.
120. Mt 6:15.
121. *A Path to Peace: Prayer, Fasting and Works of Charity*, by Joseph M. Champlin (Los Angeles: Franciscan Communications, 1983).

was good enough, only to leave her feeling terribly lonely the morning after. For her, birth control was out of the question; it only affirmed that part of herself she hated most.[122]

This deep-seated inclination to view ourselves poorly, with the subsequent hurtful behavior patterns that follow, as a consequence, finds fertile grounds in contemporary society with high divorce rates and abandoned children.

We noted earlier that very young children in troubled marriages tend to blame themselves for the conflict between their parents. The published personal account of such a girl and woman's tragic early years illustrates this point.

As a small child, she told her Cuddly Duddly, "It's all my fault my daddy and mommy don't love each other any more." During fierce battles between her parents prior to the breakup, she would reflect that the trouble surely was "all her fault" and that "she won't be the cause of their troubles any more." After the divorce, the little girl judged that the fact that mother and father never came to visit or take her back "could be only because she was bad. Mommy and Daddy had sent her away because she was a bad girl."[123]

The poor self-esteem engendered by these reflections created within her deep fears: fear of loss and fear of punishment; fear of being left, cut off; fear of being an extension of nothing; fear of being dead, killed, abandoned, alone, and unwanted.[124]

These dreadful fears gradually led her to two destructive activities: lying and promiscuity. She lied to avoid punishment and to be able to do what she wanted. "Elaborate lies, she found, sounded more truthful." She later also began experimenting sexually. She enjoyed the attention, never remembering from the past being hugged or touched or told she was loved. "Those sexual experiences gave me something to be good at, or at least that's what I told myself. And I felt sort of loved. Stupid, isn't it?"[125]

Those who are adopted can easily experience a similar questioning of their lovableness. While adoptive parents make a most praiseworthy loving choice from the beginning to adopt, and usually surround adopted ones with love, the adopted girl or boy, woman or man may sometimes ponder, "Who were my real parents?" "Why did they abandon me?" "How is it I was rejected by them?"

While these are perhaps more dramatic instances of situations or people involving poor self-esteem, the following few questions generally will reveal to most of us that we do not care deeply enough about ourselves and that our self-image needs strengthening:

- How well do I take compliments?

- Do I have a tendency to find fault with myself or my work? When I or my accom-

plishment is praised, do I point to something imperfect in me or the product?

- Is there a double standard within me? To qualify for a virtue, must there be a perfect performance on my part? To place a vice after my name, is one lapse, one poor choice, one mistake, one sin sufficient?

- Am I comfortable allowing people to love me? Or must I always be the lover, the giver, the doer?

- Do I tend to be excessively competitive or ambitious rather than genuinely compassionate and concerned?

- How often am I anxiously seeking reassurances or support from others?

- Am I preoccupied with pleasing others or fearful someone will not like me or what I am doing?

Recognizing this deeply rooted inclination to see ourselves poorly is actually the first step to healing that wound within us. The ultimate source or remedy for a poor self-image is to comprehend how God loves us in an unconditional way; to believe that we are unique creatures of this loving Maker; to grasp

122. "Finding Solutions to Teen Sexual Activity," by Most Rev. Howard J. Hubbard, in the Albany *Evangelist* (January 8, 1987).
123. *Forgive Me*, by Cathleen Crowell Webb and Marie Chaplan (Old Tappan, N.J.: Fleming H. Revell Company, 1985), pp. 13, 20, 22, 30, 32.
124. Ibid., pp. 32, 37, 48.
125. Ibid., pp. 53, 62, 74-75.

just how many gifts Yahweh has given us; and to accept Jesus' saving, forgiving, and sanctifying grace in our lives.

A religious priest, active in the preaching and healing ministry, suggests that those suffering significantly with negative self-concepts spend five minutes each day reflecting on scriptural passages that remind us of how unique we are in God's sight. For those who feel hurt or troubled by another's words or actions, he recommends that they also allocate another daily five minutes pondering God's unique love for that person. [126]

The following phrases from the prophet Isaiah can be especially helpful in that type of meditation. God speaks to the prophet and to us in these words: "Fear not, I have redeemed you; I have called you by name; you are mine. You are precious in my eyes and glorious . . . I love you."[127]

Aware of these contemporary alienations from God, others, and ourselves—understanding their root causes and knowing practical ways for bringing about needed reconciliations—is a major function of the proximate preparation for marriage. It must be carried on first and primarily in the family, at home, but it also should happen in the other settings and circumstances we will examine in the next and last part of this section.

 ## Teachable and Touchable Moments

We have examined many substantive issues that need to be treated at various times, on different levels, and in distinct ways during the remote and proximate marriage preparation periods. Obviously, religious education classes for both public and private school Catholic students are natural opportunities to cover them in repeated fashion over a period of years.

But there are numerous other unique occasions at which audiences of youth or adults, children or parents are particularly disposed to hear or to experience a message about God and God's relationships with us. These opportunities may be a birth or a death, a first communion or a wedding, a first penance or a confirmation, a *Quinceañera* celebration for a young girl or a personal tribulation in some extended family, a weekend retreat or a special Eucharist, a community celebration or a global tragedy.

These are potentially rich, religious opportunities. For the past few decades, generally, we have called them "teachable" moments because people on such occasions are frequently open to learn more about God, to grasp better with their heads the divine plan as it unfolds in their lives. But we would also term them "touchable" moments because people are, likewise, often anxious to experience God's presence in those significant circumstances, to grasp with their hearts, as well, the Creator's love manifested in their lives.

In the midst of those deeply positive or negative events, they want to understand the confusing developments, to express their joys, to share their sorrows, and to find strength for their struggles. They wish to reach out, as it were, and touch God and be touched by God at those crucial moments. They seek to establish contact with God and, by doing so, to gain divine insight and power to cope with these crises or turning points in their lives.

Astute pastoral leaders can capitalize upon those teachable and touchable occasions by integrating within them some of the pertinent notions we have outlined in these first two sections of the manual.

We ask that those pastoral leaders who are in direct contact with the Hispanic community be even more attentive to these touchable moments. We need your creativity and initiative. There are many fertile areas for pastoral action, some of which are Scriptural Circles, *Communidades Ecclesiales de Base*, Novena of *Rosarios* after the death of a family member, house blessings, the "churching" of women ceremony, fulfilling promises or *Mandas*, and *juramentos* or taking of oaths so as to change one's behavior.

A few of those opportunities or moments are as follows:

Parental preparation programs. Most parishes have, since the Second Vatican Council, developed fairly well-organized programs involving parents whose children are preparing or being prepared for baptism, first penance, first communion, and confirmation. While these sessions normally deal with the immediate matters at hand, other relational issues we have discussed in this manual could easily, and without contriving, be incorporated into the sessions.

For example, simple explanations and demonstrations of communication skills, the nature of intimate relationships, the growth of self-esteem, the very real concern of alienation or reconciliation, and proven techniques for encouraging chastity are vital issues for parents. As we have suggested, they should welcome help in these areas, and we urge the producers of parental preparation programs to develop creative methods of accomplishing this.

Sunday worship. Since this is the major occasion when the Church, including and especially families, gathers, it should not be overlooked as an opportunity to preach about and dramatize ideas we have explored in these sections. Occasional homilies, handouts, and bulletin blurbs or articles can proclaim these notions. Involvement of young people as readers, gift bearers, ushers, and greeters, as well as mention of or stories about them in the homily or prayer of the faithful, helps establish contact and moves our youth. Such integration, however, requires consid-

---

126. *The Healing Power of the Sacraments*, by Jim McManus, CSSR (Notre Dame: Ave Maria Press, 1984), pp. 42, 118-121.
127. Is 43:1,4.

erable advance planning, but the fruit yielded merits the effort.

Sunday worship for Hispanics is also a social gathering. They expect that there will be time for the community to socialize, and thus, it offers pastoral leaders an opportunity to establish direct contact with the Hispanic families. In this way, they can build friendships with their people, develop credibility as pastoral leaders, and discern the needs of the community. Generally, Hispanics do not make appointments. This time connected with Sunday worship is, thus, an opportunity to arrange such commitments for the rest of the week.

The wedding ceremony. The liturgical celebration and the homily, especially, may be more instructive for the guests present than for the couple being married. Their excitement and nervousness about the event often keeps them from anything but a superficial hearing of the words. Other participants, however, will normally pay strict attention to the homily and the ceremony if they are done well and speak to vital concerns for them. Affirming married couples for their heroism in being faithful during an age contrary to commitment and fidelity; rekindling their ideals and dreams; stressing the importance of love, communication, and forgiveness are ways of reaching others in addition to the bride and groom.

Anniversaries. Special events such as celebrations of twenty-fifth and fiftieth wedding anniversaries provide a natural occasion to address the ideals and concerns about marriage included in this handbook.

Campus ministry. Those engaged in ministry to collegians have unique opportunities and challenges before them in regard to the proximate or immediate preparation for marriage. With the young people's natural interest in these subjects and their general homogeneity as a group, the campus minister can influence them significantly and forge helpful relationships with them. At the same time, efforts, difficult as they may be, should be made to preserve and support their links with the parish back home. Some pastors have had success in attempting to maintain a newsletter or form letter connection several times yearly with young parishioners away at school. We strongly urge that close communication ties between parish and campus ministers be maintained.

Confirmation. In dioceses where confirmation is delayed until later in the teens, the preparation efforts provide exceptional opportunities for instruction and formation in all the notions we have described. This, for example, would be a nearly ideal situation in which to present natural family planning, with all its relational aspects and, as we have mentioned, to offer a process for vocational discernment.

Young adult ministry. Attention needs to be given to facilitating contact between young Catholics around the age of thirty or under. This may require something on the regional or diocesan level. Current experience indicates that many young people are attracted to specialized retreats and liturgies designed for them. Those liturgies, with socializing periods connected and opportunities provided for service to the needy, will usually attract young people and indirectly place them in contact with one another. These events and exchanges can provide valuable support to them and enable them to meet others of similar ideals. It is presently often difficult for such persons to discover suitable partners outside the "bar scene."[128]

Remote and proximate marriage preparation efforts somewhat directly, but more indirectly, set the stage for the joining of bride and groom in matrimony. We will now explore immediate marriage preparation, which explicitly concerns itself with them and with the sacrament.

---

128. There are programs available and in print to help with this ministry. One sample is *Matrimony—Jesus Invites Us to Love,* a program designed for teenagers as a vehicle to facilitate their thinking about marriage, commitment, values, and the role of Jesus and the Church in marriage. Available from Pastoral and Matrimonial Research Center, 67 Prince Street, Elizabeth, NJ 07208.

Section III: Immediate Preparation

"My experience has generally been that when a couple approaches me for marriage, they are largely unaware that there is any church preparation to do other than reserving the building and the priest for the rehearsal and the ceremony. The requirements to obtain baptismal certificates and affidavits of freedom, as well as to attend programs, weekends, or retreats are all perceived as a complicated 'hassle.' This is further compounded if a dispensation form must also be gone over. The couples are insulted when informed that the decision to marry will need to be evaluated by the Church, through use of an instrument or counselling. Even meeting with an already-married couple at the latter's home for dinner, Mass, and discussion on marital communication, sexuality, finances, and spirituality is viewed as a waste of time on topics that are unnecessary, since the engaged couple feels they are already so satisfied in those areas that they are prepared to commit to marriage. However, all engaged couples enjoy and find of value the planning of the wedding ceremony. They realize their own ignorance on this topic; they also want their wedding to be as meaningful and impressive an experience as possible. Again, while they may feel that the priest is not too credible or informed personally in such areas as marital sexuality, marital communication, and marital finances, he is, to them, the theological, liturgical, and scriptural expert on the wedding ceremony. They delight in being involved with the priest at the decision-making level in selecting the readings, the vows, the blessings, and other options for the ceremony. There may still be 'hassles' over photography and music at the wedding, at whether they can ride down the main aisle on a horse or wear bathing suits in the sanctuary, but the liturgical rites are so defined in print that the couple is able to perceive at once 'where the lines are,' and they are able to stay within the lines. Moreover, I invite the couple to come to the rectory, where we sit comfortably while I read aloud to them the entire wedding ceremony (with its variations), and, if Mass is intended, the prefaces and collect-type prayers. I also take the time to read aloud to them each of the possible readings authorized for weddings. In so doing, I use the opportunity for catechesis since not only do the readings, the parts of the Mass, and the ceremony itself instruct by their very verbal content, but I can pause and offer personal comment. The couple is also able to interject a question or comment. I explain to them that, at the time of the ceremony, they may be too nervous, tired, and preoccupied to be as receptive as at this time in advance. They are, thus, in the best position to make their selections for the ceremony, while I know that they have received preparation for the sacrament of matrimony.

"What I have found throughout the years is that problems related to the ceremony can be largely eradicated by the priest getting to know the couple in his own personal preparation of them. Sadly, though, the priest is prevented from achieving that by the volume of work in his parish or the marriage preparation 'system' at work there. This can happen if the priest only sees the couple for canonically related tasks and the ceremony itself, while delegating everything else to parish secretaries, marriage encounter couples and wedding-rehearsal coordinators.

"I have found that my going over the wedding ceremony and readings to be of value and appreciated by all couples, whether they are young, old, already married invalidly, widowed-getting-married again, or interfaith couples. The wedding liturgy is relevant to all of them, whereas other topics of marriage preparation may seem superfluous."

(California)

Definition of Immediate Preparation

T he immediate preparation for the celebration of the sacrament of matrimony takes place in the months and weeks immediately prior to the wedding, with the hope that it will give new meaning, content, and form to the prenuptial investigation required by canon law.[1]

While necessary in every case, this preparation is more urgently needed for couples about to marry who manifest shortcomings or difficulties in Christian doctrine and practice.[2]

This is a journey of faith, similar to the Catechumenate, and there are certain elements that should be instilled during these days of preparing: a deeper knowledge of the mystery of Christ and the Church; a fuller understanding of grace and the responsibility of Christian marriage; a practical preparation for taking an active and conscious part in the rites of the marriage liturgy.[3]

We could summarize the overall thrust of this immediate marriage preparation, flowing out of the teachings of the Second Vatican Council, as threefold:

To communicate an attitude of openness toward the couples seeking to marry. Those famous phrases from the opening paragraph of the *Pastoral Constitution on the Church in the Modern World* are pertinent here. The joy and hope, the grief and anguish of men and women in our time, especially of those who are poor or afflicted in any way, are the joy and hope, the grief and anguish of the followers of Christ as well. Nothing that is genuinely human fails to find an echo in their hearts.[4] The contemporary women and men who approach the Church for matrimony, in fact, bring with them all their joys and hopes as well as their anxieties and fears. We trust that those involved in marriage preparation will seek to develop an attitude of mind that wishes to identify with the couple; to grasp what are these joys, hopes, anxieties, or fears; and to echo them in their own hearts. We would like the engaged pair to complete their program elated by the reception they have received and the possibilities before them rather than deflated by judgmental questions or crushed by complicated requirements.

To establish as a goal of marriage preparation efforts the identification and deepening of the couple's faith. The *Constitution on the Sacred Liturgy* noted that the sacraments not only presuppose faith, but by words and objects they also nourish, strengthen, and express it.[5] There is, therefore, a double task involved in achieving this goal: to discover the essen-

tial faith demanded for a sacramental celebration and, through different ways, to deepen the level of that faith.

To involve a variety of personnel in the task of marriage preparation. The *Dogmatic Constitution on the Church* explicitly calls the laity, as living members, to the task of building up the Church. Through birth, they possess unique gifts from God our Creator; through the initiation sacraments of baptism, confirmation, and the Eucharist, they receive a special vocation from the Redeemer to make the Church present in those places and circumstances particular to their own lives; through the Scriptures, they can be assured of the Sanctifier's wisdom and power in carrying out their tasks.[6] Subsequent passages and other documents apply this general vocation of lay persons in a specific way to the preparation of engaged couples for marriage.[7]

While the *Code of Canon Law* places the responsibility for marriage preparation upon the pastor, it also mentions that he should see to it that the "ecclesial community" furnish assistance in these efforts.[8] Pope John Paul II, likewise, urges that the Christian family and the whole of the ecclesial community be involved in the different phases of marriage preparation.[9] What we seek, therefore, is a collaborative effort among the clergy, religious, and laity in all facets of this work.

We envision, in summary, that marriage preparation programs will not so much convey information as communicate inspiration. They will not so much have others judge a couple's capability or commitment as provide tools that enable bride and groom better to assess their own relationship and their own promises about the future. They will not so much stamp a seal of approval upon a couple's readiness to enter marriage as offer ways for the man and woman to facilitate their communication, enhance their understanding, deepen their love, reflect on the sacramental mystery itself, nurture their faith, strengthen their commitment, and consider their marriage as a real apostolate within and for the Church.

This section on immediate preparation is composed of four major parts: (1) several general observations; (2) some practical dimensions of immediate marriage preparation; (3) a theology and spirituality of marriage; and (4) suggestions for celebration of the nuptial liturgy.

---

1. *On the Family*, no. 66.
2. Ibid.
3. Ibid.
4. "Pastoral Constitution on the Church in the Modern World," *Vatican Council II*, no. 1.
5. Ibid., *The Constitution on the Sacred Liturgy*, no. 59.
6. Ibid., *Dogmatic Constitution on the Church*, no. 33.
7. Ibid. See also, *Decree on the Apostolate of the Laity*, no. 11.
8. *Code of Canon Law*, c. 1063.
9. *On the Family*, no. 66.

Part A
Several General
Observations

 Comments for the Clergy

THE IMPORTANCE OF HOSPITALITY

Contacting the parish to arrange for one's marriage is a very significant event for couples, in most cases a moment highly charged with emotion and some anxiety, as the priest from California noted at the start of this section.

There are very significant touchable and teachable moments that are taken quite seriously by the Hispanic community. It is a formal presentation by the parents of their son or daughter for marriage. There is also connected with it many customs for which we should have an open sensitivity, for example, *pedir la mano* (asking formally for the bride's hand), a custom that begins the formal courtship and formal process for church procedures. At times *padrinos* (sponsors) are already involved in these arrangements.

Hospitality should be a hallmark not only to the young couple but, above all, to the entire retinue that accompanies the couple. The sense of community is already implicit in these beginnings.

Even regular churchgoers, with no exceptional circumstances or difficulties surrounding their request, normally have many questions of great practical concern for them. For example: Will we get the date and time desired? Who will officiate? What about the organist? Are there classes to attend and documents to be obtained? These are all unfamiliar areas, leaving the couple uncomfortable until inquiries have been answered.

For some, moreover, this may be the first time in their lives that they have made an appointment and sat down with a member of the clergy to discuss any important matter. The prospects of such an encounter may cause them to feel a bit overwhelmed or at least unsettled.

Finally, when there exist unusual problems, challenges, or situations, the anxiousness intensifies, for example: if one or both have slipped from faithful church attendance; if one is not Roman Catholic; if they are already cohabiting; if one or both have previous marriages; if the bride-to-be is pregnant; if they seek something unique or special, such as having a favorite priest or deacon from outside the parish preside at the liturgy.

In those cases, they may nervously wonder: Will he scold or reject us? Will my partner like the priest or deacon? Will he ask us if we are living together?

Will we be turned down because of the divorce(s)? Will the pregnancy make a difference? Will he go along with our request?

Add to these high-risk elements the very complexity of any three persons developing a cordial relationship to one another in a relatively brief period. Furthermore, include as well the cultural differences and traditions that enrich the moment with great potential for a lifetime of good. Combine all those factors and the critical importance of that initial as well as subsequent encounters becomes evident.

A warm and caring, positive and joyful attitude of hospitality is called for on these occasions. We offer the following suggestions to help create that climate of warmth and acceptance:

Initial arrangements or questions should be handled in personal interviews and not over the telephone. Expectations for a personal interview are especially true for Hispanics since personalism is one of those characteristic Hispanic values. In the case of Hispanic couples, insisting upon an appointment is, therefore, unrealistic and pastorally unwise because 95 percent of Hispanic ministry happens without appointments. The possibilities for good from personal interviews and harm from telephone exchanges are simply too enormous to do otherwise. Human experience teaches us that misunderstandings can occur easily when people deal with delicate matters through printed correspondence or telephone calls. In neither case can we see the person's face, sense the individual's feelings, or catch the meaning behind or underneath the words written or spoken.

The priest or deacon who will preside over the wedding liturgy ideally should conduct the initial interview, not a parish secretary or even a person supervising the parish marriage preparation effort. As we have mentioned and will further stress in later portions of this manual, the involvement of lay persons in this ministry is crucial for its most effective implementation. Nevertheless, the liturgical presider needs to establish a close and comfortable relationship with the engaged couple. Meeting them at the very onset, during this critical first encounter, helps forge that bond in ways very likely beyond our comprehension.

The clergy, as we noted earlier, need to be in touch with their own family backgrounds and thus recognize, as far as possible, any conscious or unconscious personal bias they may possess that will affect their approach to the couple.

Similarly, the clergy should be aware of the contemporary cultural forces, also outlined in previous portions of this handbook, that may influence the engaged couple's words, actions, and attitudes toward the priest, deacon, or Church. Some of these forces such as personalism, no appointments, *pedir la mano,* cohabitation, civil marriages, illiteracy, community, family, and *padrinos* or sponsors are challenges to our awareness that we represent the Church.

There will be occasions when the couple seeking to marry hold values or follow practices contrary to the teaching of the Church. *The clergy,* in this context, have a difficult and complex responsibility. On the one hand, they *must avoid a defensiveness* that takes the engaged pair's contrary opinions or behavior as a personal attack and *forego making judgments* about the couple's own culpability in these matters. On the other hand, they must *uphold the teachings of the Church and challenge the potential bride and groom* to be more. Their role is to condemn the sin, but love the sinner or, in the words of Pope Paul VI, to act as Jesus did who was "indeed intransigent with evil, but merciful toward individuals."[10] As ministers, we must believe more in ourselves—what we represent to the couple—and, culturally, have greater faith in the efficacy of the anthropological or *Kairos* moment to enhance the faith of the couple—even in cases of cohabitation.

In proposing to the couple a course of marriage preparation, *the clergy need to be positive and flexible.* They can do so by congratulating the couple and expressing joy and happiness in their newly found love for each other, then stressing the values of the various facets of the program and offering them as many options as possible. The clergy ought to assist the particular bride and groom in determining just what specific alternatives will be most helpful to them. Arbitrary tests or rules of a negative nature should, to the extent feasible, be avoided.

During that initial interview, *the clergy ought to retain* in their minds *an overall plan* of what they hope to accomplish then and not seek to achieve too much during this first encounter. A little later in this manual, we will propose a sample procedure for conducting the initial exchange, which translates into practice the concepts sketched here and elsewhere.

CONCERN ABOUT THE COUPLE'S FAITH AND READINESS FOR MARRIAGE

There are two concerns that very much press upon bishops, clergy, and those actively involved in marriage preparation: the presence of faith in the couple, or at least in the Catholic partner; and the readiness of the pair for marriage. Similar and related, but separate issues, we will examine first the faith and then the readiness question.

Marriage is a sacrament and, as such, requires the presence of faith in its recipients. All sacraments "presuppose faith" and are called "sacraments of faith."[11] But what level of faith is required? And how do we determine if there is the necessary faith present in the couple or the Catholic partner?

Pope John Paul II addressed this issue in detail and provides us with these helpful, but tightly reasoned, norms—guidelines that may run counter to current pastoral practice in some areas:[12]

- The faith of the person(s) seeking marriage in the Church can exist in varying degrees. It is the primary duty of pastors to facilitate a rediscovery of this faith, nourishing it and bringing it to maturity.

- The Church, however, also admits to the celebration of marriage those who are imperfectly disposed.

- A couple who decides to marry according to the divine plan, that is, to commit their whole lives in unbreakable love and unconditional faithfulness by an irrevocable nuptial consent, are reflecting, even if not in a fully conscious way, an attitude of profound obedience to God's will, an attitude that cannot exist without God's grace. This would appear to indicate that they possess a seminal and sufficient, although perhaps only semiconscious faith.

- With such a decision or consent, the couple have entered upon a journey toward salvation, a journey that, with their upright intention and through the immediate preparation and celebration of the sacrament, can be complemented and brought to completion.

- The fact that couples often request marriage in the Church for social or cultural rather than genuinely religious reasons is understandable. However, the fact that motives of a social nature are present is not enough to justify refusal by the pastor

10. *On the Regulation of Birth,* no. 29.
11. *The Constitution on the Sacred Liturgy,* no. 59.
12. *On the Family,* no. 68.

to celebrate the marriage. The social nature of motives in Hispanics has a different value. These need to be judged more favorably because those social motives are more closely connected with the faith and the Church. The couple is in the midst of communal and familial values and do not present themselves as mere individuals.

- Engaged couples, by baptism, are already really sharers in Christ's marriage covenant with the Church. Moreover, by their right intention, described above, they have accepted God's plan for marriage. Therefore, given these two points, they at least implicitly consent to what the Church intends to do when she celebrates marriage. This would indicate sufficient faith is present for the sacraments.

- Insisting on further criteria that concern the faith level of the couple as a requirement for admission to the Church's celebration of marriage involves great risks. It leads to the danger of making unfounded and discriminatory judgments, as well as to the peril of causing doubts about the validity of marriages already celebrated. Insistence on Sunday Mass attendance, formal parish registration, and other similar external behavioral patterns, however desirable in themselves, would seem to fit into this category of further criteria. The Hispanic Catholic identity, for example, is deeper than insistence on Sunday Mass attendance and especially upon formal parish registration. Hispanics defy these measures.

- Nevertheless, when engaged couples explicitly and formally reject what the Church intends to do in the marriage of baptized persons, the pastor cannot admit them to the celebration of the sacrament.

- The pastor, in such circumstances, must indicate to the couple his reluctance to defer the marriage and stress that they are placing the obstacles to such a celebration—not the Church. Nevertheless, as a sign of his good will, he can offer another kind of help to their marriage or suggest ways to deepen their love for each other.

In the years since the Second Vatican Council and major reforms of the liturgy, we have expended enormous and praiseworthy efforts to enhance our appreciation of the faith dimension in worship. The sacraments are not merely magical or mechanical sacred signs, but rather actions of the Risen Christ that "presuppose" or demand our faithful participa-

tion if they are to bear fruit. A minimal level of faith is required for a valid and licit celebration of the sacraments.

But the sacraments also nourish, strengthen, and express faith.[13] As we have remarked in another context: "Faith grows when it is well expressed in celebration. Good celebrations foster and nourish faith. Poor celebrations weaken and destroy it."[14] The preparation for and celebration of the nuptial liturgy should, as a consequence, build upon and build up the fundamental faith of the engaged couple.

An extensive and relatively recent survey of marriage preparation programs throughout American Catholic dioceses revealed that in eighty-three dioceses, the couple's commitment to the Church and their religious practices were strong elements of the marital evaluation process. Those committed and faithful, obviously, were welcomed to a celebration of the sacrament; those not committed or faithful could be asked to defer the church marriage.[15]

In addition to the tension and conflict such examinations and postponements create, this emphasis runs counter to a cultural phenomenon among youthful Catholics. Another study discovered that young Catholics today typically loosen their connections with the Church in late-adolescence and do not renew or strengthen them until their late-twenties.[16] Since most couples who marry fit into that age category, linking the depth of religious commitment and fidelity to church practice to the celebration of marriage raises evident difficulties.

There are some persons, deeply involved in the Church's marriage preparation efforts across the United States, who question the wisdom of so tightly connecting church commitment and practice with evaluation of the couple for marriage.[17] Teaching and encouraging the ideal is one thing; insisting upon perfect adherence as a condition for the sacrament of matrimony is quite another.

If discerning the presence and level of faith in a couple about to marry is a complex matter, determining their readiness for marriage is even more so. The first issue deals more with their here-and-now attitude and intention; the later directs its attention more to the future.

With the current massive number of marital disruptions and divorces, we wish to do all within our power to assist couples in building successful marriages and avoiding such disasters. To achieve that

---

13. *The Constitution on the Sacred Liturgy,* 59.
14. *Music in Catholic Worship,* NCCB Committee on the Liturgy (Washington, D.C.: USCC Office of Publishing and Promotion Services, 1983), no. 6.
15. *Preparing for Marriage: A Study of Marriage Preparation in American Catholic Dioceses* (St. Meinrad, Ind.: Abbey Press, 1983), p. 20.
16. Ibid.
17. "Unfair Assessments," by David K. O'Rourke, in *Church* (Fall 1985): 24-26.

purpose, over 90 percent of all dioceses within the United States presently provide marriage preparation programs, and about 60 percent not only offer but also require participation in them.[18] Moreover, as Pope John Paul II has mentioned, "experience teaches that young people who have been well prepared for family life generally succeed better than others."[19] Later, we will outline some analytical statistics, indicating the positive value of these various programs in our country.

Nevertheless, it remains simply impossible to predict which marriages will succeed and, therefore, to judge with certainty that any couple is, in this sense, "ready" for matrimony.

One psychologist who does extensive testing of candidates for the religious life and, likewise, serves as a consultant for his diocese's Tribunal states quite frankly that he cannot predict the successful futures of clients, but he can project with moral certitude their forthcoming failures.[20] One of the authors of a premarital discussion instrument maintains that there are no means to measure a couple's potential for making their marriage successful, because it is not possible to measure future potential.[21] Those testimonies would seem to infer that "readiness" cannot be determined, but that "nonreadiness" may be ascertained.

The rather wide variety of common marriage policies that have developed in our country over the past decade appear to center on that point of "nonreadiness" or the presence of difficulties that project to marriage failure. A series of common major obstacles to readiness for marriage are usually stated and a process of resolving them established.[22]

The revised *Code of Canon Law* does not address directly the issue of a couple's relational readiness for marriage. Conscious of the couple's natural right to marry, it only succinctly decrees that all persons not prohibited by law can contract marriage, and that before marriage is celebrated, it must be evident that nothing stands in the way of its valid and licit celebration.[23] It does, nevertheless, empower the local ordinary to prohibit a person's marriage, but only for a time and for a serious cause—for as long as that cause exists.[24] Dioceses with a common policy of selective postponement for the ill-prepared cite this empowerment as the legal basis for such a procedure.[25]

While our marriage policies and programs are well intentioned, a decade or more experience with them prompts us to offer a few cautions:

Any regulation or policy needs to have flexibility built into its statement and application. The human condition is so varied and each person so unique that rigid rules and inflexible interpretations can cause more harm than good for the Church and, ultimately, for the engaged couple.

Two common policies reflect that flexible approach in their directives. One policy, encouraging

an early start for a couple's marriage preparation states that "ideally" it should begin with the proper minister, one year prior to the wedding date. It goes on to state that the "one year" requirement will, at times, admit flexibility for a reasonable cause if, in the prudent judgment of the pastoral minister, marriage preparation can be completed adequately.[26]

One situation in particular calls for some flexibility and understanding. If an American citizen is marrying an alien, the alien is admitted to the United States on a special K-1 visa, which is valid for ninety days. The marriage must be celebrated before the ninety-day period has expired. Obviously, the period of immediate preparation will be foreshortened under these circumstances. However, the couple's willingness to fulfill all of the necessary requirements in a brief period of time is, itself, an indication of their readiness to marry.

A second policy, elevating the minimum age requirement to nineteen, states that "generally" marriages between teenagers are to be discouraged since statistical evidence indicates that the probability of permanence in such marriages is greatly reduced. Nevertheless, it provides options for those under nineteen or even eighteen.[27] We must also be aware of the cultural backgrounds of some Hispanics whose age for marriage is closer to the canonical minimum. That should not surprise us. Still, we need to uphold and strive toward the ideal projected within the United States, especially since these couples intend to be integrated into this society.

A sense of reverent tentativeness should surround the treatment of obstacles or difficulties. As we have seen and pastoral experience confirms, the predictability factor of any marriage's success or fail-

18. *Preparing for Marriage*, p. 13.
19. *On the Family*, no. 66.
20. Personal conversation with Rev. Jeffrey Keefe, OFM Conv., Ph.D. (Syracuse, N.Y.: July 22, 1987).
21. *Preparing for Marriage*, p. 21.
22. See: "Marriage in the Church: A Common Policy for Ministry to the Engaged, Archdiocese of Louisville" (1986); "Draft Common Policy for Marriage Preparation for All Catholic Dioceses in the State of Minnesota" (1985); "Common Marriage Policy for the State of Missouri"; "A Revised Common Policy for Marriage Preparation for the Catholic Province of New Jersey" (1986).
23. *Code of Canon Law*, cc. 1058, 1066. It should be noted, however, that the *Code of Canon Law* directs the ecclesial community to furnish "assistance so that the matrimonial state is maintained in a Christian spirit and makes progress toward perfection" (c. 1063). A canon also urges that confirmation be received before marriage and strongly recommends that the engaged "approach the sacraments of penance and the Most Holy Eucharist so that they may fruitfully receive the sacrament of marriage (c. 1065). Finally, two canons require that those in special circumstances (e.g., a person who has notoriously rejected the Catholic faith; underage youth) need the ordinary's or pastor's permission (see cc. 1071-1072). In sum, the local church community also has a right and a responsibility to uphold the sacrament of matrimony; the natural right to marry is not absolute.
24. Ibid., c. 1077.
25. "A Revised Common Policy for Marriage Preparation," art. 39.
26. Ibid., art. 12.
27. "Marriage in the Church: A Common Policy for Ministry to the Engaged," p. 40.

ure is quite low. Moreover, evaluating inner attitudes or even external behavior patterns leads us perilously close to the arena of judgments reserved to God. Finally, we believe in the always present possibility of conversion or change for every person.

Premarital instruments are not tests, and we should avoid employing them as measurements to determine the readiness of a couple for marriage. The authors of one instrument stress that it is a discussion guide, not a test. It has been designed to bring out areas of agreement and disagreement between the engaged couple, as well as their attitudes toward a number of problem areas, so that they and the people preparing them for marriage may discuss these areas in a structured and focused way.[28]

The couple themselves are the persons to determine their readiness, not the clergy or delegated parish ministers. Bride and groom minister the sacrament to one another; because of their natural right to marry, they should be the ones to judge their readiness to receive this gift.

Once again, there are those with many years of involvement in marriage preparation in the United States who question the wisdom of a process that places the assessment or discernment of a couple's readiness in the hands of another—clerical, religious, or lay.[29]

The *Common Marriage Policy for the State of Missouri* seems to recognize this privacy of the couple's judgment by establishing as one goal for marriage preparation the provision of a framework within which "the couple has the best possible opportunity to assess their individual readiness to marry. . . ."[30]

The Church's role, as well as the primary task of clergy and others in marriage preparation it seems, is to assist the couple in making a judgment about their relational readiness and personal faith, not to make those judgments for or about them. That function, besides assisting them in making a judgment on readiness, is also to provide an environment of support and love for the couple to succeed. The Church wishes to surround them with love.

Pope John Paul II places this delicate issue of the engaged couple's faith and readiness in perspective when he both urges better and more intense programs of marriage preparation and stresses their necessity and obligation, yet cautions that omitting them is not an impediment to the celebration of marriage.[31]

Concern about a couple's faith and readiness has caused great anxiety for clergy and pastoral leaders in the United States, particularly during the years since the Second Vatican Council. We hope these observations and guidelines may, by placing such responsibilities in a slightly modified perspective, lift some of those burdens and ease that tension. Moreover, we trust that, through a better understanding of the cultural differences and languages, the clergy and those involved in marriage preparation programs can better assist couples at their weddings.

COLLABORATIVE LEADERSHIP

The priest, generally speaking, handled every aspect of marriage preparation before the Second Vatican Council. He instructed the couple, completed the paper work, conducted the rehearsal, and then, of course, presided over the liturgical celebration. In recent years, that has changed, basically for two reasons: practical necessity and pastoral value.

The increasing shortage of priests and growing number of weddings compel the clergy to look for ways of delegating tasks simply in order to survive. But even if there were ample clergy, we still would or should be involving lay persons in marriage preparation efforts because of the unique and positive contribution they can provide. We will expand upon that point in the very next portion of this handbook.

However, such a shift entails an adjustment for the priest. His role has changed. Previously, he did everything in marriage preparation; now he does some things and facilitates or enables others to do the rest. We could call this new position one of *collaborative leadership.*

In the beginning, that diverse function of facilitator, enabler, or collaborating leader may be uncomfortable and less satisfying for the priest accustomed to taking care of all the tasks himself. But in the words of one parish priest who has made that transition and made it well, once the clergy get on to this kind of facilitating and promoting, it is "positively joyous" and "truly exciting and fulfilling."[32]

The first function of the clergy as collaborative leader in marriage preparation is *to assess the needs of the parish.* The larger the community and the more marriages that take place in that church, the greater will be the demand for a well-organized system, involving a considerable number of religious or lay persons. These could include such people as a music minister, rehearsal coordinator, liturgy committee representative, sponsor couple, corps of married couples giving informational/formational presentations, administrator of the premarital discussion instrument, and director of an aftercare program for those recently married.

The above recommendations may well be possible in parishes that are solvent. However, many Hispanic faith communities are needy or supported by grants and subsidies. Consequently, the pastoral response must, in those circumstances, rely more on the inner cultural values of the community and develop different suggestions.

Once the needs are established, the next task is

---

28. *Preparing for Marriage,* p. 21.
29. "Unfair Assessments," p. 26.
30. "Common Marriage Policy for the State of Missouri," p. 4.
31. *On the Family,* no. 66.
32. *Take Heart, Father,* by Rev. William J. Bausch (Mystic Conn.: Twenty-Third Publications, 1986), p. 193.

to identify persons in the parish with both the gifts and the willingness to fulfill those roles. Bulletin announcements may draw forth a few volunteers, but personal invitations from the pastor and a time-and-talent, volunteer, or stewardship Sunday event have proven to be the most effective methods of securing the needed personnel.

Those volunteer or paid persons must then be motivated properly and trained adequately. Sometimes, this can be done on the local or parish level; often it requires regional or diocesan resources.

Once underway, the clergy will need *to coordinate the operation, sustain the people's enthusiasm, and deepen their spirituality.* For example, if the parish has a corps of couples who serve as "sponsor couples" or who give informational/formational sessions locally, presumably, the clergy will want to have a lead couple that assign the engaged pair to appropriate members of the team. Moreover, these married couples have a real necessity for getting together several times each year to share their experiences, receive fresh input, and gain renewed inspiration. Whether this takes the form of a "reward" dinner or a combined social-work session, the pastor or his delegate may well be the one who prompts the gathering, obviously underwrites the costs, and certainly makes an almost essential contribution by being part of the actual discussion.

The priest or deacon as collaborative leader of the marriage preparation program has before him the task of harmonizing the talents and energies of all those in or outside the parish who assist with that effort. However, the priest or deacon as eventual presider of the nuptial liturgy has before him a simultaneous task of establishing, maintaining, and deepening a cordial relationship with the engaged couple. He cannot, therefore, totally delegate all these functions and, thus, almost as a stranger meet the bride and groom at the altar for the wedding celebration.

He will need to care for certain details himself, share some responsibilities with others, and keep informed about the activities fulfilled totally by still others. An illustration of that multiple role might follow this hypothetical scenario: the priest or deacon conducts the initial interview and completes the investigation form; he greets the wedding party at the rehearsal, leads them in a scriptural reading and prayer, introduces to all the paid or volunteer coordinator, and turns the rest of the details over to that person; he receives a report and feedback about the engaged pair from the sponsor couple, music minister, liturgy director, and coordinator of the premarital discussion instrument.

While this sounds complex and does require certain organizational skills, ultimately, it both saves considerable time for the clergy and, more, actively involves lay persons in the preparation program. That conservation of time may be essential for clergy called

upon to preside over several dozen weddings each year. When the parish community is much smaller and the marriages fewer, the process could be greatly simplified. In such a context, the priest or deacon might, for example, directly help the couple in planning the liturgy, work with them through the discussion instrument, and care personally for all the rehearsal details.

Nevertheless, even when the priest or deacon has very few weddings and could, time-wise, fulfill all the tasks by himself, it would still be crucial for him to involve lay persons in some of the functions, for the reasons we will now discuss.

 The Involvement of Lay Persons

BASES FOR MINISTRY OF LAITY IN MARRIAGE PREPARATION

Our contemporary understanding of the Church's nature as the Mystical Body of Christ and, since the Second Vatican Council, as the holy People of God, envisions all members—clergy, religious, and laity—laboring together for the building up of God's kingdom.[33] In this concept, every Christian through birth and baptism bears both a right and a responsibility to engage in this fundamental work. Young couples already have been recruited for this new ministry; we trust many more soon will be added to that group. In fostering this development, we recommend that leaders stress or model the Church as a community, a service of families assisting each other.

However, the Church also explicitly mentions and calls for such an involvement of lay persons in various activities. For example, one document notes that the initiation of adults is the responsibility of all the baptized.[34] More specifically, with regard to matrimony, another names as a suitable task of the family apostolate the work of assisting engaged couples to make a better preparation for marriage.[35]

That directive has been reinforced by subsequent Vatican texts. These encourage this kind of like-to-like ministry, matching married and engaged couples for instruction and discussion; they cite the valuable witness of husbands and wives who manifest their respect for the unity of life and love in marriage through periodic continence; those decrees, finally, urge that the Christian family and the whole of the ecclesial community should become and feel involved in all phases of marriage preparation.[36]

33. *Dogmatic Constitution on the Church*, ch. IV. "The Mystical Body of Christ," Encyclical of Pope Pius XII (June 29, 1943).
34. *Rite of Christian Initiation of Adults*, no. 9.
35. *Decree in the Apostolate of the Laity*, no. 11. See also, *Code of Canon Law*, cc. 204ff, 1063.
36. *On the Family*, nos. 35, 66; *On the Regulation of Birth*, no. 26; *Dogmatic Constitution on the Church*, nos. 35, 41; *Pastoral Constitution on the Church in the Modern World*, nos. 48-49.

In addition to the essential nature and official teachings of the Church, pastoral wisdom dictates that we actively involve lay persons in marriage preparation. Married couples who serve in this capacity regularly testify that their encounters with an engaged man and woman seem to enrich them as much as those exchanges benefit the couple about to marry.

Moreover, the engaged couple cannot but be helped by the example as well as the words of the married persons guiding or instructing them. The clergy could utter almost the same words in preparation session as the married couple; the impact, however, can often be quite different. The engaged pair may consciously or unconsciously presume that the clergy are supposed to speak about God, Church, love, commitment, and other similar concerns. In their perception, this is simply the job, the function, the responsibility of the clergy. But to the engaged persons, the lay couple assisting them are under no such obligation. They do this freely, merely out of conviction. Furthermore, the married couple can speak from personal experiences, while the clergy—at least the priest or celibate deacon—cannot.

As a consequence, the married couple's evident happiness, example of faith in God, commitment to one another, and loyalty to the Church may tremendously influence an engaged pair. It can give them strong hope for their own future and, likewise, spur them right now to become reconciled or allied more deeply with the Church.

The contribution of lay persons in marriage preparation efforts over the past two or more decades has been so outstanding that Family Life Directors now consider that any such program without lay involvement will be inferior and inadequate.

Successfully married couples, for obvious reasons, should form the core of a marriage preparation team. Nevertheless, spouses abandoned by their partners, single parents, those in legitimate second marriages, widows and widowers, as well as single persons are also people whose insights and talents can make a valuable contribution to marriage preparation.[37]

THE RITE OF CHRISTIAN INITIATION OF ADULTS AS A MODEL

The *Rite of Christian Initiation of Adults* offers in its pattern of implementation several ingredients that could be applied to marriage preparation.

First of all, marriage preparation, like adult initiation, is a gradual process and a spiritual journey of adults. As such, it will and should vary according to the many forms of God's grace, the free cooperation of the individuals, the action of the Church, and the circumstances of time and place. It must, likewise, provide opportunities for making inquiry and for maturing.[38]

The entire local Church and parish community must be prepared fully to help those who are preparing for marriage. Not everyone, of course, will be actively involved in diocesan, regional, or parish preparation programs. But all can lend their prayer and concern. A little creative effort, from time to

---

37. *On the Family*, no. 20.
38. *Rite of Christian Initiation of Adults*, no. 4-6.

time, with the parish bulletin, the banns of marriage, the general intercessions, the homily, and comments at Mass could help in this regard by raising the consciousness of the faith community and stimulating their prayerful interest.[39] In addition, some formal recognition of parishioners who take an active part in the marriage preparation program accentuates the importance of this ministry for building up the Church.

A sponsor couple who know or come to know the man and woman about to marry can assist them in practical ways and also serve as inspirational models for the engaged pair by their faith, example, good qualities, and friendship. Ideally, if that relationship should continue after the marriage, the sponsor couple can sustain newlyweds in moments of hesitancy and anxiety, in times of difficulty and doubt.[40]

Sponsor couples, or *Padrinos de Matrimonio* in Hispanic marriages, have had a traditional role that was both social and religious. We wish to challenge the Hispanic community to develop that role, especially in line with the suggestions noted here from the *Rite of Christian Initiation of Adults.* Hispanics possess many riches related to marriage and family, which need to be exploited.

Lay women and men as instructors will be needed to reinforce and expand the counsel of the clergy in the many facets of married life, including topics such as communication, finances, and natural family planning.[41] For Hispanics, the grandparents or *Abuelos* naturally fulfill this role, especially imparting the wisdom of the ages. Some instruction to them would enhance their culturally given natural role.

The preparation process should include reflection on the mysteries of our faith, be filled with the spirit of the Gospels, flow out of the Scriptures, have a connection with the symbols of the liturgy, relate to the Church's year of grace-filled celebrations, and respond to the varied needs of each engaged couple.[42] The development and use of simple or solemn paraliturgical celebrations of the Word throughout the preparation program could aid in translating these ideals into realities for those involved.

PARISH-BASED EFFORTS

The *Code of Canon Law* seems both to call for parish-based marriage preparation programs and to imply that regional or diocesan assistance will be required as well.[43] We will note some of the more common extraparochial types momentarily, but here wish to recommend that every parish have a functioning marriage preparation committee. Even with multiple and superb regional and diocesan programs, there is a need on the local scene for people who can complete what has been accomplished, for example, during an Engaged Encounter weekend. Moreover, given the mobility of our society today, couples frequently

cannot meet the relatively fixed schedule of regional, diocesan, or even parish-formed programs. In these cases, the availability of parish-based people who can adjust rather easily to the couple's time limitations and schedule a personalized arrangement becomes critical. It is both unrealistic and unfair to mandate participation in some preparation program as a requisite for marriage unless we have developed this kind of flexible capacity within every parish.

Parishes across the United States have incorporated into their marriage preparation programs, among others, the following types of persons:

Sponsor couples. These persons may conduct one-to-one sessions with engaged couples, join with others in small group presentations, participate in a larger parish program, or assist with regional or diocesan courses. It is of crucial importance that the pastor or his delegate provide both training and support for them on a regular basis.

Coordinator of premarital instrument. This person (or persons) has a familiarity with the chosen instrument (see our discussion, to follow, of the more common ones), administers the document, arranges for its scoring, and either shares this with the couple or facilitates the priest or deacon doing so.

Music minister. Normally the organist, this individual meets with the engaged couple and discusses the music for their nuptial celebration.

Rehearsal director. A few parishes have paid or volunteer persons who care for the actual details of the rehearsal. She or he clearly needs to work in close concert with the priest or deacon who will preside over the liturgy.

Liturgical facilitator. This person presents the liturgical options available for the couple and helps fashion a personalized, integrated nuptial service for them.

Investigation clerk. This delegate of the pastor completes the prenuptial investigation form.

Coordinator of aftercare. Not many parishes provide organized programs for couples in the first years after marriage, but their desirability and importance have been clearly demonstrated.

In all probability, few churches have individuals for each of these ministries. The more common procedure would be for those various tasks to be carried out by one or two persons, including the pastor. As we mentioned earlier, the priest or deacon who will preside should collaborate closely with those different ministers so that he may establish a very personal and aware relationship with the couple preparing for marriage.

39. Ibid., no. 9.
40. Ibid., nos. 10-11.
41. Ibid., no. 16.
42. Ibid., nos. 4, 16.
43. *Code of Canon Law,* cc. 1063-1064.

3 Statistical Support for Marriage Preparation Programs

When pastors or their delegates—following either a diocesan mandate or a parish policy—inform couples seeking to marry in the Church that they are required to participate in a formal marriage preparation program, the engaged pair's response may not always be positive and enthusiastic. If they strongly object, the pastoral leaders can appeal to the bishop's or pastor's authority. However, that procedure, while legitimate and perhaps necessary, nevertheless leaves much to be desired. On the other hand, if they could cite solidly scientific statistics that indicate that those who complete marriage preparation programs are happier and enjoy more successful marital lives than those who do not participate in them, then the task of persuading or insisting on these courses would be much easier.

Unfortunately, we do not possess that kind of predictability data. Still, we do have statistical surveys that conclude that marriage preparation programs make a constructive difference and promote growth in a couple's relationship.

First of all, research scholars in the United States have concluded that no empirical data exist to support the notion that marriage preparation programs reduce the incidence of divorce or separation of those couples who participate in them. Similarly, no data exist that indicate that couples who participate in premarital counseling programs are more satisfied or successful in their marriages than those who do not. Finally, no data exist to determine whether or not such marital preparation programs prevent bad marriages.[44]

A Canadian research project does present some data that indicate that couples are more likely to resolve conflicts and take other positive and preventive actions as a result of marriage preparation programs: five years after marriage, couples are more successful if they had completed the program surveyed by the research.[45]

The reasons for this lack of or limited data should be fairly evident. Earlier, we mentioned the impossibility of predicting marital success, although acknowledging it may be possible in a tentative fashion to project marital failure. Moreover, such studies will need to be long-term and the testing in them very rigorous. Premarital counseling is relatively new (first appearing in the 1930s), and thus, we are not able to examine marriages of sufficient length to draw valid conclusions about the impact of preparation efforts upon them. Finally, the complexity surrounding every couple, especially the family system from which each person comes, makes it exceedingly difficult—if not impossible—to isolate a marriage preparation program as the determinant of marital success or failure.[46]

Having made that disclaimer, we can, however, cite statistical studies that reveal that marriage preparation programs have been well received by engaged couples and appear to exert a positive influence upon them.

One study of a premarital assessment program concluded from its preliminary evaluation that the partners' relationship expectations became more congruent as a result of participation in the program.[47]

A midwestern diocese's marriage preparation efforts, examined in 1985, led the researcher to conclude that the program fulfills its stated mission "by effecting noteworthy improvements in attitudes and values concerning marriage." Those attitudes or values touched upon children, finance, in-laws, interests and activities, interpersonal communication, marriage readiness, personal adjustment, religion and philosophy, role adjustment, sexuality, and critical items. There was improvement in each of those areas.[48]

The evaluation of a parish marriage preparation program in a West Coast diocese, also conducted in 1985, came to similar conclusions. Of the newly married respondents, 91 percent judged that the program was either much or very much worthwhile, and 86 percent considered the program either much or very much personally enriching. The majority of respondents termed it enlightening, practical, and positive, as well as helpful in drawing couples closer together, strengthening their commitment, and confirming their faith beliefs.[49]

Consequently, while we do not have data that prove premarital preparation ensures better and more successful marriages, there is good scientific research that indicates that such programs are well received and positively impact the engaged couple's relationship. It is in this fashion that we interpret Pope John Paul II's observation: "Experience teaches that young people who have been well prepared for family life generally succeed better than others."[50]

44. "Premarital Counseling: Appraisal and Status," by Dennis A. Bagarozzi and Paul Rauen, in *The American Journal of Family Therapy* 9:3 (Fall 1981): 13-30; "A Theoretically Derived Model of Premarital Intervention: The Building of a Family System," by Dennis A. and Judith I. Bagarozzi, in *Clinical Social Work Journal* 10:1 (1982): 52-64.
45. Cf. Rev. Donald Conroy, National Institute for the Family, 3019 4th Street, N.E., Washington, D.C. 20017.
46. "Premarital Counseling," and "A Theoretically Derived Model of Premarital Intervention."
47. "A Premarital Assessment Program," by Lynn P. Buckner and Connie J. Salts, in *Family Relations* (October 1985): 513-520.
48. "Attitude and Value Changes of Participants in the Springfield-Cape Girardeau Diocese Marriage Preparation Program," by William H. Datema, a seminar report presented to the faculty of the Department of Guidance and Counseling, Southwest Missouri State University (April 1985).
49. "Parish Marriage Preparation Program: 1985 Evaluation," conducted by Office of Family Life Ministries, Diocese of San Jose.
50. *On the Family*, no. 66.

Part B
Some Practical Dimensions of Immediate Marriage Preparation

In this section, we will include an outline of the more common formats in existence for parish, regional, or diocesan marriage preparation programs. Each of them, however, should touch upon all of the practical items treated here, as well as pertinent points discussed in other portions of the marriage manual. For example, any formal or informal method or system of preparing couples for the sacrament of matrimony necessarily must cover topics such as commitment and communication skills (Section I); intimacy and responsible childbearing (Section II); the couple's faith and readiness (Section III). In other words, organizers of marriage preparation efforts ought to compare their course outlines with this manual's content in order to discern areas for possible addition or adjustment.

 Instruments to Facilitate Dialogue

In the 1982 study of marriage preparation programs we cited earlier, eighty-eight dioceses reported that they used some form of instrument or inventory to facilitate dialogue as part of their efforts.[51] New and revised instruments have appeared on the market since then. Moreover, additional dioceses have begun to employ them in their programs. Furthermore, there are experts in the medical field who recommend that a family health history of the bride and groom could also, in our time, be especially valuable for better discussion and decision making.

Because of their widespread use and significant importance, we would like to examine at some length the purpose of marital instruments or inventories; offer criteria for evaluating those that are available; suggest ways that they are to be employed properly; sketch several positive effects from their use; issue a few cautions about them; and identify the three most commonly used versions.

THE PURPOSE OF MARRIAGE PREPARATION INSTRUMENTS

To give an engaged couple concrete means to look at their particular relationship in light of the factors and issues that are usually involved in all marriages. Through matching and comparing the man's and woman's separate responses to questions, the instruments are designed to provide the couple with an individualized profile so that, subsequently, they engage in a process of discussion, problem solving, decision making, and shared study/growth, which can have maximum usefulness because its starting point is the particular couple themselves.

To allow clergy, married lead-couples, and counselors who work with the engaged to tailor their facilitation or teaching appropriately. The instrument does so by its individualized focus on the specific couple with their strengths, developing areas, and other tendencies in need of growth. The resulting profile also enables those in marriage preparation ministry to maximize their teaching, counseling, or modeling by avoiding a need to present every topic or issue generically or equally.

To increase the engaged couple's felt need and appreciation of subsequent preparation by raising the consciousness of the potential bride and groom about their unique needs, problems, and issues. Working through the instrument before formal preparation programs can make them more ready to listen and to learn.

To give straightforward education and/or evaluation by providing the couple with both a broad and specific checklist of the issues/concerns/topics that impact marriage. The educational purpose of such a checklist is to teach a couple about the range of attitudes/factors/responses that they need to consider and discuss as they prepare for marriage. The evaluative purpose of the instrument as checklist is to help the engaged couple and those working with them to determine the process or the amount of work to be done in preparation for the marriage.

CRITERIA FOR EVALUATING MARRIAGE PREPARATION INSTRUMENTS

They should reflect the body of common knowledge about marriage: what makes good matches; what skills are needed; what causes breakups; what are bonders in successful marriages; how people get through difficult periods; plus such basic areas as background, personality, sexuality, communication, problem solving, children, religion, in-laws, friends, and money. In reflecting the body of common knowledge about healthy and unhealthy marriages, instruments will provide not only relevant questions/concerns/issues but also a way of measuring the individual's and couple's responses against the "preferred" or most healthy responses. In this way, the instrument can provide the engaged couple with some objective criteria with which to evaluate their own situation.

Those used in the Catholic Church must mirror the components and ideals needed in valid and

---

51. *Preparing for Marriage*, pp. 20-21.

growing sacramental marriages such as fidelity, permanency, openness to children, forgiveness, the role of shared faith and values, and unconditional loving.

They need to address themselves to both current and specialized issues if they are to enable couples to get an accurate and useful fix on their own situations: for example, two-career marriages; older marriages; teen marriages; interreligious and "split-level faith" marriages (two Catholics who have radically different practice or belief); second marriages; and the implications for their relationship of a premarital contract, if one exists.

They ought to be easily usable by engaged couples, the clergy, and lay marriage preparation ministers. They have to be accessible, easy to use and understand, inexpensive, clear in their intentions, and almost impossible to misuse. Instruments that require a highly trained professional for appropriate use or that lend themselves to categorizing or labeling couples will not be helpful or safe as common preparation tools.

WAYS TO USE MARRIAGE PREPARATION INSTRUMENTS

Marriage preparation instruments should be used, first of all, to help the engaged couple look at their relationship; learn about each other; and grow in their skills of relating, good decision making, and problem solving; as well as deepen their understanding of marriage, especially a Christian sacramental marriage. Second, they should also assist the marriage preparation minister in the task of enabling an engaged couple to accomplish these things.

There are several levels of ways that an instrument can be used to achieve both of those purposes:

At the simplest level, *it can serve the engaged couple as a private checklist and a starting point for their own personal thoughts and discussions.* If used in this manner, its intent and limitations need to be explained clearly to them so they do not make it into a test or a way to label one another. A marriage minister (clergy or lay) will know that at least a couple has been exposed to all pertinent topics for discussion if the instrument is employed in this manner. Not every instrument lends itself to this level of use.

Most commonly, *the marriage preparation instrument is used with both engaged couple and marriage minister studying the results to determine areas that need special discussion, problem solving, or growth/education.* Either clergy or married lead-couples can facilitate that study. This mode includes the value of the simple checklist as a starting point for the engaged couples but goes beyond to deepen teaching, point out patterns, and facilitate problem solving. Such an approach usually leads to the highest satisfaction on the part of couples and those preparing them for marriage.

In many situations, the study of the couple's results, with the marriage minister, is followed by an educational program such as Evenings for Engaged, Engaged Encounter, or Pre-Cana. Sometimes, such study is included in the work with a Sponsor Couple program. In all of these instances, use of the instrument readies the engaged couple for maximizing the effectiveness of the educational program. It has created in them a felt need for the modeling, teaching, and personal couple processing that the educational component provides.

On occasion, both the study and discussion of the instrument results will make it clear that *a given couple requires referral for specialized counseling before marriage.* In these instances, the instrument itself is only a first indication; it does not provide the complete grounds for such a decision. It can, however, bring to light issues or patterns that allow both couple and preparation minister to begin to see substantive reasons for more intense work, postponement of the marriage, and/or special assistance.

SEVERAL POSITIVE EFFECTS OF MARRIAGE PREPARATION INSTRUMENTS

Couples appear to make more reflective choices of partners. The Archdiocese of Omaha (Nebraska), currently using FOCCUS and before that PMI, finds that approximately 17 percent of the couples who begin the marriage preparation process in this archdiocese, using the marriage preparation instrument, decide to postpone or not to marry. Before the archdiocese began to use an instrument for all marriages, an average of 3 to 7 percent of couples who began marriage preparation decided to postpone or cancel their wedding plans.[52] Developers of PREPARE have approximately the same results.[53]

Marriage preparation ministers, particularly clergy, find that the use of instruments makes them more comfortable and satisfied in this work. They judge that they have a better handle on the areas of emphasis and concern and that the engaged couples feel the ministry is more personally directed and appropriately applicable to them. Overgeneralized teaching—a little bit of time on every topic—is avoided and moments with the engaged couple are better utilized.

All areas are covered in each preparation to the degree that they touch carefully and thoroughly the fundamental topics of marriage preparation. To the degree of thoroughness that instruments raise specific and general questions in areas necessary for engaged couples to ponder, they make it possible for

52. Data from yearly marriage statistics, Archdiocese of Omaha, Family Life Office, 3214 North 60th Street, Omaha, NE 68104.
53. David Olson, *Prepare*, Inc., P.O. Box 190, Minneapolis MN 55440.

the marriage minister to be reasonably sure that all essential topics have been covered adequately.

Longitudinal research, still needing to be done, could reveal further benefits from the use of these instruments.

A FEW CAUTIONS ABOUT MARRIAGE PREPARATION INSTRUMENTS

It is most important that the marriage preparation instruments not be employed as a pass/fail test, as a fixed diagnostic measure of a couple's potential for a good marriage, or as a single measure of whether or not a couple may be married in the Church. The three major instruments, commonly used in the Church throughout the United States today, all clearly state for engaged couples and marriage ministers that they are not intended to predict the future or to determine if a couple should be married. Instead, they are designed to help a couple examine, understand, and communicate. They have been conceived to facilitate a process. The danger still exists, however, that couples or marriage ministers will use instruments inappropriately. This may be because of format (question-and-answer responses, measured against "best" or "preferred" responses); because of an overall "test mentality"; or perhaps, because of confusion over the difference between "predictive" data (which the instruments do not provide) and "descriptive" data about healthy and less healthy responses (which the instruments can provide).

It is important that instruments fit the times and the culture of the couples using them. This means updating. It also implies that instruments have to be studied to see if, even with a translation, they can or cannot be used with minority or certain ethnic groups. For Hispanics, who suffer a high index of illiteracy, these instruments are not necessarily the most desired tools to facilitate discernment and discussion. Moreover, the cost at times becomes prohibitive. While not placing heavier burdens upon the couples, we still need to become creative with other communitarian supportive elements.

THREE MOST COMMONLY USED MARRIAGE PREPARATION INSTRUMENTS

The following marriage preparation instruments are the most commonly used in the United States today:

- *FOCCUS (Facilitating Open Couple Communication, Understanding, and Study) was developed in 1984 by the Archdiocese of Omaha (Nebraska). It has sixteen categories:*

  1. Communication
  2. Extended Family Issues
  3. Financial Issues
  4. Friends and Interests
  5. Interfaith Marriages
  6. Key Problem Indicators
  7. Life-Style Expectations
  8. Marriage Covenant
  9. Parenting Issues
  10. Personal Issues
  11. Personality Match
  12. Problem Solving
  13. Readiness Issues
  14. Religion and Values
  15. Second Marriage
  16. Sexuality Issues

Computer scoring of FOCCUS is provided through the Family Life Office of the Archdiocese of Omaha, at $5.00 per couple. Hand scoring materials are also available. Personal computer scoring diskette for FOCCUS can be obtained through Parish Data Systems, 3140 North 51st Avenue, Phoenix AZ 85031. Scanner diskette and licensing for individual diocesan scoring of FOCCUS may be secured through the Omaha Family Life Office.

Spanish, Braille, and audio-tape versions of FOCCUS are available. In considering the Spanish version, pastoral leaders will need to examine the text to see if it is a transliteration or if it has been culturally adapted. Finally, a Counselor Manual can be purchased for $9.50.

Contact: FOCCUS
Family Life Office
3214 North 60th Street
Omaha NE 68104

- *PMI (Pre-Marital Inventory) was developed by BESS Associates in 1975, and revised as PMI Profile from Intercommunications Publishing, Inc., in 1984. It has ten categories:*

  1. Children
  2. Family Issues
  3. Finances
  4. Interests and Activities
  5. Interpersonal Communication
  6. Marriage Experience
  7. Personal Adjustment
  8. Religion and Philosophy
  9. Role Expectations
  10. Sexuality

Scoring of PMI Profile is provided through the Central Office, at $5.00 per couple. Hand scoring was available with PMI, but not with the PMI Profile.

Contact: PMI Profile
Intercommunications Publishing, Inc.
1 Valentine Lane
Chapel Hill NC 27514

- *PREPARE (Premarital Personal and Relationship Enrichment) was developed in 1977, by Dr. David H. Olson and his colleagues. It has twelve categories:*

1. Children and Marriage
2. Communication
3. Conflict Resolution
4. Equalitarian Roles
5. Family and Friends
6. Financial Management
7. Idealistic Distortion
8. Leisure Activities
9. Personality Issues
10. Realistic Expectations
11. Realistic Orientation
12. Sexual Relationship

Computer scoring is provided through the central office of PREPARE-ENRICH, at $20.00 per couple. Clergy, counselors, or married couples working with PREPARE are encouraged to complete the training, which is available through one-day workshops or through a Counselor Manual. Counselor Manual is available for $47.50. A special edition of PREPARE MC is available for couples entering second marriages.

Contact: PREPARE-ENRICH, Inc.
        P.O. Box 190
        Minneapolis MN 55440

 ## The Question of Cohabitation

Premarital sexual intercourse and cohabitation without marriage are not identical issues or questions. One can exist without the other. Couples may engage in sexual intercourse without living together; other couples, particularly those sharing homes for financial reasons, may live together without having sexual intercourse.

Premarital sexual intercourse, as we discussed in an earlier portion of this manual, violates an objective moral code that the Church officially teaches and is not, in our judgment, a recommended or wise way to prepare for marriage.

Cohabitation, on the other hand, especially for those couples bound by affection or even contemplating marriage, establishes a situation in which avoidance of premarital sex becomes exceptionally difficult. Moreover, when a couple move in together without exchanging formal nuptial vows and live externally as husband and wife, they create an occasion of scandal for others by weakening the sanctity of marriage itself. In addition, as we will observe below, empirical data raise doubts about cohabitation as a healthy preparation for marital life. For these and other reasons, we reject a cohabitation that simulates marriage as appropriate behavior for Roman Catholics.

Before exploring the question of cohabitation, we first must define our understanding of the term. For this discussion, we accept in general the definition of two scholars and educators who have researched the matter: *cohabitation* means a couple who have been living together at least four nights a week for an extended period of time in which there is a commitment to each other and a recognition that together they form, in a certain sense, a "family."[54]

In Hispanic communities, there is the phenomenon of civil marriages, marriages without cohabitation for the sake of getting legal immigration status, and a special understanding of concubinage. Concubinage or common-law marriages and even mere civil marriages have been a common practice in Latin America. These do not arise out of a popular trend, but arise more so from poverty, lack of clergy or social status, and sometimes *machismo*. Rather than trying to set a social trend, these marriages or unions, though not gone into as a preparation or trial basis for marriage, have deep ingredients of faith. These are open to the sacramentality of the Church. Consequently, the pastoral leader's attitude should be one of acceptance, leading the couple to complement their status with the sacrament. It will be more profitable pastorally to convince them about the grace of the sacrament, the Church, the Eucharist, the will of God for them and the blessings of marriage, than to stress the wrong or sinful character of their current state. In fact, many couples who are cohabiting and approach the Church to be married are by this very action indicating that they are seeking something more profound and deeper in their relationship and see the Church and Christ as a means whereby they can respond to that inner, spiritual yearning.

We will now examine what personal experiences and the behavioral sciences have to say about cohabitation and, then, outline certain pastoral approaches to cohabiting couples who come to the Church seeking marriage.

INPUT ON COHABITATION
FROM PERSONAL EXPERIENCES
AND THE BEHAVIORAL SCIENCES

The number of unmarried couples living together in 1984 totaled 1,988,000 —a tripling since 1970. That represents an estimated 4 percent of all couples or family units residing in the United States.[55] Both parents and those involved in marriage preparation could testify from personal experience to this rapid

---

54. *Family Communication*, p. 257.
55. Ibid. In the consultation process, one advisor judged that this section on cohabitation would not have relevance for the urban black community, with a presumed high incidence of cohabitation. In that connection, the *Journal of Marriage and the Family* 49:3 (August 1987): 131, contained this pertinent information: "Contrary to the findings of previous research, black women today are not more likely to be cohabiting or to have cohabited than white women."

growth, although their impressions might lead them to raise that percentage higher than those statistics indicate.

Many, including good parents, who have witnessed or experienced the terrible trauma of divorce in their own families or within the surrounding society accept, even if reluctantly, the "common sense" arguments behind cohabitation. From a surface point of view, it seems to make sense that living together on a trial or free basis would screen out less compatible couples. In this fashion, the man and woman are enabled to recognize their fundamental mismatch and to break up before marriage. Thus, they avoid the emotional and psychological wounds and scars that tend to accompany divorce. The reasoning behind that argument might be stated in this pragmatic way: "I wouldn't dream of marrying someone I hadn't lived with. That's like buying shoes you haven't tried on."[56]

A full-page newspaper advertisement for one popular national magazine features a smiling young woman whose comments reflect this argumentation:

> I still can't believe it. . . . Jeff and I are married! We eloped last week . . . and I'm weak with joy! A lot of our friends say why get married? . . . Why not just live together? Well we did that and the time comes when you have such a deepening friendship and such a commitment to each other you want to spend your lives together officially. . . .[57]

The estimated facts are that among such cohabiting couples from one out of four to one out of eight eventually do marry.[58] Those figures could be used both to justify this "common sense" argument that cohabiting screens out poor prospects for marriage and to indicate the fear that a cohabiting couple may have that their relationship will not last.

Earlier studies in the behavioral science field also tended to support this reasoning and growing phenomenon. Several of those surveys in the 1970s suggested that cohabitation effectively sifted out incompatible couples, served as a training/adjustment period for couples, improved mate selection, and enhanced the chances of avoiding divorce. In addition, other research efforts discovered little evidence that cohabiting couples had more difficulty remaining married than those who had not lived together prior to marriage.[59]

However, more recent studies in the mid-1980s have produced quite opposite conclusions. One noted that couples who had not cohabited had higher marital adjustment scores one year after marriage than did those who had cohabited.[60] A second investigation showed that cohabitants, when compared with noncohabitants, scored significantly lower in both perceived quality of marital communication and marital satisfaction. Those differences were signifi-

cant for wives in the area of communication and for both spouses in the area of marital satisfaction. The authors conclude that the "common sense" argument as well as the previous sociological contentions that cohabitation serves as an effective training period for marriage and will result in improved mate selection are not supported by the most current statistical data. In sum, cohabitation, despite its increasing popularity, has no particular advantage over more traditional practices in assuring couple compatibility in marriage.[61]

For the Hispanic couple, the question of civil law in many Latin American countries contributes to the increase of cohabitation. Frequently, Hispanics must contract marriage first with the civil judge before they can proceed with the church ceremony.

The statistical data cited above and even the increasing popularity of cohabiting do not exert much of an impact upon the Hispanic couple. The faith and teachings of the Church carry more appeal and convincing value. In addition, since Hispanics tend to possess a more philosophical bent, arguments of that type are more influential. Thus, for example, the criticism that there is no possibility for total self-surrender when the other in the relationship can leave, that cohabitation may lead to abuse or selfishness, and that the arrangement lacks permanency may be more impactful argumentation for Hispanics.

In reality, cohabitation may reduce the possibility of eventual marriage and of greater marital satisfaction for those who do marry. Why is that so?

There appears to be some connection between premarital sex, obviously facilitated by cohabitation, and marital disruption.

One diocesan Tribunal official, for example, testifies that in a high percentage of the approximately 300 annulment cases he has studied in detail, premarital sex emerged as a common element. While he acknowledges that premarital sex may not have been a direct cause of the couple's problem, this coincidence seems to suggest a correlation with their marital unhappiness.[62]

56. "When Unmarried Couples Live Together," by Dr. Joyce Brothers, in *Reader's Digest* (March 1986): 11.
57. The *New York Times* (April 16, 1975): 34-M.
58. *Family Communication*, p. 258.
59. Ibid.
60. Ibid.
61. "Cohabitation with the Future Spouse: Its Influence upon Marital Satisfaction and Communication," by Alfred De Maris and Gerald R. Leslie, in *Journal of Marriage and the Family* (February 1984): 77-84. *Time* Magazine (December 21, 1987): 51, reported on a study of 4,996 Swedish women, ages 20-44, conducted for the National Bureau of Economic Research in Cambridge Massachusetts. The report found that couples who had lived together and then married were 80 percent as likely to separate or divorce as those who had lived apart. Application of those findings to the United States, however, should be done with great caution because of differing cultural circumstances.
62. "Pastoral Letter Orders Immediate Separation of Cohabiting Couples," by Jeff Ethen, in *National Catholic Reporter* (September 28, 1984): 25.

To maintain the cohabiting relationship, couples often hide from each other important aspects of their lives.

The couples frequently withhold or conceal from each other their self-surrender, permanent commitment, and faith in the Church. Because fear lurks in the back of their minds, there is no chance to build a strong relationship. This may pose a fatal hazard by postponing the inevitable adjustments inherent in the transition from cohabitation to married life. It avoids dealing in an honest and intimate fashion with issues and relationship building dynamics that are integral to forming a committed relationship. In fact, one researcher observes that the movement from dating to "sleeping together more, staying over, preparing meals" to cohabitation and possibly to marriage is experienced more as a developmental process rather than a "conscious decision." In order to make the kind of commitment necessary to form and sustain a marriage, a free and conscious choice is essential.[63]

One scholar researched 100 couples who had lived together, married, and within five years, divorced. The majority had discussed the vital issues of finances, careers, leisure activities, and children only in the most general terms. They avoided those areas because they were afraid their differences might spoil the relationship.[64]

Cohabiting couples may tend to speak and behave cautiously to avoid criticizing each other and to repress anger, lest the relationship disintegrate.

The very tentative nature of the arrangement, as well as the statistical probability of a breakup, can cause the couple to be very cautious and tread lightly. The real person does not emerge in such a situation. If they, for some reason, judge that all irritating characteristics will somehow magically disappear after marriage, the eventual disillusionment will be devastating. Even if they are not such mistaken dreamers, their repressed anger and true selves must eventually surface and create serious conflicts.[65]

The handling of finances during cohabitation and after marriage may be quite different and a source of discord.

While living together, money earned is seen as "his" or "hers." They generally share expenses, but personal extravagances are not seen as a cause for jeopardizing their future. That shifts after marriage, when saving for a home, children, and other joint projects means that superfluous spending by one partner necessarily impacts and, thereby, can annoy the other.[66]

Relationships with members of their families and with others may be strained during the period of cohabitation.

When the couple knows or presumes that their parents and family members do not accept the living-together arrangement, they may lie or mislead people to conceal the situation. That lack of authenticity or honesty always produces inner anguish. Similarly, when the relationship is openly acknowledged but frowned upon by the parents, the distancing pain or open conflicts create difficulties for the cohabiting couple.[67]

Violation of their religious tradition may produce a guilt that, whether acknowledged or repressed, disturbs inner peace and can surface later in other destructive ways.

For Roman Catholics, the teaching about premarital sex and cohabitation is very clear and publicly recognized. While the couple may, on the surface, reject those norms, the breaking of moral codes inculcated since one's youth is not accomplished without some misgivings or adjustment problems.

The absence of unique marital graces bestowed by God through the sacrament of matrimony, presumably not present in a couple cohabiting without nuptial promises, must weaken, even if in intangible fashion, their efforts to build a stable relationship.

Marsha, a twenty-two-year-old graduate student moved in and out of a cohabiting relationship and finally on to marriage. She illustrates the "common sense" argument behind cohabitation, its pitfalls, and a surprising resolution of the matter:[68]

My own parents divorced 15 years ago, so I was determined not to jump into marriage. That's why I moved in with Tom—so we could develop our relationship and get to know each other first.

It went from beautiful to miserable in about four months. I was knocking myself out to please him, feeling insecure whenever the arrangement seemed the least bit shaky. And I was using sex in a way that was false to myself. Intercourse was my way of reiterating, "The relationship is still on"; of asking, "Is the relationship still on?" It was my way of saying, "Keep me, I'm good!" (even when sex wasn't always that good), and of reassuring myself, "See, he still loves me."

---

63. *Paths to Marriage,* by Bernard Murstein (London: Sage Publications, 1986), pp. 91, 93.
64. "When Unmarried Couples Live Together," p. 12.
65. Ibid.
66. Ibid.
67. *Family Communication,* p. 259.
68. "Unmarried Couples Shouldn't Live Together," by Juli Loesch, in *U.S. Catholic* (July 1985): 16-17.

Important questions were never settled, things such as: "What if I get offered a good job in another state?" or "What if he decides to go back to school?" or "The Pill is making me depressed—should I stop taking it?" We'd just end up in bed again, without resolving things. I got to the point where I felt like yelling, "Sex, schmex! I just want you to talk to me!"

I told Tom I wanted to move out and think things over. I wanted him to really see me and hear me as a person—something our sexual involvement made it hard for him to do. I wanted perspective—and friendship.

I must say that—after the initial shock— Tom rose to the challenge. We spent a whole year getting to know each other every way but horizontally. We must have logged 1000 hours just talking. And I knew I wasn't sliding into something through compliance and neediness and emotional fuzziness: I was exercising real sexual intelligence. That gave me new respect for myself—and for Tom.

We're getting married. It took a while, but now we know we're committed.

PASTORAL APPROACHES TO COHABITATING COUPLES

When a man and a woman who have been cohabiting come to the parish clergy and wish to marry, with a typical and solemn wedding ceremony, they present a delicate and difficult pastoral problem or dilemma.

To confront the couple immediately and directly condemn their behavior starts the entire marriage preparation process off in sour fashion and risks further alienating perhaps already marginal Catholic persons. A confrontational and condemning approach would be very detrimental, for example, to the Hispanic community. It would be interpreted as rejection—the opposite of compassion and understanding, where faith is at the root of their relationship.

On the other hand, the clergy must be faithful to the teachings of Christ and the Church. Being pleasant and welcoming, accommodating and understanding, as well as overlooking the living-together aspect of the couple's relationship may relieve their anxieties and win popularity contests, but does it amount to tacit approval of the cohabitation?

In the past ten to twenty years, Catholic clergy have struggled with considerable anxiety over this question. Up until recently, probably most tended to overlook the situation, not pressing the couple too hard, even when their cohabiting status surfaced. They judged that, after all, the couple had asked for a sacrament, were rectifying their wrongful state, and might draw closer to the Church through the marriage preparation program and a beautiful nuptial celebration.

Some church leaders and clergy, in the last few years, have begun to take a more challenging, confrontational approach with cohabiting couples. The negative statistics and harmful effects of cohabitation outlined above certainly contributed to that new development, as well as the question of scandal to others and the potential injury to the sanctity of marriage.

In 1984, the pastor of the Bismarck (North Dakota) Cathedral wrote a letter to cohabiting couples that explained both his policy and position. It was subsequently picked up by a syndicated religious news service and received widespread publicity, certainly indicative of interest in the topic. We reprint the letter in its entirety:[69]

Dear Friends,

You have asked me to witness your marriage and I am pleased that you wish to be married in the Church. Before I give you my answer about witnessing your marriage I want to share a few thoughts with you.

I am sure that you know that the Church does not approve of your living together before marriage, and I hope you are not surprised that I also disapprove of it. By asking me to witness your marriage with the usual kind of wedding celebration, you are putting me in an awkward position. I feel that if I do witness the vows in a big celebration I am giving tacit approval to your present behavior. I would be treating you in the same way as I would treat a couple who has not been living together. I am uncomfortable with that because I want to encourage young people to live up to Catholic Christian standards before marriage.

Let me try to explain why I think that what you are doing is wrong. I don't want to talk just in terms of the commandments, though I believe what you are doing is contrary to them. I would rather talk about your relationship to the community—both the civil community and the church community. Both these communities disapprove of couples living together prior to marriage.

By your living arrangements, you are saying quite publicly that you don't care very much what these communities think. And yet, now you come to me, an official in the church community, and ask me to treat you in the same way I would treat a couple who had respected the community's customs and rules.

Putting it another way, you have been living as if married, in effect saying to the

69. "Living Together: What's a Pastor to Do?" by Rev. Thomas Kramer (Bismarck, N.D.: Cathedral of the Holy Spirit).

community, to your friends and your families, that you wish to be treated as if married—at least you want to live that way. But now, you come and say you want to be treated as unmarried and have a big celebration of the fact that you are now marrying. There is some kind of contradiction here, and it puts me in a difficult spot. If I say yes, I seem to be saying that what you are doing is okay. If I say no, I am refusing to help you get back into the community.

I think that living together and sexual relations prior to marriage are wrong. Sexual relations is a sign and symbol of a total gift of one person to another. That total gift is made in the marriage vows in which two people give themselves publicly and irrevocably to each other for life. To engage in sexual relations before making that formal, public, permanent gift and commitment in marriage is to falsify the sacred symbol that sexual intercourse is. It is to give yourself in this act that symbolizes total giving, but which in this case can be reversed because you haven't given yourself to each other in marriage. We don't like people who give gifts and then take them back. Even children see the error in that; but premarital sex can too easily become such a gift, which can be taken back.

God's laws regarding sexual behavior are not whimsical nor arbitrary. They are guidelines to the deep significance of sexuality in our lives. They recognize the profound sacredness of our sexuality and are directly opposed to the cheap, selfish and shallow view of sexuality that is found in so much of our culture.

I think I can understand the social and economic pressures and your own feelings that have led you to live together. I would like to hear your reasons, but I am convinced that another solution could have been found—and even still can be—that will permit me to witness your marriage.

I would be happy to witness your marriage in a simple, quiet ceremony with two witnesses and perhaps your immediate families. That is what I would do if you had been married in a civil ceremony and now wished to have the marriage validated in the Church.

By your living together you seem to be saying, "We want to be like married people." I would be very happy to treat you like married people, and witness your vows simply and quietly.

But I have serious difficulties with treating you like any other couple wishing to be married, who has not been living together.

Another possible solution might be for you to live separately from now until marriage. That would be a public statement to your family, your friends and to me that you are trying to live your courtship in a Catholic way.

I hope you will think about these things. I also hope you will come to see me again and that we can work out some way that will allow me to witness your marriage.

I am happy that you love each other, and that you wish to marry. I hope that we can work out the difficulties that I have had with your present living arrangements.

I hope to hear from you soon.

Shortly after publication of the Bismarck letter, also in 1984, Most Rev. George H. Speltz, then bishop of the Diocese of St. Cloud (Minnesota), issued a "Pastoral Letter on Cohabitation."[70]

Responding to a study and recommendations from his Presbyteral Council, Bishop Speltz, in the lengthy document, made these major points: cohabitation is no preparation for marriage; sexual intercourse is for marriage only; intercourse is a sign of self-giving; and cohabitation can be a deterrent to good communication, as well as to marital fidelity. He then established the following diocesan policy:

With the sanctity of the Sacrament of Matrimony in mind, in the name of the Church, I wish to affirm her traditional position that living together outside of marriage is immoral and is a scandal to the community. At the same time, I wish to convey, as strongly as possible, the Church's deep concern for the spiritual well-being of couples living together before they are married and about their continuing participation in the life of the church community. The Church, in her wisdom and compassion, knows that premarital chastity engenders marital chastity and, therefore, a greater chance for genuine fulfillment and happiness within Christian marriage. Mindful of that wisdom and compassion, I affirm the following policy regarding couples wishing to be married in the Diocese of St. Cloud:

1. When marriage preparation begins, the priest is to determine whether or not the couple is living together.
2. If couples intending marriage are living together, they are to begin living separately immediately.
3. If they do not comply, the priest shall refuse to witness the marriage. If, however, the

---

70. *Pastoral Letter on Cohabitation*, by Most Rev. George H. Speltz (September 4, 1984). Available from: Family Life Bureau, 305 North 7th Avenue, Suite 102, St. Cloud MN 56301.

priest deems it advisable for compelling pastoral reasons that the marriage should take place:

a) The celebration of the sacrament shall be in private in the presence of the witnesses and the immediate families.

b) The parish facilities will be available to the wedding party and the immediate families only.

c) The couple is bound to all the guidelines of the existing marriage policy of the diocese.

About a year afterward, the Family Life Office of the Diocese of St. Cloud conducted an informal survey among the clergy about the document's impact. They learned that approximately 150 out of the 1600 couples in marriage preparation courses were living together. Of those 150, 77 agreed to live apart, 51 refused to comply, and 22 were involved in special circumstances. Some of the clergy have opposed the policy from the beginning but do comply with the regulations.[71]

Few other dioceses have explicitly adopted the Bismarck or St. Cloud regulations, even though there has been good support for both statements.[72]

Several dioceses have issued documents on cohabitation that offer fairly detailed suggestions on how to respond pastorally to this question.[73]

For example, the current marriage policy for the Diocese of Cleveland, with its companion resource book, explores in some depth reasons why couples do live together and includes several operational criteria or guidelines to assist the clergy and others who work with cohabiting couples. They recommend, among other suggestions, that a special premarriage inventory be given to all cohabiting couples and that, as a general pattern, a full nuptial Mass would not be celebrated for couples who are living together.[74]

The Diocese of Peoria, as another illustration, in its guide for pastoral counseling on the matter, stresses that this is a "teachable" moment for the cohabiting couple. The Church's minister, in such a situation,

should strive to respond with pastoral sensitivity, lest a positive motivating factor on the part of the couple be frustrated. The minister should try to meet the couple where they are, accepting them as persons who may well be in the process of spiritual growth and leading them toward reconciliation with God, the Church and their families.[75]

This guide recommends that the minister explore a number of areas about marriage with the couple and offers these questions for assistance in that process:

1. Why did they choose to live together (e.g., fear of permanent commitment, testing the relationship, convenience, need for companionship, financial reasons, escape from home)?

2. What have they learned from their experience of having lived together?

3. What is it that is causing them to want to commit themselves to marriage at this time?

4. Was there a previous reluctance/hesitation to marry? If so, why? Are they now at a new point of personal development?

5. What is it that prompts them to marry in the Roman Catholic Church at this time? In other words, why have they approached a Catholic minister?

6. What does marriage as a sacrament/sacred union mean to them?

7. How do they see their faith and love and the continued growth of that faith and love for one another as being an intimate part of their marriage?[76]

The guide then provides these concluding practical directives:

If, after the pertinent issues have been discussed, the minister is pastorally satisfied that the couple is acting in good faith, he or she should prepare them for marriage in accordance with this Common Policy. At this time, the minister might suggest to the couple that they separate. In making this suggestion, the minister should relate that separation would best reflect the Church's understanding of their situation and could be in their own personal best interest in that separation could allow them the space needed to be more objective about their relationship.

Since cohabitation is not a canonical diriment impediment to marriage, the minister need not postpone or refuse the continuation of their marriage preparation because the couple does not separate. However, if there is not sufficient awareness on the couple's part of the essential commitments in the marriage they are entering, the marriage

71. "Bishop Says Ban on Cohabitation before Marriage a Success," by Karen Mills, in Syracuse *Herald-Journal* (January 18, 1986): A-9.
72. Most Rev. Joseph A. Fiorenza, bishop of the Diocese of Galveston-Houston, issued a somewhat similar pastoral letter on October 8, 1987.
73. For example: "Guide for Pastoral Counselling with Couples Cohabiting before Marriage" (Diocese of Peoria, 1987); "Diocesan Policy for Cohabiting Couples Seeking a Church Marriage," including "A Pastoral Approach to Cohabiting Couples Seeking Matrimony" (Diocese of Galveston-Houston, October 8, 1987); "Marriage Policy for the Diocese of Cleveland" and "Department for Marriage and Family Ministry Resource Book" (Diocese of Cleveland, April 3, 1988).
74. "Marriage Policy for the Diocese of Cleveland," pp. 17-18; "Department for Marriage and Family Ministry Resource Book," Part III, pp. 1-8.
75. "Guide for Pastoral Counselling with Couples Cohabiting before Marriage."
76. Ibid.

should be postponed until such an awareness has developed.[77]

Another possible pastoral approach would be to use the information in this section on cohabitation as a basis for discussion during religious education classes, for inserts or comments in the parish bulletin, and for occasional homilies on appropriate Sundays. Even if the parish does not establish a blanket policy like those described above, such an education program creates a climate suitable for one to emerge and may cause future couples to ponder before moving in together.

Pope John Paul II offers an overall approach toward cohabiting couples. Pastors and pastoral leaders should, he recommends, examine each situation case by case. Moreover, they ought to make "tactful and respectful contact with the couples concerned and enlighten them patiently, correct them charitably, and show them the witness of Christian family life in such a way as to smooth the path for them to regularize their situation."[78]

The following testimony from a young military officer from Texas describes the initial sexually active courtship days with his girlfriend and a subsequent change in that pattern. The shift materialized after personal reflection upon their developing relationship and extended discussions with a priest advisor:

I was involved in a relationship that was really pretty good in all respects. After six months, the growth of this relationship stopped. I really was not sure what I should do, but I knew that I liked this relationship and that it could possibly develop as a lasting one.

My girlfriend and I decided not to "sleep" together any more. It really took a lot of discipline, but we figured it would pay off in the long run, no matter what became of the relationship. Time passed and the desire to be "together" was strong, but because we had committed ourselves to this special agreement we were successful. It felt like we were doing something together, as one, to strengthen our relationship. We found that our relationship had grown more in one month than over the first six months combined. We had discovered a new life within our relationship.

A month had passed when I realized that I did indeed love my girlfriend. The love was strong and had grown stronger by the week. We developed a great deal of respect and found many new and wonderful things about each other. The relationship had come alive. Sex no longer seemed as desirous because we were having so much fun learning new things about each other and ourselves.

The next great thing to happen to us was our new relationship, together, with God. This really put our relationship on an even stronger foothold. We could barely believe how great a relationship we had. We were so proud of ourselves and of each other. When our relationship did hit a low point, which I feel all relationships will at some time, we had recalled experiencing the beauty and gratification of a full relationship. The low point quickly passed and the relationship actually became stronger. With a strong faith in our relationship and God we realized that our life together could and can overcome anything.

From a small agreement and commitment between two adults came an incredibly wonderful relationship based upon mutual respect for each other and upon a faith that God will be with us at all times. My girlfriend will no longer be my girlfriend, she will be my wife in a few months.

3 Interreligious Marriages

There exists an awkward ambiguity about terms used to describe marriages between Catholics and those who are not Roman Catholic. For example, one hears or reads of "mixed," "ecumenical," or "interfaith" marriages. But since, for example, marital unions may involve a Catholic and a baptized Christian; a Catholic and a Jewish person; a Catholic and a Muslim (a growing phenomenon in the United States); or a Catholic and a nonbaptized, nonchurch-affiliated individual, each of those labels fails to encompass all of today's situations. We have chosen, therefore, the word *interreligious* as a generic term in this handbook to cover any marriage that involves a Catholic and a partner who is not Roman Catholic. The cases in which the latter possesses absolutely no faith or religious belief are relatively few in number. Almost all partners who are not Roman Catholic would consider or categorize themselves as "religious" to some degree at least, even if not affiliated with any particular religion or faith. Consequently, the term *interreligious* appears to be sufficiently accurate, provided we understand that the various types of marriage under consideration here vary greatly from one another—from both a theological and pastoral viewpoint.

Theologically, the marriage of a Catholic and a person who is validly baptized is a sacrament and enjoys all of the characteristics of a sacramental marriage. Pastorally, the differences of religious affiliation and beliefs require special attention in the process of marriage preparation. Those differences can introduce profound strains, not only in terms of the marriage ceremony itself but, more important, in the

77. Ibid.
78. *On the Family*, nos. 80-81.

community of life, which is one of the ends of marriage. For this reason, the Church requires a special dispensation for a Catholic to marry a non-Catholic.

CURRENT STATISTICS

Interreligious marriages are common among Roman Catholics, and the number, percentage-wise, is growing. At the present moment, about 40 percent of American Catholics enter into an interreligious marriage when they marry.[79]

The following trends from another body of research on interreligious unions may be helpful background for those in marriage preparation work:[80]

- In 50 percent of interreligious marriages, one of the spouses converts to the other spouse's religion. In previous periods, a Protestant spouse normally became Roman Catholic. Today, that trend has been reversed and evened out. Conversions are the same in both directions.

- The strength of one spouse's religious conviction is the most important factor influencing the conversion process. Persons of weaker conviction generally convert to the religion of the individual with a stronger conviction.

- Nearly all conversions take place at the time of the marriage or before the first child is ten years old.

- Interreligious marriages are often most successful when one spouse converts to the other's religion. The continued presence of religious differences definitely can reduce marital satisfaction and decrease church involvement.

- Lack of companionship and disagreement over children's religious upbringing are the most common causes of strife in interreligious marriages.

- As far as Christian religions are concerned, the mother has a stronger influence on the children's religious identification than the father, but the religious practice of the father is a very important predictor of the long-term religious commitment of the children, especially of the sons.

- Interreligious marriages—at least those of Protestant-Catholic unions—are more likely to end in divorce than either Protestant or Catholic same-faith marriages. However, it is not clear if that religious difference is the cause of the disruption or one of several factors behind the breakup.

PASTORAL APPROACH

These statistics clearly indicate the importance and delicacy of marriage preparation for those who seek to enter an interreligious union. The large and growing number of such couples tells us that we have here a major reality in the Church—a reality to which we must respond in as positive a way as possible. The shift in religious affiliation and the high rate of marital discord or divorce within interreligious marriages also tell us, in sobering terms, that in the preparation program, we are dealing at a most critical moment with relationships that are quite fragile in many ways. The marriage preparation process may well have a direct impact upon both the religious and marital future of the bride and groom.

We offer the following suggestions about the proper pastoral approach in such situations:[81]

The priest or deacon who conducts the initial interview with the couple seeking an interreligious marriage needs to do so with a delicate and confronting realism. As we have seen, the woman and man approaching the Church for marriage come with considerable anxiety—yet, also, with dreamy expectations. To be confronted at once with negative statistics or comments about an interreligious marriage will probably prove very unproductive and even generate hostility. On the other hand, the facts are the facts, reality is reality, and the couple must ultimately face both.

Perhaps, the best approach is to place the detailed discussion of these facts and realities after the initial stages of the encounter. By then, the couple's anxieties about arrangements should have been reduced and a cordial relationship established between the clergy and the couple. At that point, the priest or deacon can, in gentle fashion, introduce some of the statistical observations above and other commonly understood obstacles involved with an interreligious marriage, especially the promises to be made by the Catholic party. That introduction may lead them to confront reality now; to realize the generous efforts required for a successful interreligious marriage; to think about their differences; to decide about the children's religious upbringing before the marriage; and to undergo more eagerly the various facets of the marriage preparation program.

In other settings, such as religious education classes and occasional homilies, an explanation of

79. Rev. Eugene Hemrick, NCCB/USCC Office of Research (Washington, D.C., 1987).

80. *To Love and to Honor: A Pre-Marriage Ministry Resource Manual* (Lansing, Mich.: Diocesan Liturgical Commission, 1983), p. 134; quoting from *Empirical Research on Interfaith Marriage in America*, by Dean R. Hoge and Kathleen M. Ferry (Washington, D.C.: USCC Office of Publishing and Promotion Services, 1981).

81. For a helpful diocesan booklet, see *Your Marriage and the Catholic Church, A Guide for Interfaith Couples* (Diocese of Cleveland, January 1986).

the challenges in interreligious marriages need to be given to our Roman Catholics. This type of instruction is not as potentially volatile as the exchange with the couple about to marry, but nevertheless, it requires great tact.

Because of the factual data we have sketched earlier, and for other reasons, the Church continues to encourage Catholics to marry Catholics.[82] Nevertheless, such encouragement and instruction, however informative and accurate, easily becomes interpreted or relayed as disapproval of those many Catholics actually living out an interreligious marriage.

While these negative dimensions of interreligious marriages need to be faced, we also must stress their positive potential. Pope John Paul II has discussed some of those possibilities, for example, in connection with the sacramental nature of Christian marriages or marriages between the baptized, with the religious upbringing of children and with a shared sacramental life in marriage.[83]

The Holy Father even explicitly comments on the positive aspects of interreligious marriages. In speaking about unions between Catholics and other baptized persons, he remarks:

> They contain numerous elements that could well be made good use of and developed, both for their intrinsic value and for the contribution that they can make to the ecumenical movement. This is particularly true when both parties are faithful to their religious duties. Their common baptism and the dynamism of grace provide the spouses in these marriages with the basis and motivation for expressing their unity in the sphere of moral and spiritual values.[84]

The interreligious couple will, of course, require an informational and formational preparation that concerns itself with marriage. However, we also encourage strongly the offering of an optional, but carefully designed, minicourse in major Catholic teachings and practices.

While this is no longer a required element for the permission or dispensation to enter an interreligious marriage, it remains highly desirable. Such a brief overview could be beneficial to both spouses and represent an effective tool of evangelization. It should renew and deepen the faith of the Roman Catholic; at the same time, it promotes better understanding within the one who is not Roman Catholic and may, even under grace, lead to that person's acceptance of Catholicism. The statistics we have cited clearly testify that at the time of marriage, couples are often open to a new or different religious experience; they also note that the strength of their religious convictions will influence greatly the couple's future church behavior or affiliation. Such data would seem to support our recommendation for some kind of a minicourse for the interreligious couple.

Those in marriage preparation must ensure that both spouses enjoy total freedom with regard to their own beliefs and practices. While partners who are not Catholic are, of course, most welcome to enter the Church—and the interreligious relationship may well be the situation that leads to that decision—there should be no undue pressure to do so or any interference in the free manifestation of beliefs through religious practice by either spouse.[85] In fact, many clergy discourage conversion at the time of marriage, lest the pressures to be Catholic in time for the wedding unduly influence the decision or foreshorten the process of investigation and reflection. An interreligious marriage may be the occasion, but must never be the cause of any conversion.

An up-front statement of this point can be a pastorally wise procedure for those working with the interreligious couple. It immediately dissipates any fears about being forced to convert, which those who are not Catholic may possess. At the same time, the priest or deacon should encourage both spouses to learn about and be familiar with the teachings and practices of each other's religion.

Efforts should be made to establish cordial and cooperative relations between the Catholic and non-Catholic clergy, both during the marriage preparation process and within the wedding ceremony itself, when such steps would be pastorally wise and are expressly desired by the engaged couple.[86]

The couple should be urged strongly to arrive at an agreeable decision about the religious upbringing of the children before the actual marriage. Otherwise, it will be a source of stress for the couple and lead to the religious confusion or neglect of the children.[87] In so doing, the promise required of the Catholic should be kept in mind. "I promise to do all in my power to share the faith I have received with our children by having them baptized and reared as Catholic."

The interreligious couple will need to explore ways in which they can develop a life of shared prayer, devotion, and service in their households while still being members of distinct religious communities. The possibilities will vary, depending on

82. "Guidelines for Ecumenical and Jewish-Catholic Relations" (Diocese of Trenton, 1981); "Guidelines for Ecumenical and Interreligious Affairs" (Archdiocese of Los Angeles); "Working with the Intermarried: A Practical Guide for Jewish Community Workshops," by Andrew Baker and Lori Goodman (New York: The American Jewish Center, 1985).

83. *"Familiaris Consortio*—New Light on Mixed Marriages," by Rev. John F. Hotchkin, executive director, Secretariat, NCCB Committee for Ecumenical and Interreligious Affairs; address delivered at a symposium on Marriage in Washington, D.C.

84. *On the Family,* no. 78. See also, Pope John Paul II's address in Columbia, South Carolina (September 11, 1987), in which he stressed the common vocation of Christian couples to work for unity in the Church and in society.

85. Ibid.

86. Ibid.

87. "Vatican Council II and Pastoral Care," *Dictionary of Pastoral Care and Counseling,* by Rev. John F. Hotchkin.

how divergent are their religious backgrounds and communities.

Since personal religious discussion may not have been a prominent feature of their conversations while dating, they need to be alerted to the fact that many people sense their religious interests, commitment, and fervor rising in the early years of marriage. Otherwise, when this phenomenon occurs, it may be misinterpreted as a distancing factor in the marriage and be misconstrued as an attempt of each partner to assert a distinct identity over the other in a competitive way.[88]

CANONICAL REGULATIONS

We summarize here the major provisions of the current *Code of Canon Law* concerning interreligious marriages, while also including references to earlier universal and national church documents that touch upon those directives:[89]

a) The Catholic Church holds that a valid marriage between two baptized Christians is a sacrament.[90] Priests and deacons may wish to inform and educate couples on the consequences of this point—that marriage to a nonbaptized person is not a sacrament.

b) The marriage of a Catholic and a Christian of another communion calls for special pastoral concern. The Catholic Church shows particular care for these marriages and treats them in a way that is distinct from its treatment of the marriage of two Catholics.[91]

c) Such marriages require permission from the local bishop. They require a just and reasonable cause as well as the following conditions being fulfilled:

(1) The Catholic party is to declare that he or she is prepared to remove dangers of falling away from the faith and is to make a sincere promise to do all in his or her power to have all the children baptized and brought up in the Catholic Church;

(2) The other party is to be informed, at an appropriate time, of these promises that the Catholic party has to make, so that it is clear that the other party is truly aware of the promise and obligation of the Catholic party;

(3) Both parties are to be instructed on the essential ends and properties of marriage, which are not to be excluded by either party.[92]

d) The declaration and promise by the Catholic party, necessary for permission to enter any interreligious marriage, is to be made in the following or similar words:

I reaffirm my faith in Jesus Christ and, with God's help, intend to continue liv-

ing that faith in the Catholic Church. I promise to do all in my power to share the faith I have received with our children by having them baptized and reared as Catholics.[93]

The pastoral minister should draw the attention of the Catholic to the communion of spiritual benefits in a Christian marriage. The declaration and promise should be made in the light of the "certain, though imperfect, communion" of the non-Catholic with the Catholic Church because of his or her belief in Christ and baptism:[94]

It is evident that in preparing for a mixed marriage, the couple will have to reach decisions and make specific choices in order to fulfill successfully the responsibility that is theirs toward their children in this respect. It is hoped for their own sake that in this matter, the couple may reach a common mind ... if this issue cannot be resolved, there is a serious question whether the couple should marry.[95]

e) The declaration and promise are to be made in the presence of the priest or deacon. The one who submits the request for permission or dispensation to enter an interreligious marriage shall certify that the declaration and promise have been made by the Catholic party and that the other party has been informed of this requirement and fact. This is to be done in the following words:

The required declaration and promise have been made by the Catholic in my presence. The non-Catholic has been informed of this requirement so that it is certain that he/she is aware of the promise and obligation on the part of the Catholic.

f) The instruction on the ends and essential properties of marriage, which are not to be excluded by either party, is in addition to the customary

88. Ibid.
89. This summary is based upon the "Province of Chicago Ecumenical Guidelines," revised in 1986.
90. Eph 5:30; *Dogmatic Constitution on the Church*, no. 11; *Code of Canon Law*, c. 1055.
91. *Code of Canon Law*, c. 1124.
92. Ibid., c. 1125.
93. *Apostolic Letter on Mixed Marriages*, no. 7; *Statement on the Implementation of the Apostolic Letter on Mixed Marriages*, National Conference of Catholic Bishops (Washington, D.C.: USCC Office of Publishing and Promotion Services, 1971).
94. *Decree on Ecumenism*, no. 3. "To do all in one's power," recognizes the religious convictions of the non-Catholic party and implies that a decision is reached that respects those beliefs. It does not mean an absolute promise at the risk of jeopardizing the marriage itself. Decisions of the Sacred Congregation for the Doctrine of the Faith (May 17, 1966; June 18, 1966; July 9, 1966; December 10, 1966; December 12, 1966; February 17, 1967).
95. *Statement on the Implementation of the Apostolic Letter on Mixed Marriages*.

marriage preparation program and should be done on a direct and individual basis.[96]

g) Each one preparing couples for an interreligious marriage should emphasize that such a marriage is an opportunity to live the principles of ecumenism deeply and intensely on a day-to-day basis.

h) In the assistance that is given to prepare for a marriage between a Catholic and one of a church or ecclesial community not in full communion with the Catholic Church, and in the continued efforts to help all married couples and families, the priest (or deacon) should endeavor, where wise and requested, to be in contact and to cooperate with the minister or religious counselor of the other party.[97]

i) The impediment of disparity of cult, holding invalid the marriage between one who was baptized in the Catholic Church or received into it and another not baptized, even though such may claim some Christian affiliation, remains in force.[98]

j) The Canonical Form of the celebration of marriage, required for validity (i.e., that the marriage take place in the presence of the Catholic pastor of the place [or his delegate, either priest or deacon] and two witnesses) is to be observed in interreligious marriages.[99]

k) The local ordinary may grant permission for an interreligious marriage, dispensation from the impediment of disparity of cult, and dispensation from Canonical Form for reasons such as the following: "to achieve family harmony or to avoid family alienation; to obtain parental agreement to the marriage; to recognize the significant claims of relationship or special friendship with a non-Catholic minister; to permit the marriage in a church that has particular importance to the non-Catholics."[100]

l) In an interreligious marriage, for which there has been granted a dispensation from Canonical Form, an ecclesiastical record of the marriage shall be kept in the chancery of the diocese that granted the dispensation and in the records of the parish from which the application for the dispensation was made.[101]

m) It is forbidden to have, either before or after the canonical celebration of marriage, another religious celebration of the same marriage either to give or receive matrimonial consent; nor may there be a religious celebration of the marriage in which the Catholic priest or deacon and a non-Catholic minister, each performing his or her own rite, ask for the consent of the parties.[102]

n) A marriage between a Catholic party and baptized non-Catholic party is to be celebrated in the parish church. With the permission of the local ordinary or the pastor, it may be celebrated in another Catholic church or oratory. The local ordinary can also allow it to be celebrated in some other suitable place.[103]

o) At an interreligious marriage in a Catholic church, when the party who is not Catholic expresses the wish to have his or her minister present, the Catholic pastor (or his delegate) should issue an invitation, giving an assurance of a cordial reception. When issuing such an invitation, the Catholic pastor (or his delegate) should advise the guest minister to wear whatever is deemed appropriate and that a place of honor will be reserved either in the sanctuary or in the body of the church. However, it should be kept in mind that this invitation will not be accepted in every case and, perhaps, not even be welcome because of either an official church policy or the specific minister's personal preference. The couple, thus, may need to be alerted that even though we will extend the invitation in accord with their wishes, it may be declined by the other minister for reasons of church policy. That will spare them the feeling that they are personally being spurned.

p) The guest minister may be invited to participate in the Catholic marriage service by giving additional prayers, blessings, or words of greeting or exhortation. If the marriage is not a part of a eucharistic celebration, the minister may also be invited to read a lesson and/or preach. For him to preach as part of a eucharistic celebration, a special dispensation from the diocesan bishop is required in individual cases.[104]

q) In a marriage between a Catholic and a baptized person who is not Catholic, the *Rite for Cele-*

96. *Apostolic Letter on Mixed Marriages*, no. 6; *Code of Canon Law*, c. 1125:3; *Statement on the Implementation of the Apostolic Letter on Mixed Marriages*, no. 3.
97. *Statement on the Implementation of the Apostolic Letter on Mixed Marriages*, no. 4.
98. *Code of Canon Law*, c. 1086.
99. Ibid., cc. 1108; 1127:1.
100. *Statement on the Implementation of the Apostolic Letter on Mixed Marriages*, no. 10; *Apostolic Letter on Mixed Marriages*, no. 9; *Code of Canon Law*, c. 1127:2.
101. *Statement on the Implementation of the Apostolic Letter on Mixed Marriages*, no. 12.
102. *Apostolic Letter on Mixed Marriages*, no. 13; *Code of Canon Law*, c. 1127:3. *Directory for the Application of the Decisions of the Second Vatican Council concerning Ecumenical Matters*, Part I, no. 56; *Statement on the Implementation of the Apostolic Letter on Mixed Marriages*, no. 15.
103. *Code of Canon Law*, c. 1118:1 and 2.
104. *Ecumenical Directory*, Part I, no. 56; *Statement on the Implementation of the Apostolic Letter on Mixed Marriages*, no. 15; *Bishops' Committee for Ecumenical and Interreligious Affairs Newsletter* I:3 (July 22, 1972).

brating Marriage outside Mass or, when available, *A Christian Celebration of Marriage: An Ecumenical Liturgy* may be used. The latter rite has been developed by the Consultation on Common Texts and approved by the National Conference of Catholic Bishops in November 1987; approval from the Holy See is pending. If circumstances justify it, and providing the couple request it, and provided that no undue pressure has been exerted and the party who is not a Catholic does not have to act against his or her conscience . . . , "the rite for celebrating marriage within Mass may be used, except that, according to the general law, communion is not given to the non-Catholics." For exceptions to the general law, see below.[105]

r) In a marriage between a Catholic and one who is not baptized, the *Rite for Celebrating Marriage between a Catholic and an Unbaptized Person* is to be used.[106]

s) In the case where there has been a dispensation from the Canonical Form and the priest or deacon has been invited to participate in the marriage service, his participation should be the same as outlined above, for the minister of a church or ecclesial community not in full communion with the Catholic Church at a Catholic rite of marriage.

t) Members of a church or ecclesial community not in full communion with the Catholic Church may act as official witnesses (i.e., best man and maid of honor) at a Catholic marriage, and Catholics may do so at marriages in churches or ecclesial communities not in full communion with the Catholic Church, except when there is reason to believe that the marriage to be witnessed is invalid in the eyes of the Catholic Church.[107]

u) The banns for an interreligious marriage may be announced. However, the publication of banns should be omitted if it violates the norms of the other church or ecclesial community.[108]

v) In a marriage between a Catholic party and a separated Eastern Christian, the Canonical Form obliges only for lawfulness; for validity, however, the presence of a sacred minister is required, with the observance of the other requirements of law.[109]

w) The ordinary of the Catholic party in a Catholic-Orthodox marriage may dispense from observing the Canonical Form for lawfulness if there is a pastoral reason that, according to his prudent judgment, requires this dispensation.[110]

x) Catholic-Orthodox marriages are to be entered carefully into the prescribed registers as soon as possible.[111]

EUCHARISTIC SHARING

In 1986, we issued several brief guidelines that, in popular terms, convey the regulations of the Church on extending general invitations for those who are not Roman Catholics to receive Holy Communion at our eucharistic celebrations. To other Christians, we said:

We welcome to this celebration of the Eucharist those Christians who are not fully united with us. It is a consequence of the sad divisions in Christianity that we cannot extend to them a general invitation to receive Communion. Catholics believe that the Eucharist is an action of the celebrating community, signifying a oneness in faith, life, and worship of the community. Reception of the Eucharist by Christians not fully united with us would imply a oneness that does not yet exist, and for which we must all pray.

To those not receiving Communion at a Roman Catholic Eucharist, we commented:

Those not receiving sacramental Communion are encouraged to express in their hearts a prayerful desire for unity with the Lord Jesus and with one another.

To those participating at a Eucharist who are not Christian, we explained:

We also welcome to this celebration those who do not share our faith in Jesus. While we cannot extend to them an invitation to receive Communion, we do invite them to be united with us in prayer.[112]

This prohibition of general invitations to receive Holy Communion, extended toward those who are not Roman Catholic, mirrors the legislation in the *Code of Canon Law* (c. 844). It would, therefore, be inappropriate for a priest or deacon, during the course of a nuptial Mass, to invite all participants or even to welcome simply anyone who is Christian to receive Holy Communion.

At the same time, the identical canon and other earlier church decrees do allow instances in which individual Christians, under certain conditions, are welcomed to receive penance, Eucharist, and anoint-

105. *Rite of Marriage*, Introduction, no. 8, and ch. II; *Apostolic Letter on Mixed Marriages*, no. 11.
106. *Rite of Marriage*, no. 8, and ch. III.
107. *Ecumenical Directory*, Part I, no. 58.
108. *Code of Canon Law*, c. 1067.
109. *Decree on the Catholic Eastern Churches*, no. 18; *Decree on Catholic-Orthodox Marriages, Code of Canon Law*, c. 1127:1.
110. *Decree on Catholic-Orthodox Marriages; Code of Canon Law*, c. 1127:2.
111. *Decree on the Catholic Eastern Churches*, no. 18; *Decree on Catholic-Orthodox Marriages; Code of Canon Law*, c. 535:1.
112. "Guidelines for Receiving Communion," National Conference of Catholic Bishops (Washington, D.C., November 8, 1986).

Petition for Marriage Permission or Dispensation

BRIDE		**GROOM**
_____	Name	_____
_____	Address	_____
_____		_____
_____	Age	_____

Religion

☐ Catholic	☐ Catholic
☐ Baptized Non-Catholic	☐ Baptized Non-Catholic
Denomination: _____	Denomination: _____
☐ Unbaptized	☐ Unbaptized
_____ Parish	_____
_____ Place	_____

Scheduled date for Marriage Ceremony _____

Because of the following circumstances, this couple petitions the Diocesan Bishop to grant permission and/or dispensation from impediment(s) to permit their marriage:

☐ **Mixed Religion** (c. 1124) and, if necessary, **Disparity of Worship** (c. 1086.) See reverse side.

☐ Dispensation from the **Canonical Form of Marriage** (c. 1127:2). See reverse side.

☐ Other reason(s) in law necessitating permission and/or dispensation (cc. 1071, 1083-1094)

Explain: _____

_____

_____

_____ **RESERVE FOR CHANCERY USE** _____

The above indicated petition is hereby granted.

_____   _____
Date   Delegate

In cases involving **Mixed Religion** or **Disparity of Worship,** the Catholic party is to make the following promise, either in writing or orally:

"I reaffirm my faith in Jesus Christ and, with God's help, intend to continue living that faith in the Catholic Church. I promise to do all in my power to share the faith I have received with our children by having them baptized and reared as Catholic."

_____
Signature of Catholic Party

Affirmation by the Priest/Deacon:

"The required promise and declaration have been made by the Catholic in my presence. The non-Catholic has been informed of this requirement so that it is certain that he/she is aware of the promise and obligation on the part of the Catholic."

_____   _____
Date   Signature of Priest/Deacon

FOR DISPENSATION FROM CANONICAL FORM

Church: _____

Address: _____

Name of Officiant: _____

Date of Marriage: _____

Names of Witnesses: _____

Dispensation from the **Canonical Form of Marriage** is requested for the following reason(s):

- ☐ To achieve family harmony or avoid family alienation.
- ☐ To obtain parental agreement to the marriage.
- ☐ Significant relationship or special friendship with non-Catholic minister.
- ☐ Religious edifice has particular importance to non-Catholic.
- ☐ Other reason(s)—explain: _____

_____

I request that the above petition(s) be granted for the following reason(s):
- ☐ Spiritual welfare of the couple.
- ☐ Convalidation of existing marital union.

_____
Signature of Priest/Deacon

_____
Rectory Address

_____   _____
Date   Place   Zip Code

ing of the sick.[113] Because in addition to the bond of baptism, Christians married to Catholics also have a further sacramental bond of matrimony linking them with the life of the Catholic Church, their requests for admission to these sacraments merit altogether particular attention. Cases envisioned for this participation at weddings are necessarily rare; the documents in the above footnote explain the requirements for such a possibility.

Given the restrictions on general invitations to eucharistic sharing, it often is a wise policy for an interreligious couple not to celebrate their wedding in the context of a nuptial Mass.[114] That could serve to stress the split that exists between their own and their families' religious beliefs and practices rather than highlight the harmony of their love.

More satisfactory, normally, is the scriptural marriage ceremony without Mass. It eliminates the problem of division that we mentioned and provides greater options for participation. In addition, the Catholic party naturally can participate in the Eucharist at an earlier time during the day.

Having mentioned these things, however, we wish to note the positive effect a well-prayed eucharistic liturgy can have upon an interreligious couple who are marrying, as well as upon their families and friends. Moreover, such a nuptial celebration in the context of a Mass does underscore our desire to relate all of the sacraments more closely to the Eucharist.

PETITION FOR PERMISSIONS OR DISPENSATIONS

Given the ever-increasing mobility of our society, there are distinct advantages to having standardized marriage forms or questionnaires for the United States. We offer the following sample application for permissions or dispensations, as well as the subsequent Prenuptial Inquiry Form, to help in that process. Each diocese, of course, is free to develop its own or to adapt those presented in this manual.

The comments that follow may assist the pastor or his delegate in using the petition in a more easily efficient and pastorally effective manner.

a) *Fact of baptism.* To determine the validity of the baptism of the partner who is not Roman Catholic, these guidelines should be kept in mind:

- Baptisms and confirmations in Orthodox churches are always valid.

- Some Christian churches do not baptize infants, but "dedicate" or "enroll" them at that time. Later, actual baptism needs to be verified.

- Other Christian churches officially hold to a valid formula and ritual (flowing water and Trinitarian formula), but actual observance of the essential form and rite may

be ignored or substantially altered by the baptizing minister. That, too, will require verification.

- However, the petition form covers this situation by requesting, if necessary, dispensation from Disparity of Worship should the baptism prove invalid.

b) *Other reasons necessitating permission and/or dispensation.* These include (c. 1071) the local ordinary's permission for the marriage of transients; people who cannot be recognized or celebrated in accord with civil law; one bound by natural obligations toward another party or children arising from a prior union; one who has notoriously rejected the Catholic faith; one bound by a censure; a minor child, when the parents are unaware of it or are reasonably opposed to it; those entering the marriage by proxy, mentioned in c. 1105. These also include the local ordinary's dispensation from invalidating or diriment impediments (cc. 1083-1094) such as: age (The *Code* sets for a valid marriage the completion of the sixteenth year for the man and of the fourteenth year for the woman. However, many—if not most—dioceses have raised the age requirement for a licit marriage to eighteen or nineteen.); impotency; a prior bond; Holy Orders; religious profession; abduction; crime; consanguinity; affinity; public propriety; and relationship.

c) *Promise.* Note that the promise can be given orally, as well as in writing. In those cases, the Catholic party does not need to sign the document.

d) *Canonical Form.* The "church" is the church or place (e.g., a Protestant church or hotel ballroom) where the marriage is to take place. The "officiant" is the minister or rabbi who will witness the vows.

e) *Spiritual welfare of the couple.* This could include, for example, a well-founded hope of conversion for the partner who is not a Catholic; the pregnancy of the bride; the danger of marrying outside the Church; legitimization of children; regularization of an already sexually intimate relationship.

By following the pattern of the initial interview provided below, the need for a dispensation should surface early and, consequently, the petition should be sent early in the preparation process and not at the last moment. The petition or dispensation will need to be noted in the marriage registry of the parish.

---

113. In addition to c. 844, the following documents address this issue: *Decree on Ecumenism* (1964); *Ecumenical Directory* (1967); *Instruction concerning Cases When Other Christians May Be Admitted to Eucharistic Communion in the Catholic Church* (1972); *A Note about Certain Interpretations of the 1972 Instruction* (1973).

114. From the *Rite of Marriage,* Introduction, footnote 13. According to the words of *The Constitution on the Sacred Liturgy,* repeated in no. 6 of the aforementioned Introduction, the celebration of marriage normally takes place during Mass. Nevertheless, a good reason can excuse from the celebration of Mass (cf. *Inter Oecumenici,* no. 70: AAS 56 [1964] 893), and sometimes, even urges that Mass should be omitted. In this case, the *Rite for Celebrating Marriage outside Mass* should be used.

Working Together

Two interrelated matters, if dealt with well, can contribute greatly to the success of a marriage and, on the contrary, if dealt with poorly, can almost certainly doom the union of husband and wife. Those issues are the handling of finances and the differing roles of women and men in a marital relationship.

FINANCES

An East Coast savings bank placed a large advertisement in the daily newspaper, featuring pictures of Presidents Washington, Lincoln, Jackson, and Hamilton excerpted from dollar bills.[115] Underneath those four images was the headline, "These Four Guys Are Responsible for a Lot of Broken Marriages." The text went on to state:

> If money could talk, these four would have some tales to tell. Because more than half the marriages in America break up over money. The real problem, though, is that most couples start yelling before they ever try talking. So here, in the public interest, are four tips for domestic tranquillity.

The bank goes on to offer the following practical suggestions about money matters in a marriage:

1. Talk about money. Especially if you're newlyweds, or about to be. You've got a lot to learn about each other.

2. Both of you must feel that you're contributing your fair share. If your incomes are wildly different, then contribute proportionately. Be sure to recognize the value of unpaid work.

3. One person—the one with the better money sense—should keep the family checkbook and say the two most important words since "I do": "We can't."

4. Set financial goals. If you don't know where you're going, it's hard to get there.

The married couples that we have consulted on this topic would agree with those recommendations from that savings bank and add these observations:

Establish and adhere to a budget. From the very beginning of the marriage, this type of planning seems critical. That means knowing how much is coming in and how it is going out, including assigned amounts for recreation, church, and savings.

Agree upon and follow priorities. Deciding upon the important and essential, as well as upon the attractive but nonessential, may prove particularly crucial in the first years of marriage, when significant adjustments in spending habits have to be made for a variety of reasons.

Determine who best handles the financial details. Clear and loving communication is needed both to establish the priorities and to determine who most enjoys handling money matters. Always talking through major expenditures such as a new refrigerator, car, or house, of course, should be an understood and expected procedure. However, managing the actual budget, writing checks, and paying bills may be the free choice of one spouse or the other. In one household, to illustrate, the husband keeps track of the budget while the wife writes all the checks and monitors the bills. In another, the wife takes care of both the budget and its implementation.

Always save something. From the start, and even in hard times, the setting aside of an amount, however small, for a savings account has some kind of subtle positive value for the marital relationship—beyond the sum accumulating in the bank.

Be wary of credit cards. Writing a check or paying out cash keeps the limitation of one's income clearly in perspective; that vision somehow gets lost or blurred when persons use credit cards too spontaneously.

Distinguish between wants and needs. Our consumer culture constantly seeks to transform wants into needs. Falling victim to this societal pressure can cause serious difficulties in both personal and marital lives.

We have indirectly addressed this question of family finances in several parts of our recent pastoral letter, *Economic Justice for All.*

First of all, we urged all the People of God, including spouses and families, to adopt sacrificial giving or tithing as a way of life for supporting the Church's mission and helping the world's poor.[116] In this concept, the person or family initially decides what percentage of total income—ten percent in the case of tithing—will be given back to God through donations to Church and charity in gratitude for gifts received from the Creator. Then, they keep the rest of that income for their own needs and wants.

This is, consequently, a priority-type procedure that places spiritual relationships or one's connection with God first in the decision-making process. It requires establishing a decided upon location for church and charitable contributions in the budget, not leaving these donations to the category of habit, leftover amounts, or spontaneous out-of-pocket giving. Finally, sacrificial giving or tithing facilitates an understanding of the difference between needs and wants.

Second, in the delicate, complex matter of making decisions about responsible childbearing and

---

115. The Wilmington *News-Journal* papers (July 10, 1986): A-4.
116. *Economic Justice for All,* no. 351.

childrearing, as noted earlier, we urged husbands and wives to "weigh their needs carefully and establish a proper priority of values as they discuss the questions of both parents working outside the home and the responsibilities of raising children with proper care and attention."[117]

In that section, we raised questions about needs and wants. Do both spouses have to work outside the home to garner necessary income or do both work simply to make it possible to acquire or enjoy desirable, but unneeded items?

Finally, the section on "Biblical Perspectives" of the Christian vision of economic life discussed, at length, the responsibility we possess as stewards of God's creation and gifts to share our time, talent, and treasures with others, especially the poor.[118]

In addition to its evident use for purchasing goods and services, money also possesses symbolic value and power. It can be employed to dominate people, to make another feel helpless, and to exercise control over spouse or children. It can also be employed to free people, to give persons a sense of worth, and to provide independence for spouse or children.

All Christian couples, likewise, need to face the issue of poverty. Even if they do not experience what it is to be actually impoverished, spouses are called by the gospel message to live in a spirit of poverty, to cultivate a simplicity of life style, and to reach out toward those in need. Many, however, like a great number of Hispanics, truly live in poverty or close to the poverty line. That represents a challenge both for them and for those who could assist them.

As we said, money matters, if dealt with well, can contribute greatly to the success of a marriage; if finances are dealt with poorly, they can almost certainly doom the union of husband and wife.

DIFFERING ROLES

Over the past two decades across the United States, the enormous shift in the roles of women and men within marriage has, understandably, exerted a tremendous impact upon marital relationships. The following are illustrative of that change in roles or attitudes and some of its consequences for marital life:

Today, 60 percent of women with children under eighteen work outside the home, most of them out of economic necessity.[119]

Recent university studies at Yale, the University of Illinois, and the University of Michigan reveal how differently men and women perceive marriage. According to this research, the main attraction for men is "her looks"; for women, "his earning potential." The important or essential element in a marriage for men is her ability to make love and their shared interests; for women it is how well he handles her parents, how well each gets along with the other's friends, and marital fidelity. Men tend to judge that a marriage relationship is doing well in communi-

cation, finances, relationship with parents, listening to each other, tolerating each other's flaws, romance; women tend to judge that a marriage relationship is not doing well in all the above.[120] While these may not be new differences between women and men, the studies do highlight a diversity of views or attitudes that will have a decided influence upon their roles and relationships.

Within the family unit, men and women are learning to help one another according to their gifts and talents rather than limiting themselves to traditional roles of father and mother. Both are willing to cook, clean, earn money, and care for the children. In broader society, also, both men and women are developing new skills and confidences in a variety of roles that were once the exclusive domain of the other sex. Now, both men and women can be doctors and nurses, politicians and scientists, workers and managers.[121]

More and more women see themselves as gifted, fully autonomous persons, able to define themselves in ways other than in relation to men. Their self-concept has been enlarged.

There is a growing demand, mostly initiated by women, that there be a more equitable sharing of the duties of family life and recognition by society of the importance of equal opportunity for meaningful work outside the home.

Women are stronger in their refusal to accept low pay, low status, poor working conditions, and blocked access to executive-level jobs. They resent the expectation that they share in the financial support of the family, while carrying alone the full burden of child care.

There is a marked change in the pattern of interpersonal relationships between men and women. Women are no longer content to be passive.

Work place and schedule are being altered: flexible hours in the work place; part-time work with benefits; parental leave with pay so that both fathers and mothers can leave their work temporarily to care for their infants; flexible work arrangements so that they can work at home, and so forth.

There is an increased sensitivity to "sexist" language in all areas of society—secular and religious.

Many of our Hispanic Catholics have different experiences and many Hispanic women may not be in these trends and patterns of our society. Moreover, the role of women in Church is, perhaps, more important for the transmission of our faith and catechetics.

117. Ibid., nos. 332-336.
118. Ibid., nos. 28-60; see also, nos. 61-95.
119. "Poverty Striking Women at Different Life Stages," by Jo VandenBerg and Ellen McKay, in *Charities USA* (December 1986): 21-24.
120. "Two Views of Marriage Explored: His and Hers," by Daniel Goldman, in *New York Times* (April 1, 1986): C-1, C-11.
121. These societal changes and the seven others that follow were noted in "Changing Roles of Women and Men," the intervention of the National Conference of Catholic Bishops at the 1980 Synod of Bishops, as reported in *Origins* 10:19 (October 23, 1980): 299-301.

In the face of these massive and impactful shifts, we would like to make a few comments or suggestions:

We view co-equality, interdependence, and complementarity of men and women in marriage and in the institutions of society as the will of God. It is a fact that major tasks in society—government, medicine, education, religion, childrearing—can be best accomplished by men and women in co-equal and complementary cooperation and partnership. The world, in fact, needs the benefits of this total creative energy in all areas. The Holy Father affirmed and encouraged this when, in his exhortations, he asked women to transpose the exercise of their qualities from the private sphere to the public one . . . and when he asked men to allow the nuturing sides of their personalities to enrich their family life and child care.

Those changes in the roles of sexes that reflect gospel values and the teaching of the Church are legitimate and respond to the inspiration of the Holy Spirit. As parents discover that certain values traditionally deemed "feminine" or "masculine" can be reappraised and adopted by both men and women on behalf of the family, children will develop a broader and deeper range of mental and emotional reactions to functions they may later have to perform. They will also be in a better position to evaluate critically the meaning of personal qualities as opposed to "sex-determined" functions. In this way, both Church and civil society will be enriched by a proper appreciation and use of God's gifts.

The importance of work in Christian life must be understood adequately, and women must be given free access to meaningful work and equal pay. Work must be seen not only as a means of earning one's living, but also as a means for persons to develop their own creative capacities and skills; to take part in the process of building up a more just society as a link whereby people can experience and develop solidarity with others; and as an opportunity for broader dialogue and self-fulfillment. This way the private and social aspects of people's lives will be linked.[122]

In these matters, the variety and individuality of each person, as well as the age-level of the family, should be recognized. Today, for example, the woman who is very comfortable with and deems extremely valuable a full-time role as homemaker and mother may feel great pressure from peers and the surrounding culture to seek employment outside the home, even when no added income is necessary. We judge it regrettable that the economic situation in our society also compels many who would prefer to give their total energy and attention to tasks at home to work full or part time. On the other hand, many feel a need to work outside the home not for economic necessity but for other reasons of personal growth or community service. They find that such a part-time break from home and child care gives them a fresh perspective and renewed enthusiasm, as well as curbing

---

122. Ibid. These proposals were, likewise, made at the 1980 Synod of Bishops.

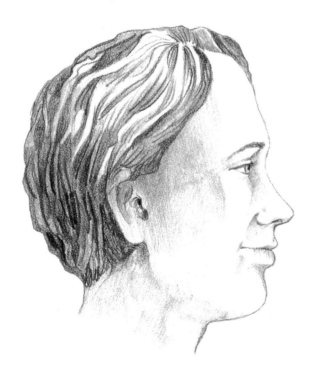

the development of an excessive dependence of their children upon them. Nevertheless, those who work outside the home, especially on a full-time basis, seem to experience real concern about their inability—due to a lack of personal energy or immediate availability—to be actively present and attentive listeners to their daughters and sons at important moments. Wrestling with those conflicting demands appears to cause a certain amount of guilt among some and a tender defensiveness among others.

The following story illustrates, in a real way, these shifts in roles and the struggles that can accompany those changes:

> A husband and father was watching professional football one night on television, folding diapers as he did so. The man's father stopped in for a visit, felt stunned by what he saw, expressed annoyed shock at his son, and angrily pulled the basket of diapers away from him.
>
> "What are you doing? That is her job!"
>
> After a long and painful silence, the son quietly, but firmly reached for the basket of diapers, pulled it back to him, resumed his task, and responded, "But they are my children, too."
>
> His father never raised the issue again.

The integration and adjustment of old and new roles for men and women in marriage continues to be a shifting, complex, and highly personal phenomenon in the contemporary world. But dealing patiently, openly, and wisely with the concerns involved is crucial for the success of any marriage.

 A Variety of Preparation Programs

We will sketch now the major types of formal marriage preparation programs, evaluating at the end their strengths and weaknesses, advantages and disadvantages. An important consideration—apart from the format of any specific program, as such—which is not treated here, is the question of proper screening of those presenting the programs. Couples seeking sacramental marriage have the right to a full, authentic witness to the doctrine and discipline of marriage as expressed in the previous pages. Therefore, presenting individuals should be identified who clearly espouse in word and deed with joy and gratitude the authentic teaching of the Church regarding marriage, including fidelity, indissolubility, and birth control.

ENGAGED ENCOUNTER

This weekend experience for engaged couples grew out of the Marriage Encounter format and follows its fundamental concepts. Conducted by a priest and two married couples—the junior couple married five years or less; the senior couple married five years or more—it can serve as few as three to four engaged couples, up to as many as twenty to twenty-five, depending upon the need and the facilities available.

After each presentation, the engaged couples are given a list of pertinent questions and asked to select several that are particularly relevant to them. During a ten-minute period, each person then writes out her or his individual responses to the questions. At the signal, everyone seeks out her or his partner, and together, they share the responses and discuss them.

The main thrust of the weekend is to facilitate couple communication on a wide range of topics such as self-knowledge; obstacles to relationships; current concerns (e.g., children, in-laws, sex, drugs); making decisions; sexuality; the sacramentality of marriage; service to the Church and to others; careers; parenting; a plan of life; and the healing of relationships.

There is an optional Mass Saturday morning; a candlelight prayer service Saturday night; a discussion of betrothal on Sunday morning, with encouragement to compose such a formula; and a concluding Eucharist on Sunday night, during which those who wish to do so read the betrothal texts they have written.

Evaluation: This weekend program offers the couple an intense, three-day experience away from their environment and free of distractions, which forces them to examine their relationship in some depth. The fact that, following an Engaged Encounter weekend, some couples break off their engagement speaks about its effectiveness in helping them come to grips with the realities in their relationship.

The possibility of providing Mass and other prayer services is a plus for Engaged Encounter, as is the deep sharing of the couples and priest. The length of time available and the location provide a climate of honest, extended communication on tough issues, which usually is not feasible in some other marriage preparation formats.

On the negative side, the weekend, despite use of modest facilities, may seem a relatively large expense to the engaged couple. In addition, it represents more of a time-and-energy commitment than many couples are willing to give to their marriage preparation. Moreover, its intensity may frighten away some couples.

Engaged Encounter is judged by many to be a fine marriage preparation program, but should not be the only format available.

DIOCESAN OR REGIONAL "PRE-CANA" CONFERENCES

These vary, of course, from diocese to diocese and from region to region, but the fundamental approach would parallel the arrangement of the following sessions offered in an eastern seaboard diocese:

The Family Life Office there provides a six-hour experience, either on a Sunday afternoon or split between a Sunday afternoon and Tuesday evening. The number of conference participants will range from thirty to sixty couples. The presenting team is comprised primarily of married couples and a priest or deacon, but some are single persons with expertise in particular fields. There is no eucharistic celebration, but a few of the teams conclude their conferences with a brief paraliturgical celebration.

For the engaged couples, leaders propose numerous workshops on typical topics such as communication, spirituality, finances, sexuality, adjustments and ideals, career and marriage, parenting and natural family planning. Only the last one is obligatory; from the others, each couple selects several workshops that appeal to them and respond to their needs.

Emphasis is more on facilitating communication between the engaged couple, through written and shared exercises following each presentation, rather than on giving extensive input from the speakers. Printed materials—excellent for stimulating discussion and taken from contemporary commercial publications—are distributed to participants following each brief talk. The engaged couple are never allowed quite enough time to exhaust their discussions. Some moments are scheduled with the entire group to permit sharing of thoughts and feelings by each engaged pair, but this type of disclosure remains totally optional. The cost for this type of conference is $20.00 per couple.

Evaluation: This experience gives the engaged couple an opportunity to see that they are part of a wider picture. The presence of so many other couples, all reaching for the same goal, has a certain motivational power in itself. Moreover, the testimony and expertise of several married couples are valuable. These sessions lightly cover the crucial topics and promote good dialogue between each couple. They are relatively inexpensive. Shy and retiring couples may be more comfortable in the anonymity of the large group. Those not motivated to attend or not at ease with Engaged Encounter should find these sessions acceptable.

On the negative side, the exchanges are less intense than in Engaged Encounter. The relationship that develops between the engaged and married couples, likewise, cannot be as close nor the modeling by the married couple as potent. The individualism of the engaged couple can be lost. Of necessity, these sessions are scheduled early in advance and, therefore, do not admit of much flexibility. An alternative is needed for those with conflicts in dates and places. The many limitations in these types of conferences with large groups have led many Family Life Directors to judge them as hardly adequate.

PARISH "PRE-CANA" CONFERENCES

Some parishes or clusters of parishes sponsor conferences very similar to the typical one outlined above. They have all the advantages and disadvantages noted for the diocesan or regional events.

Evaluation: With regard to speakers, the parish has less to draw on in terms of resources and will presumably not attract as large an audience. However, the parish has a local flavor, which possesses its own value, and it may be more convenient. Finally, the subsequent modeling (e.g., seeing the presenters at Sunday Mass) is more liable to occur in the parish than after diocesan or regional conferences.

PARISH "ONE-TO-ONE" OR "COUPLE-TO-COUPLE" PROGRAMS

An increasing number of parishes have developed a corps of committed married couples who will host the engaged in their homes for an evening or several evenings of sharing on marriage. The sessions are mostly informal, but with an outline or framework that ensures that they cover the key issues of sex, communication, in-laws, careers, parenting, religion, finances, forgiveness, friends, and prayer. In some situations, the engaged and married are matched one-to-one. In others, the married couple may host several engaged couples at a single session.

There are a few commercial texts that provide guidance and help with this format, but generally speaking, the married couple simply share from their own experiences and carry on considerable dialogue with the engaged pair throughout the encounter. The following outline, used by a large suburban parish in Arizona that celebrates about ninety weddings each year, is illustrative of this approach:

- A priest interviews the couple at the start to put the pair at ease, to learn about their background, and to determine what type of preparation will be best for them.

- He then arranges for them to complete the FOCCUS instrument and, when the results are available, spends several sessions with the engaged couple, reviewing the areas of agreement and disagreement that have surfaced.

- Next, the couple join four or five other engaged pairs for six nights of the "Evenings for Engaged," conducted by married parishioners trained for this task.[123] The priest attends the last session to present a talk on the theology of marriage, to cele-

---

123. The booklet *Evenings for the Engaged* is available from: Pastoral and Matrimonial Renewal Center, 67 Prince Street, Elizabeth, NJ 07208.

brate Mass in that home, and to share in a potluck supper.

- The engaged couple return for another meeting with the priest who will preside at their wedding. He takes care of technical details, discusses the ''Evenings for Engaged'' with them, offers the further option of an Engaged Encounter weekend, supplies ideas and materials for their preparation of the wedding liturgy, and gives them a personalized plaque.

- After developing the celebration itself, they come back to visit with the priest to talk about the liturgy and are introduced to one of the four wedding hostesses who will guide them through the rehearsal and be present for assistance at the wedding itself.

Evaluation: The willingness to share, the depth of care, the ability to listen, the testimony of experience, and the wisdom from years of reflection will vary from married couple to married couple. Those factors largely determine each encounter's effectiveness or ineffectiveness. Persons uncomfortable with large crowds may find the intimacy of these sessions much more to their liking. The possibility exists for great modeling in marriage and faith. Personal follow-up after the marriage, likewise, becomes feasible. The possibility of adjusting schedules to resolve conflicts, which many of today's couples face (e.g., being separated by careers and only occasionally being together) is a unique and crucial benefit of this format. The married couples also appear to profit greatly from these sessions with the engaged couples.

As we mentioned earlier, the unique contributions that ''one-to-one'' or ''couple-to-couple'' encounters offer have led us to urge the establishment of a corps of such committed married people in every parish.

COMBINED PARISH AND REGIONAL OR DIOCESAN PROGRAMS

One Canadian diocese developed a marriage preparation program that combined the best features of the above formats.

For example, when there are twenty-five engaged couples preparing for matrimony, the system works in this fashion: The engaged are divided into groups of five, with each unit assigned to a particular married couple. They meet for three consecutive Sunday nights to discuss certain marriage matters. On the fourth weekend, the five groups (twenty-five couples, plus five leaders) assemble for a weekend experience similar to Engaged Encounter. There, they cover additional matters—including the wedding ceremony—and celebrate reconciliation on Saturday night.

Evaluation: This seems to be an almost ideal program, merging the best of all the above formats. However, it represents a significant expenditure of time, energy, and money for all concerned.

INTERRELIGIOUS PROGRAMS

For many years, one diocese featured a conference for those facing interreligious marriages. The married couples were all interreligious; both priest and minister participated. However, in recent years, this specialized program ended due to lack of registrations. Despite the increasing number of interreligious marriages, the couples simply do not find religious differences a problem or challenge for them. For many reasons, that reaction is a bit ominous, indicating almost a lack of interest in religion, rather than the sign of a remarkable ecumenical harmony.

Evaluation: A regrettable loss.

SPONSOR COUPLE

In this system, a married couple is specially trained by a regional or diocesan office and assigned in the parish to the marriage ministry. They may, for example, meet with the engaged couple, administer the chosen premarriage inventory, score and discuss the results afterward, assist in the preparation of the liturgy, and, finally, seek to provide aftercare following the marriage.

While such a ''sponsor couple'' often, likewise, take part in the ''couple-to-couple'' or ''one-to-one'' encounters described earlier, their training and function move them beyond that stage of marriage preparation ministry. Thus, they may keep a closer, more personal and continuous contact with a particular engaged pair than do the married couples who simply host the ''one-to-one'' experiences. Moreover, as we noted, the sponsor couple may also oversee or administer much of the parish premarriage preparation efforts.

Evaluation: A praiseworthy development, providing it does not eliminate or diminish the clergy's critical role, which we have discussed elsewhere.

It is for the priest or deacon, during the initial interview, to sketch for the engaged couple the nature of the programs available—with an evaluation of each—then to help them select the one or the combination of them that best fits their circumstances.

6 The Initial Interview

As we have mentioned in several contexts, the initial interview with the church representative is a high-risk, emotionally filled, critical moment for the engaged couple. We also urged the priest or deacon who will preside over the liturgical celebration to conduct this first meeting. Here, we offer to that priest or deacon an outline format for the beginning session, which seeks to establish a cordial and relaxed, but still challenging and profound relationship between the engaged and the clergy. At the same time, it tries to provide, in an efficient way, the desired practical wedding information; to secure deftly some needed data; and to handle in delicate, but forthright fashion, sensitive issues that may arise.

Having ensured that, wherever possible, there will be no interruptions during the interview except for emergencies, and having greeted the engaged couple in a warm, welcoming way, the priest or deacon could proceed with the initial encounter along this route:

- *"Where do you work?"*

The object, at this point, is to begin by a non-threatening question with which one or both of the engaged are very comfortable and about which they feel knowledgeable. The place and type of employment fit into that category. The discussion that follows the question can prove both interesting and informative for the clergy and serve as an icebreaker for the couple. Later, after the engaged depart, it would be helpful to make a few notes about each one and insert those recollections into the inquiry form. This will prove useful at subsequent meetings as a means of recalling highlights of their background.

For Hispanics, this could be a sensitive question and might be better phrased: "What is your trade or work?" ("*¿En qué trabaja?*"). An additional inquiry, similar in purpose, would be: "Where do you come from?"

- *"How did you meet?"*

This edges the exchange ever so slightly into a more personal, intimate area. A little humor may aid in taking any edge off the question for them: "You probably met at the college bar, but you are going to tell your children it was at a church picnic, right?"

- *"What was your first impression of her? Of him?"*

The discussion, while still on a light level, nevertheless, now delves a bit deeper and becomes somewhat more revealing. In fact, the couple may never have shared with each other this particular information. Obviously, the responses will vary greatly ("I didn't like him at all"; "She seemed stuck up"); routine at times, but on other occasions touching or laughable.

- *"Why do you think you fell in love with each other?"*

We are now plunging rather swiftly and profoundly into the matter of their relationship. For most, this question will leave them puzzled, unable

to answer. A few remarks can be both educational and facilitating at this point. For example:

> That is a tough question. Contemporary psychologists tell us that, in our complex society, the reasons why we fall in love are so complicated and hidden that only an in-depth analysis would reveal the hidden reasons behind this phenomenon. Some scholars, however, say we tend to fall in love with our ego complement—a person who helps complete us, who helps fill up what is lacking in ourselves. For example, a hot-tempered, excitable person may fall in love with an even-mannered, quite controlled individual; a superorganized person with one who is more comfortable simply letting things happen; an outgoing person with a more shy, retiring individual. Do any of those combinations fit the two of you?

In many instances, the couple will nod and quickly describe some of their differences. The goal, however, is not to complete an instant analysis of the relationship, but simply to engage them in a deeper discussion about relationships in general, with their own as a starting point.

The priest or deacon will find the earlier section on a quest for loving intimate relationships valuable in formulating and pursuing this particular question.

- *"What is his most endearing quality for you, right now? Hers?"*

We have now taken them to a surprising and affirming moment in the interview. This normally brings forth a personally positive comment that, quite naturally, warms the heart of the other and prompts a similar remark in return.

These five questions and the dialogue they elicit may require from five to fifteen minutes, depending upon how articulate the couple is. Nevertheless, they give the priest or deacon a better awareness of the couple and more important, help establish a warm, positive connection with the engaged pair and the clergy. This will be especially important should difficult issues surface later in the exchange.

- *"So you wish to get married. Wonderful! Would you tell me a little about your religious upbringing?"*

This inquiry can produce an extensive response or a few short sentences. However, it will surface the matter of an interreligious marriage—should that exist—and perhaps, also reveal some careless church attendance. Rather than deal with those issues at this juncture, the priest or deacon might make a mental note, knowing he will come back to them later in the interview.

If the interreligious situation does arise, this

additional question could be useful: "Have you talked about those religious differences?" That will sometimes disclose that they have already resolved appropriately all the issues; in other circumstances, it will be clear that they have not discussed them at all or that serious problems are present. Normally, it would be best to postpone moving into a fuller discussion of the interreligious matter until later in the interview, unless a major obstacle or impediment to the marriage has emerged and must be worked out before proceeding with arrangements.

A short positive welcome or mere word of encouragement to the one who is not Catholic would be in order before initiating the next question.

● *"Are there any serious obstacles standing in the way of your marriage in the Church, such as either one or both of you having been married before?"*

Obviously, this is designed to surface any impediment, especially a previous bond of marriage. Should that arise, the whole interview procedure clearly has to halt and assume a different direction. In many—if not most—cases, that difficulty would have been addressed earlier by the person affected and resolved before the engaged come to set the date for a church wedding. If not, however, the priest or deacon must interrupt the marriage preparation process and move to a discussion of the necessity of an annulment. All of those previous relationship-building questions now become especially significant, since some negative and disheartening news may need to be given to the engaged couple.

● *"What date and time do you wish for your wedding?"*

Having ascertained, in an informal manner, that there are no invalidating impediments or major obstacles, the priest or deacon can now reserve the date and time in the parish marriage book and in his own personal appointment book. As the priest observed in the letter introducing this section of the manual, we have now reached the issues of high interest for the engaged couple. Establishing and reserving the time and date for the church is a major move in their preparation process. Making a little ritual out of that by securing the actual marriage reservation book and writing the information into the volume as they observe dramatizes this important event. Should they have planned the rehearsal time at such an early date, that hour could also be noted in the two books.

Here would be the moment to secure a copy of the Prenuptial Inquiry Form and complete several items. On the cover page, the first four lines and, if known, the fifth line (rehearsal), could be completed. On the inside, questions 1 and 2, but without the oath, might be asked in order to provide future information. If these appear to reveal a cohabiting rela-

tionship, that should be noted mentally, for possible discussion at the end. If there is a policy about a cohabiting arrangement, then the priest or deacon needs to explain and discuss that matter now before proceeding. Then, by flipping to the back page of the inquiry form (the checklist page), the priest or deacon can also check off items 1 and 2 (Mass Book and personal appointment book).

All of these steps help to ritualize a major decision and moment for the engaged couple.

● *"After I explain some of the practical details about a wedding in our church, would you be sure to tell me if I have missed anything?"*

Since the pressing concern for the couple at this moment are matters such as the organist, offerings, and so on, the priest or deacon might skip over the marriage preparation program information for the time being and explain the wedding details, as outlined.

As we have observed, efficiency could dictate preparing this information on a duplicated sheet to be distributed to the couple. On the other hand, jotting down the data as a handwritten note to be given to the engaged has a more personal flavor to it.

Understandably, each parish possesses its own practical rules and regulations. We would, however, like to make a few observations about three particular concerns:

Banns of marriage. These can be explained not only as a legal process to ensure freedom to marry, but more as an announcement to the community to rejoice over and pray for the engaged couple in their preparation.

Liturgy booklet. Description of this could wait until presenting them with a text from which to read over the scriptural, prayer, and blessing options.

Offerings. The following introduction may assist in presenting the connected money matters more positively:

> It does not cost anything to be married in our church. Still, if you will be spending a considerable sum of money on other items such as the reception, flowers, and formal dress, it seems fitting to make a proportionate gift or offering to God, through the church and through those who will serve you at the wedding. To help you in this regard, here are the usual amounts that people give to the church, the organist, the servers, and so forth. If you wish to make these offerings, simply put them in envelopes, mark them, give them to me at the rehearsal, and I will see that each one receives your gift.

The names and standard amounts would be added to that list of items to be cared for by the couple.

Each priest or deacon develops his own style of

treating the items on the checklist. Listing those matters on the form is simply an aid to remembering what major practical concerns require some explanation.

Hispanic couples will often require a pastoral leader's personal help in gathering the baptismal certificate, whether from Mexico, Cuba, Puerto Rico, etc. The leaders may need to assist directly and even make personal contact for those records. Thus, more time is needed to gather this documentation. It may be necessary to explain the civil requirements for obtaining the marriage license and then to repeat it.

- *"Are you wondering about any preparation classes that we have available or require before marriage?"*

Much of the couple's defensiveness and anxiety should now have been reduced substantially through these discussions and explanations. The engaged pair, as our introductory letter attests, have obtained what they came for: the reservation of the church and information about practical details. Consequently, we trust that they are, at this time, more relaxed and better disposed to hear about the marriage preparation program—the instrument used, the variety of classes, the sponsor couple, and so forth.

The priest or deacon should find useful for his presentation the statistical data about the value of marriage preparation programs covered in the previous part of this section. Also, as we have noted, he needs to discuss with the couple what program best fits their circumstances.

- *"Did you know that we invite you to plan a wedding celebration that will be very much your own and personal to you?"*

Nearly two decades of experiences with couples actually planning their wedding liturgies have made this possibility fairly common knowledge to engaged couples today. Nevertheless, the formal description of alternatives and actually giving copies of a booklet to the couple to help them read through the options and select their preferences continues to be surprising and pleasant news for them. It represents a gift from the Church and symbolizes a climate of openness to their individual creativity.

In a subsequent section, we will make some pastoral suggestions about this moment in the interview.

- *"Do you have any questions?"*

Having now cared for all the details and distributed the materials, the priest or deacon can wrap up the interview with one final question. It is also the time to sit back and, in a less-pressured way, discuss delicate issues that have surfaced earlier (e.g., inactive church attendance, an interreligious marriage, cohabiting). Any specific steps to be taken, such as the optional minicourse in Catholic teachings and practices, can be worked out then.

- *"When would you like to come again?"*

The back page of the inquiry form provides space for two appointments. While each parish, priest, and deacon works these matters out quite differently, we would recommend setting a date after the completion of the instrument/marriage preparation course portion and at least one month before the wedding. They will then have had an opportunity to ponder comments made at the interview; perhaps, change their current religious practices; read the liturgy preparation text; benefit from the instrument results and the preparation experiences; secure the necessary documents; determine the time of the rehearsal; and be in a better frame of mind to complete the full investigation form.

- *"Would you care to pray before leaving?"*

A spontaneous prayer and a reading from the Scriptures taken out of the liturgy preparation text conclude the session on a spiritual note.

7 The Prenuptial Inquiry

A RECOMMENDED FORM, WITH PASTORAL SUGGESTIONS FOR ITS USE

The revised *Code of Canon Law* directs the conference of bishops to issue norms concerning the examination of the parties and other appropriate means for carrying out the necessary investigations that are to precede marriage.[124] Moreover, there are good reasons that suggest that a standardized Prenuptial Inquiry Form for the United States would be pastorally useful. Several bishops have spoken on this point at recent conference meetings.

In responding to this direction and recommendation, an Ad Hoc Subcommittee of the Bishops' Committee on Canonical Affairs collected samples of existing premarriage questionnaires from dioceses throughout the country. The committee judged three as the most suitable for general use. A group of pastors and parochial vicars then selected one, made several minor revisions in it, and returned the edited version to the NCCB Committee on Canonical Affairs for consultation. That committee subsequently offered two small recommendations, which are incorporated into the form included here.[125]

---

124. *Code of Canon Law*, c. 1067.
125. Most Rev. John R. Keating chaired the subcommittee that selected the investigation forms from Atlanta, Richmond, and San Francisco. The pastoral consultants chose the Richmond version and made the minor revisions contained in the form that appears here. The NCCB Committee on Canonical Affairs, under the chairmanship of Most Rev. Adam J. Maida, reviewed the proposed text and approved it—with two small suggestions—at their July 2, 1987 meeting (Pittsburgh). Those suggestions were subsequently made in the document. The three pastoral consultants field-tested samples of the proposed text with over one dozen engaged couples, whose input resulted in a few typographical improvements in the form itself.

The Prenuptial Inquiry Form being presented with this handbook has, therefore, been prepared in consultation with the NCCB Committee on Canonical Affairs. It is, however, not offered as the model, standardized, or best-available form in and for the United States. Instead, we propose it simply as a typical example, which may be useful to various dioceses when they wish to review their own forms.

Completion of the Prenuptial Inquiry is more than a legal requirement. It is also an opportunity for the Church to serve pastorally the couple preparing for marriage. We offer here some pastoral suggestions, with the hope that these comments may transform what is often a mechanical, routine, and legalistic burden into an encouraging, supportive, and catechetical moment.[126]

For easy use and storage, the complete form can be printed as a single document which, when folded, consists of six pages (8½″ × 11″). The questionnaire could also be produced as a folded four-page form, when printed without the front cover and final page. A sample of the six-page form is included in the appendix of this manual and could quite simply be adopted and adapted for diocesan use.

SOME GENERAL PASTORAL COMMENTS

Before actually completing the form itself, the church representative might offer a few remarks to the couple about the significance of the Prenuptial Inquiry. Those remarks would note:

- the public nature of marriage that leads both Church and State to have a serious concern about the marriage and to establish certain basic requirements before a couple may legally marry;

- the permanent recording of the marriage's essential facts, both in the parish marriage register and in the files of the pertinent government office;

- the need to establish, for the Church and the persons involved, that the two persons are freely giving their consent to marry and that there are no obstacles or impediments that would make the marriage invalid or illicit, according to canonical or civil law;

- the determination that the couple possesses an adequate understanding of Catholic teaching on marriage.[127]

Through these requirements, the Church wishes, as far as possible, to assure that the marriage will be beneficial—not detrimental—to the couple, to their children, to the community, and to the Church.[128]

The comments could be in these or similar words:

Now that you have completed your marriage preparation sessions and understand more clearly the great hopes the Church has for you, we need to fill out this Prenuptial Inquiry Form. As you know, because of working on the details for the wedding and making practical plans for your life after the ceremony, your marriage is a public, rather than a private, event. It will affect not only the two of you but your relatives, your friends, your coworkers, the community, the Church, and the whole world. That fact leads the Church to have a special concern about your marriage. It is anxious that your union will be truly beneficial, a blessing, and not in any way harmful to either of you, to children you may possibly have, to the community, or to the Church.

Both the Church and the State have established some basic requirements to be fulfilled before you can marry. These minimal demands are designed to ensure, as far as is feasible, that all obstacles have been

---

126. *Code of Canon Law*, c. 1063.
127. Ibid., cc. 1066-1068, 1077.
128. *Code of Canon Law: A Text and a Commentary*, James A. Coriden, Thomas J. Green and Donald E. Heintschel, eds. (New York: Paulist Press, 1985), pp. 750-752.

eliminated and that the conditions are in place for a successful marriage. The State will insist upon a few documents and ask some pertinent questions. The Church does the same with this Prenuptial Inquiry.

The questions in the Church's questionnaire are the same for both the bride and the groom. These seek to assure the Church that you are free to marry and freely wish to marry one another at this time. They also explore briefly your understanding of Catholic teaching on marriage. Those inquiries should help you appreciate better what God and the Church expect of you both now and in the future as husband and wife. In turn, the inquiries express a care and concern for you by the faith community, which you can expect will continue throughout your marriage.

After the wedding, we record the essential facts about your marriage—names, addresses, parents' names, witnesses, baptismal information, date of wedding, and presider of the liturgy—in a permanent marriage register book, kept in the parish safe. We also retain on file this questionnaire, with its documents. That will explain why we ask some of these fundamental questions. In addition, the person performing the ceremony must complete the civil license afterward and send it back to the issuing office.

As you can see, the Church takes you and your marriage seriously. It wants you to be successful as a husband and wife.

We interview you separately, even though the forms are essentially identical. This separate completion of the inquiry is a sign of respect for your individuality and surrounds the process with a climate of freedom.

Quite often, the formality and newness of this experience leave some persons slightly uneasy and even suspicious. Describing the form, as suggested above, and displaying it to both parties before proceeding with the separate interviews can ease that tension.

The pastor, with the canonical right to assist at marriages in his parish, also has the responsibility to see that the necessary marriage preparation and Prenuptial Inquiry are carried out correctly. While the actual completion of the document may be handled by another, the completion of the inquiry by the priest or deacon who will preside over the liturgy is to be highly recommended.[129] Doing so can enhance the relationship between the couple and the one who will lead their liturgical celebration. It also supplies that individual with insights and information that will prove helpful in the final preparation of the ceremony, especially in the development of the homily.

The term, "pastor or his delegate," used in the document, covers the different types of persons eligible to complete the inquiry, according to the *Code of Canon Law*, without making a suggestion as to the most appropriate one.

Using a dignified and substantial Bible for the oath, as well as a few explanatory words about the nature of that promise, intensifies the serious tone of the inquiry. While that seriousness may slightly unsettle the couple, it usually also pleases them and deepens their awareness of the sacredness of the steps they are taking. Just as establishing the actual place, date, and time accelerates their process of moving from the dream to the real world, so too this solemn oath-taking and the questionnaire itself are another step in that movement. Couples are familiar with oath-taking on a Bible during solemn ceremonies such as the inauguration of the president; employing one here adds that sacred symbol to the experience and, thus, can further dramatize the event.

Most—or at least many—couples have never taken an oath; therefore, a brief explanation in these or similar words can be a multiple teaching tool:

> In an oath, we call upon God to be a witness that what we are about to say is true. Since God's word is always truthful and never to be changed, we promise to be similarly truthful, holding ourselves responsible to God if we are not. This Bible contains the words of Scripture, which we believe are inspired by God. By placing your right hand upon these words of God, you are reinforcing by that gesture what you are agreeing to do by responding "I do" or "Yes" or "I will" to this oath.

Those who, for pastoral reasons, have had to search marriage registers and nuptial inquiries for information know how helpful it is to find entries in which the facts (names, addresses, etc.) were clearly printed. For that reason, the form itself recommends that certain items be printed, and practical experience urges that the one completing the form print legibly the given responses.

The pastor or his delegate might secure a suitable, small, popular booklet on marriage and give it to the bride for reading as the groom is being interviewed. When they exchange positions, he in turn can read the same text. This procedure has an educational or formational value and also reduces the uneasiness caused by being forced to wait for a significant period of time, without positive distractions, in a sometimes pressurized situation.

---

129. *Code of Canon Law*, cc. 530, 1070, 1112.

COMMENTARY ON THE COVER PAGE

This cover page is for the convenience of the one who completes the necessary documentation and of persons who will need the information before and after the nuptial celebration. Before the ceremony, the pastoral minister, who probably will have several couples under preparation during the same time period, can identify easily the correct questionnaire in his or her temporary file. Afterward, the cover page provides readily available data necessary for other documents (e.g., marriage license, church certificate of marriage) and, likewise, provides similar easy identification within the permanent file. Documentation (e.g., baptismal record, death certificate, annulment statement, notification return) can be stapled to the inside of the form.

At the initial meeting, the church representative and the couple might complete together the first few items on this cover page such as names, date/time/location of celebration, and presider, plus rehearsal information, if known, as well as questions 1 and 2 of the Prenuptial Inquiry Form itself. This serves as both a practical identification and a gentle, indirect, nonthreatening introduction to the legal aspects of the marriage event.

There are sound pastoral reasons for completing the rest of the Prenuptial Inquiry Form after the couple have finished their marriage preparation program and begun some of their planning for the liturgy. Normally, major obstacles or impediments will surface, in an informal way, during the first session with the church representative and can be addressed at that time. Our suggestions, given earlier, for the initial interview between the couple and the pastor or his delegate provide a pastoral way for ensuring the discovery of such possible difficulties. After their marriage preparation program and the preliminary liturgy planning, the bride and the groom will usually be more comfortable and trusting with the church representative. This creates a better climate for the inquiry experience and offers a greater possibility that it will be a positive occasion for them. Moreover, they will, through these formational and liturgical processes, generally have gained a deeper understanding of the Church's teaching on marriage, reflected personally on their own spiritual condition, and discussed some of the vital issues surrounding the marriage (e.g., children, religious differences, communication blocks). Such growth in those areas can make their subsequent dialogue with the pastor or his delegate more productive and satisfying.

Nevertheless, the completion of the Prenuptial Inquiry should be carried out sufficiently in advance (e.g., a month before the marriage) so that necessary permissions or dispensations can be secured easily and without last minute application to the Chancery Office.

COMMENTARY ON THE QUESTIONS IN THE PRENUPTIAL INQUIRY

Since the form for the bride and the groom are essentially identical, the following pastoral suggestions apply to both documents.

Question 1: Occupation. While this is not an essential piece of information, it provides additional background about the person, can stimulate further exchanges between the individual and the church representative, and normally is not a threatening question. The question of cultural identity, the place of birth, and some of the other cultural inquiries are also nonthreatening. They help give the couple assurance that the interviewing clergy will understand their concerns. For Hispanics who are not accustomed to registering, the pastor or his delegate would do well to use this opportunity as a moment to explain the reason for parish registration and the value of belonging to a community.

Question 2: Religious Affiliation. If one follows our sample initial interview, the question of religion would already have been asked informally. The inquiries here, therefore, are simply a more formal noting of that data. The deeper and more delicate matter of the person's practice of her or his religion is handled by question 7. As we mentioned above, while the practice or nonpractice of one's religion will be treated informally during the initial encounter, with appropriate encouragement and recommendations made then, the formal posing of question 7 and of all those other than questions 1 and 2 might best be carried out after the completion of the marriage preparation program and after some consideration has been given to the liturgical celebration. When a difference in rite occurs, consult the *Code of Canon Law* (cc. 111-112, 214, 372, 383, 476, 479, 1119). In addition, confer with the bishop's office about special circumstances that may develop. See the earlier section on "Interreligious Marriages" for assistance with couples in which a difference of religion exists.

Question 3: Parents' Addresses and Religion. That data will reveal whether the parents are alive or deceased; disclose if they are divorced, separated, or together; and indicate the religious background or tradition of the bride and the groom. As we have indicated in remarks under "Remote Preparation," those are all powerful factors that might possibly affect the attitude that a person brings to his or her marriage.

Question 4: Baptism. A new baptismal record, issued within the past six months and with notations concerning any previous church marriage, reception of Sacred Orders, or profession in a religious community, as well as confirmation date and place, can be stapled to the form and kept with the investigation. Should the document, a subsequent question (e.g., nos. 9 or 20), or previous discussion disclose the

Cover Page

Prenuptial Inquiry
AND
Necessary Documentation

Groom: _____ Bride: _____

Date/time of the nuptial celebration: _____ at _____

Location: _____

       ☐ Celebration with Mass   ☐ Celebration outside of Mass

Presider of the Liturgy: _____

Rehearsal on: _____ at _____

Best man: _____

Maid/matron of honor: _____

Entered in marriage register: Volume _____ page _____

Church and date of groom's baptism: _____

_____

Notification of Marriage: Sent _____ or Entered in baptismal register: Volume _____ page _____

Church and date of bride's baptism: _____

_____

Notification of Marriage: Sent _____ or Entered in baptismal register: Volume _____ page _____

Required notification sent to appropriate state agency: _____

Pastor or delegate: _____

(Each party must be interviewed alone. The pastor or his delegate will propose the questions and write the given answers.)

GROOM

The pastor or his delegate, having reminded the groom of the sacred character and binding force of an oath, will ask: Do you solemnly swear to tell the truth and nothing but the truth in answering the questions that shall be submitted to you, so help you God and these holy scriptures which you touch with your hand? _____

1. Your full name? _____
   (print)

   Address? _____
   (print)

   How long have you lived at this address? _____ Home: _____
   Phone

   Occupation: _____ Work: _____

2. Your religion? _____ To what parish and rite do you belong? _____

   _____ In what diocese do you live? _____

3. Date and place of your birth? _____

Father's	Mother's

   Name: _____ Maiden name: _____
   (print)   (print)

   Address: _____ Address: _____
   (print)   (print)

   Religion: _____ Religion: _____

4. Were you ever baptized? _____ In what religion? _____

   Date? _____ Church? _____ Place? _____

QUESTIONS 5, 6 AND 7 ARE TO BE ASKED OF CATHOLICS ONLY

5. First Holy Communion   Yes? _____   No? _____

6. Confirmation?   Yes? _____   No? _____   Date? _____

   Church? _____ Place? _____

7. How would you describe your practice of your religion? _____

   When did you last approach the sacrament of Penance? _____

   When did you last receive Holy Communion? _____

---

8. Give the names and addresses of two persons (preferably parents or relatives) who could testify to your freedom to marry: _____

   _____

9. Have you ever previously been married or attempted marriage, even a civil marriage, or lived in

   a common law union? _____ If so, how many times? _____

   Name of former spouse(s) and her (their) religion? _____

   _____

Was it dissolved by (a) Death? (give date) _____

(b) Ecclesiastical Decree? (date and Tribunal) _____

10. Has your intended bride ever been married or attempted marriage, even in a civil marriage?

    If so, how many times? _____

    Give the name(s) of her former spouse(s) _____

11. Are you related to your intended bride by blood (kinship), or by a legal relationship (in-laws), or by adoption? _____

12. Have you or your intended spouse any physical, emotional, or psychological situations which may seriously affect your marriage? _____ Explain _____

    _____

13. Is any person or circumstance forcing you to enter this marriage against your will? _____

    Is any person or circumstance forcing the bride to marry against her will? _____

14. Are you attaching any conditions, restrictions, or reservations of any kind to your consent to this marriage? _____

15. Do you intend to enter a permanent marriage that can be dissolved only by death? _____

16. Do you intend to be faithful to your wife always? _____

17. Do you understand that one of the purposes of marriage is the begetting and rearing of children, God willing? _____

    Do you accept and intend to fulfill this aspect of marriage? _____

    Does your intended bride accept and intend to fulfill this aspect of marriage? _____

18. How long have you known your intended bride? _____

    How long have you been engaged? _____

19. Have either your or her parents any objections to this marriage? _____

20. Is there any major fact about you, either in the present or the past, which you have not made known to your proposed spouse and which might affect her willingness to marry you? _____

Date: _____ Groom: _____

Church: _____ Place: _____

Pastor or his delegate: _____

Church Seal

(Each party must be interviewed alone. The pastor or his delegate will propose the questions and write the given answers.)

BRIDE

The pastor or his delegate, having reminded the bride of the sacred character and binding force of an oath, will ask: Do you solemnly swear to tell the truth and nothing but the truth in answering the questions that shall be submitted to you, so help you God and these holy scriptures which you touch with your hand? _____

1. Your full name? _____
   (print)

   Address? _____
   (print)

   How long have you lived at this address? _____   Home: _____
                                                                        Phone

   Occupation: _____   Work: _____

2. Your religion? _____ To what parish and rite do you belong? _____

   _____ In what diocese do you live? _____

3. Date and place of your birth? _____

Father's	Mother's

   Name: _____   Maiden name: _____
        (print)   (print)

   Address: _____   Address: _____
           (print)   (print)

   Religion: _____   Religion: _____

4. Were you ever baptized? _____ In what religion? _____

   Date? _____   Church? _____   Place? _____

QUESTIONS 5, 6 AND 7 ARE TO BE ASKED OF CATHOLICS ONLY

5. First Holy Communion   Yes? _____   No? _____

6. Confirmation?   Yes? _____   No? _____   Date? _____

   Church? _____   Place? _____

7. How would you describe your practice of your religion? _____

   When did you last approach the sacrament of Penance? _____

   When did you last receive Holy Communion? _____

---

8. Give the names and addresses of two persons (preferably parents or relatives) who could testify to your freedom to marry: _____

   _____

9. Have you ever previously been married or attempted marriage, even a civil marriage, or lived in

   a common law union? _____ If so, how many times? _____

   Name of former spouse(s) and his (their) religion? _____

Was it dissolved by (a) Death? (give date) _____

(b) Ecclesiastical Decree? (date and Tribunal) _____

10. Has your intended groom ever been married or attempted marriage, even in a civil marriage?

    If so, how many times? _____

    Give the name(s) of his former spouse(s) _____

11. Are you related to your intended bride by blood (kinship), or

    by a legal relationship (in-laws), or by adoption? _____

12. Have you or your intended spouse any physical, emotional, or psychological situations which

    may seriously affect your marriage? _____ Explain _____

    _____

13. Is any person or circumstance forcing you to enter this marriage against your will? _____

    Is any person or circumstance forcing the groom to marry against his will? _____

14. Are you attaching any conditions, restrictions, or reservations of any kind to your consent to

    this marriage? _____

15. Do you intend to enter a permanent marriage that can be dissolved only by death? _____

16. Do you intend to be faithful to your husband always? _____

17. Do you understand that one of the purposes of marriage is the begetting and rearing of children,

    God willing? _____

    Do you accept and intend to fulfill this aspect of marriage? _____

    Does your intended groom accept and intend to fulfill this aspect of marriage? _____

18. How long have you known your intended groom? _____

    How long have you been engaged? _____

19. Have either your or his parents any objections to this marriage? _____

20. Is there any major fact about you, either in the present or the past, which you have not made
    known to your proposed spouse and which might affect his willingness to marry you? _____

Date: _____ Bride: _____

Church: _____ Place: _____

Pastor or his delegate: _____

When the marriage is to be witnessed by a priest who is not a parochial vicar in the parish, the pastor will sign this form:

I hereby delegate Rev. _____ to assist in this marriage within my parish.

Date _____ Pastor's Signature _____

Church Seal

existence of an impediment such as a previous church marriage, Sacred Orders, or religious profession, proof of release from these vows will be needed. Documented proof of baptism is not required for persons baptized in Christian churches outside the Roman Catholic tradition. However, see our earlier treatment of "Interreligious Marriages" for a discussion not only of the fact, but also the validity of baptisms in other Christian traditions. As mentioned earlier, Hispanics may require special assistance in obtaining baptismal certificates and a longer period of time will need to be allocated for international mail.

Question 5: First Communion. Neither a document nor precise information about date, church, and place is required. The response, however, naturally does give an indication of early Catholic formation. This can be an excellent occasion for catechesis, faith sharing, and even preparation for the sacrament.

Question 6: Confirmation. The annotated baptismal record should provide information about this sacrament. However, if it does not, neither a record nor precise data is required. Catholics who have not yet received the sacrament of confirmation are to receive it before being admitted to marriage —if they can do so without serious inconvenience.[130] This fact usually will surface in an informal way at the initial session between the couple and the parish minister, as the latter explains the documentation they will need to secure. Efforts can be made then to remedy that situation.

Question 7: Practice of Religion. This three-part question, related to question 2, deals with a delicate area and should be posed in a gentle way. The answers tend to reveal the current religious state of the person and her or his spiritual readiness for marriage and the sacrament of matrimony. The first meeting between the couple and pastoral minister, described elsewhere, will, in most instances, surface an active or inactive practice of religion on the part of one or both parties. Discussions then, and subsequently, would need to deal with that issue. Normally, when the time arrives for the inquiry to be completed, we would hope that this critical matter had already been discussed at length and difficult situations satisfactorily resolved.

Question 8: Witnesses to Freedom. The pastoral minister must be morally certain that a marriage will be valid and licit. This type of certitude, practically speaking, means there is no reason to believe that the marriage would be invalid or, at least, illicit. The witnesses identified by this inquiry would be helpful in establishing moral certitude—if there were reason to doubt the proposed marriage's validity or liceity. For that purpose, a Freedom and/or Baptismal Affidavit sample form is included in the Appendix. Questions 1 to 8 of that appended document deal with the issue of freedom; subsequent questions are concerned with the baptismal status and with young persons seeking to marry. In the majority of instances,

no such doubt will exist, and such recourse to witnesses will not be necessary.[131]

Questions 9 and 10: Previous Marriage(s). A common-law union or marriage is an exchange of marital promises—without a religious or civil ceremony—followed by cohabitation. Simple cohabitation, as discussed earlier, does not include that exchange of marital promises. Documented proof of death or ecclesiastical declaration of nullity should be checked and information noted, but the document need not be retained. The requirement for such documentation would be discussed in the initial interview, described elsewhere. When a previous marriage does exist, it must be established that natural obligations toward a third party or toward children (see *Code*, c. 1071:3) and legal requirements for support of either or both have or are being fulfilled.

Question 11: Relationship. If such a relationship exists, recourse to the bishop's office for the appropriate dispensation will be required. There are a variety of cultural practices of which the pastor or his delegate should be aware. Thus, relationships such as cousins who contemplate marriage, although very much frowned upon in Mexico, may be more common and accepted socially in other Latin American countries such as Puerto Rico.

Question 12: Physical, Emotional, or Psychological Situations. In our high-stress culture, a great number of persons do experience mental or nervous illnesses. Some also live with unique physical, emotional, or psychological situations. As a result, many persons have sought immediate or long-term help through counseling, medical care, or even hospitalization. Those illnesses and situations can be relatively minor and temporary or major and lengthy, even permanent. The key word in this question is *seriously*. If this inquiry or other discussions surface a serious, major, long-term or quasi-permanent illness or situation, the pastoral minister will need to explore that matter. In doing so, the minister might suggest to the person the wisdom of consulting with his or her doctor or therapist about the proposed marriage. Some type of a statement, agreed upon by the client and counselor, would indicate the situation or illness does not appear to be an invalidating impediment and could, thus, ensure the moral certitude required for the marriage to take place. That statement should be enclosed as part of the documentation. Here again, such a serious difficulty will usually be raised at the initial interview and these steps recommended then.

Question 13: Forced Consent. If the existence of such serious pressure or force exists, the pastoral minister should consult the bishop's office for advice in this situation. The wisdom of separate interviews

---

130. Ibid., c. 1065.
131. *Code of Canon Law: A Text and a Commentary*, pp. 750-751.

for the completion of the nuptial inquiry is especially evident with this question. Occasionally, surprising incidents do occur in which one manifests a reluctance to marry or notes some type of external pressure to wed. Cultural and linguistic sharpness is needed here to discern such situations and to deal with them well.

Question 14: Conditions, Restrictions, or Reservations. If a serious condition, restriction, or reservation does exist, the pastoral minister should contact the bishop's office for consultation on the matter. For example, the existence of prenuptial contracts could indicate that the couple is putting a restriction or reservation on their marital consent. A prenuptial contract could call into question the couple's commitment to the permanency of their marriage.

Questions 15 to 17: Marital Promises. During the marriage preparation program, these issues of the permanency and exclusivity of the marital bond or promise, as well as the openness to the transmission of life, presumably will have been covered at length and in a variety of ways. These three questions enable the interviewer to review briefly the main points of those presentations with the bride and the groom before posing the actual inquiries.

Question 18: Courtship. Formal engagements—with or without a ring—are ordinary procedures in this country, but are neither universal nor required. The pastor or his delegate should be aware of certain cultural customs, particularly among Hispanics, such as *pedir la mano* of the bride and the *plazo*, which is the formal length of time for courtship established by the parents, when they give their consent.

Questions 19 and 20: Undisclosed Major Obstacle. If a major impediment or negative factor surfaces in response to questions 19 or 20, the pastoral minister should consult the bishop's office for recommendations on how to proceed.

At this point in the questionnaire, special attention should be paid to the situation of an American citizen or permanent resident marrying an alien. Unfortunately, recent changes in immigration law and regulations treat the marriage of persons in this category in a way that calls for pastoral care and vigilance. Because of the possibility that, in some few cases, the marriage is merely a fraudulent attempt on the part of the alien to gain legal entry into the United States, the INS treats the alien as a temporary resident for a period of two years, by granting conditional permanent resident status. The alien must apply for removal of the conditions within ninety days immediately preceding the second anniversary of the alien's having been granted such status. Further, the INS then investigates, by means of a most intrusive personal interview, to ascertain that the couple is indeed still married. Failure to conform to this requirement of the second-anniversary petition, or failure to satisfy the investigator on the *bona fide* status of the marriage, subjects the alien to deporta-

tion proceedings. The alien is then barred from reentering the United States under any category for a period of two years. In addition, any alien already under a deportation order must leave the United States for two years, regardless of whether or not they are marrying a citizen.

Needless to say, this situation poses serious threats to the community of life, which is one of the essential purposes of marriage. When it arises, marriage preparers should attend to the following issues:

- Any impression created by the civil law that marriage under these circumstances is merely temporary or conditional should be addressed.

- Although the kind of preparation for marriage required for Catholics greatly reduces the possibility of fraud, it is still feasible that it may be present under these circumstances.

- The couple should be reminded of the second-anniversary petition requirement and should be urged to take every step necessary to fulfill it. They may be referred to diocesan agencies that deal with immigration questions for advice and counsel.

If the verbal answer to question 20 is "No," the pastor or his delegate might first ask the bride or the groom to read through the completed document. That ensures accuracy and gives the respondent additional ownership of the process. He or she could then be invited to write "No" after question 20 and sign his or her full name on the line indicated.

COMMENTARY ON THE CHECKLIST PAGE

This page, in its naturally folded position together with the front cover, becomes a practical aid for the pastor or his delegate. For those who like such comprehensive lists of necessary steps for formal events, this page identifies those basic ingredients for the celebration of marriage and provides space to check them off as they are completed.

The heading "Wedding details explained," with its subsequent subdivisions, is intended to be a reminder for the pastor or his delegate of the various concerns to be covered with the couple in the initial interview. While efficiency may urge the printing of a standardized parish document, with details about these several items (e.g., organist's phone number), there is much to recommend that the pastor or his delegate simply write by hand notes containing salient facts as the explanation is given. That information list, transmitted to the couple afterward for their future reference, by its very personalized nature helps to communicate how unique and special these two people are to the pastor or his delegate and to the Church.

The items listed under "Any comments or questions about" are merely further areas to be raised by

A Handy Checklist for the Pastor or Delegate

☐ Marriage date, time, and banns reserved in *Mass Book*.

☐ Marriage date noted in personal *appointment book*.

☐ Marriage preparation programs *information given*.

☐ Wedding details explained.

      * Church documents required

      * Special permission if needed

      * Organist/music director

      * Servers

      * Banns of marriage

      * Liturgy booklet

      * Offerings

      * Other local concerns

      * Any comments or questions about:

      License _____ flowers _____ runner _____ photographer _____

      reception _____ invitations _____ newspapers _____ rings _____

☐ Next Appointment(s): Date _____ Time _____ Date _____ Time _____

☐ Premarital inventory instrument

☐ Copy of records (baptism, death certificate, annulment decree, special permission if needed)

☐ Prenuptial Inquiry Form

☐ Dispensations

☐ Rehearsal date and time

the pastor or delegate as a means of ensuring that the major issues involving the couple are covered. However, the state legal requirements in connection with the license (e.g., blood test, waiting period, age restrictions, etc.) will usually need to be explained and could be a suitable introduction to those other points.

The earlier section in this manual, "The Importance of Hospitality," spells out rather specifically how these matters may be done in a pastorally effective way.

The time and date of the next interview(s) can be noted on the proper line, as well as within the pastor's or delegate's own personal appointment book. Should conflicts arise, the contact phone numbers of the bride and the groom will be found under question 1 of the investigation form itself.

8 Ethnic and Regional Adaptations

Traditionally, the Catholic Church has been, for many, the welcoming party to this country, helping the immigrant make a transition to the American experiment of a community of different peoples and languages. Proud of such a record, the Church views itself as akin to the biblical tradition of welcoming the poor, the alien, the orphaned, the widowed, and the weak. Today, immigration continues—even increasing—and the Church, in many areas of the country, still performs this traditional biblical role.

The Catholic Church, true to its nature of being catholic and universal, opens her arms to embrace all. For example, on any Sunday in major cities such as Boston, New York, Philadelphia, Chicago, and Los Angeles, priests will be celebrating the Eucharist in several dozen different languages. The pride in one's cultural background and native tongue felt by contemporary people, together with the respect for the richness of other traditions, which the Church encourages, makes those kinds of Masses a pastoral necessity for our time and reflects her catholicity.

Moreover, within the vast area of the United States, there are also regional variations in accent and attitudes, in style of dress and ways of living. Those regional, ethnic, and lingual differences, quite naturally, will seek expression in the secular and sacred rituals that accompany marriage. It should be noted that the Second Vatican Council emphasized the tradition of the Church (i.e., the right of the people to express their prayers in the vernacular). While certain elements seem to occur in every wedding liturgy, other rites appeal especially to a particular ethnic group.

Thus, every bride and groom will exchange vows; but not every couple will sing a duet in their native tongue honoring the Blessed Virgin Mary, as a Vietnamese couple might do. Every couple will have pas-

sages from Scripture at the wedding; but not every bride and groom will incorporate the *arras* or silver or gold coins of the Hispanic tradition in their celebration. Each liturgy will likely incorporate the singing of a solo, but few shall have the stirring, soulful tones that arise from the African American tradition.

The Church recognizes and encourages such rich diversity. At the Second Vatican Council, the bishops employed strong words in support of these cultural and regional adaptations. After indicating that local rituals may be developed to meet the language needs of a region and to respond to other area traditions, they "earnestly desired" that other praiseworthy customs and ceremonies of any territory "by all means be retained."[132] As we noted in the Introduction, our 1983 statement *The Hispanic Presence: Challenge and Commitment* recognized the Hispanic community as a blessing from God and urged such adaptations and developments so that the special gifts of the Hispanics might be brought to the Body of Christ, Jesus' Pilgrim Church on earth.

The universal *Rite of Marriage*, implementing those directives, explicitly mentions such adaptability. Every country's conference of bishops "may draw up its own marriage rite suited to the usages of the place and people and approved by the Apostolic See."[133] Even in countries where the gospel is being received for the first time, "whatever is good and is not indissolubly bound up with superstition and error should be sympathetically considered and, if possible, preserved intact. Sometimes the Church admits such things into the liturgy itself, as long as they harmonize with its true and authentic spirit."[134] Other parts of the ritual for marriage reflect that same flexible approach.

This handbook of pastoral help for marriage preparation attempts to manifest a similar orientation. The material within the text has, for the most part, a universal relevance. However, the regional and ethnic variations that exist in the preparation and celebration of marriage within the Catholic Church throughout the United States are far too vast for inclusion in a national volume. Nevertheless, as we also stated in our Introduction, we have attempted to include in the handbook some Hispanic values and suggestions as a step toward recognizing and integrating the Hispanic community within the Church of the United States and as a fulfillment of the objectives and priorities of the *National Plan for Hispanic Ministry*.

We envision that dioceses and provinces will develop additions to this text that contain the adaptations and applications necessary for their region and for the ethnic groups within their territory. In

---

132. *The Constitution on the Sacred Liturgy*, nos. 63b, 77.
133. *Rite of Marriage*, no. 17.
134. Ibid., no. 16.

this fashion, we trust a certain unity of approach can be observed in the country—but a united effort and attitude that also preserve and promote the rich diversity of customs surrounding marriage and marriage preparation in the United States.

Part C
A Theology and Spirituality of Marriage

Introduction

Over the past few years, many publications have examined marriage from both a speculative and a pastoral point of view.[135] What we offer in this part of the manual are a few fundamental concepts about matrimonial theology and spirituality, not an exhaustive treatment of those double approaches to marital life.

The framework we will follow is based upon the four general tasks of the family—which Pope John Paul II has emphasized—that flowed from the 1980 Synod of Bishops.[136] Under each of those functions or purposes, we will suggest several related thoughts and, then, reach out to the major or standard sources of revelation for support of those thoughts. The fountains of truth we look to and cite within quotation marks are the authentic teaching of our tradition; the inspired Word of God; the Church's liturgical celebration of marriage; and the testimony of the faithful, represented in this instance by the comments of a sacramental couple from New York.

The four general tasks, functions, or purposes of marriage and the family can be categorized as: (1) forming a community of persons; (2) serving life; (3) participating in society's development; and (4) sharing in the Church's life and mission.

 Forming a Community of Persons

There is a parallel or, better, a mutuality of symbolism between the Most Holy Trinity and the sacramentally united couple. Father, Son, and Holy Spirit are absolutely different and diverse persons, but they are bonded as one through the perfect love that each divine person has for each other person of the Trinity. God, in creating every woman and man as a totally distinct and different person, nevertheless, wishes those who enter marriage to become one in body and spirit, likewise bonded by an absolute love for each other. The divine love of the Trinity is unconditional, committed, irrevocable, and exclusive or faithful; God's plan is that human marital love will be the

same. In both cases, unity emerges out of diversity through love.

Similarly, both divine and marital unity through love are sacramental—symbols of something more— and possess a unique, mysterious power within them. The Trinity symbolizes what married life can and should be; conversely, married life can mirror, even though only in faintly reflective fashion, the love and unity of Father, Son, and Holy Spirit.

The Trinity's love, however, has also reached out to us through creation and, later, through redemption. The same bonding love extends to human beings as creatures and, after fall and forgiveness, in old and new covenants of closeness. God made a marriage with humankind from the beginning and restored that union, especially through Jesus' coming, dying, and rising, as well as through his continued presence in the Church.

Once again, God's absolute, unconditional, irrevocable, and faithful love —now manifested through creation and Christ's saving life, as well as through a Church that will last until the end of time and reaches out to all—models or symbolizes what marriage can or should be. In parallel fashion, the love between spouses; between parents and children; between members of the extended family; as well as between healthy members of the family and those who are in any kind of need—from the sick or disabled young to the deteriorating and vulnerable elderly—those loves reflect and lead us to the Trinity's love, which is so vastly greater.

God's plan intends for marriage to be a community of persons, linked as one by love.

135. The following is not an exhaustive list of current books on marriage, but rather a sampling of the types of publications that are available: *Marriage among Christians*, by James Tunstead Burtchaell (Notre Dame: Ave Maria Press, 1977); *For Better for Worse*, by James Tunstead Burtchaell (New York: Paulist Press, 1985); *Marriage Studies I: Reflections in Canon Law and Theology*, Thomas P. Doyle, OP, ed. (Toledo: Canon Law Society of America, 1980); *Marriage Studies III: Reflections in Canon Law and Theology*, Thomas P. Doyle, OP, ed. (Washington, D.C.: Canon Law Society of America, 1985); *Feast of Love: Pope John Paul II on Human Intimacy*, by Mary G. Durkin (Chicago: Loyola University Press, 1983); *Embodied in Love: Sacramental Spirituality and Sexual Intimacy*, by Charles A. Gallagher, et al. (New York: Crossroad Publishing Company, 1983); *Covenant of Love: Pope John Paul II on Sexuality, Marriage and Family in the Modern World*, by Richard M. Hogan and John M. LeVoir (Garden City, N.Y.: Doubleday and Company, Inc., 1985); *Original Unity of Man and Woman: Catechesis on the Book of Genesis*, by Pope John Paul II (Boston: Daughters of St. Paul, 1981); *Theology of Christian Marriage*, by Walter Kasper (New York: Crossroad Publishing Company, 1984); *Secular Marriage, Christian Commitment*, by Michael G. Lawler (Mystic, Conn.: Twenty-Third Publications, 1985); *Marriage in Canon Law*, by Laidislas Orsy, SJ (Wilmington, Del.: Michael Glazier, Inc., 1986); *Christian Marriage*, by David M. Thomas (Wilmington, Del.: Michael Glazier, Inc., 1983); *Man and Woman, He Made Them*, by Jean Vanier (New York: Paulist Press, 1985); *Marrying Well: Stages on the Journey of Christian Marriage*, by Evelyn Eaton and James D. Whitehead (Garden City, N.Y.: Doubleday and Company, Inc., 1983). See also, *Pastoral Letter on the Sacrament of Matrimony*, by Most Rev. Raymond G. Hunthausen, Archbishop of Seattle (Elizabeth, N.J.: Pastoral and Matrimonial Renewal Center, 1982).

136. *On the Family*, Part 3, nos. 17-64.

a) OUR AUTHENTIC TRADITION

"The family, which is founded and given life by love, is a community of persons: of husband and wife, of parents and children, of relatives.

". . . Without love the family is not a community of persons and, in the same way, without love the family cannot live, grow and perfect itself as a community of persons."[137]

"By virtue of the covenant of married life, the man and woman 'are no longer two but one flesh' and they are called to grow continually in their communion through day-to-day fidelity to their marriage promise of total mutual self-giving.

". . . [I]n the Lord Christ, God takes up this human need, confirms it, purifies it and elevates it, leading it to perfection through the sacrament of matrimony: the Holy Spirit, who is poured out in the sacramental celebration, offers Christian couples the gift of a new communion of love that is the living and real image of that unique unity which makes of the Church the indivisible mystical body of the Lord Jesus."[138]

God wills and communicates "the indissolubility of marriage as a fruit, a sign and a requirement of the absolutely faithful love that God has for [us] and that the Lord Jesus has for the Church."[139]

b) GOD'S INSPIRED WORD

"For no one hates his own flesh but rather nourishes and cherishes it, even as Christ does the Church, because we are members of his body. 'For this reason a man shall leave [his] father and [his] mother and be joined to his wife, and the two shall become one flesh.' This is a great mystery, but I speak in reference to Christ and the Church."[140]

"Believe me that I am in the Father and the Father is in me. . . .

"If you love me, you will keep my commandments. And I will ask the Father, and he will give you another Advocate to be with you always, the Spirit of truth. . . . On that day you will realize that I am in my Father and you are in me and I in you."[141]

"In this way the love of God was revealed to us: God sent his only Son into the world so that we might have life through him. In this is love: not that we have loved God, but that he loved us and sent his Son as an expiation for our sins."[142]

c) THE WEDDING LITURGY

"You created us in love to share your divine life. We see this high destiny in the love of husband and wife, which bears the imprint of your own divine love. Love is our origin; love is one constant calling; love is our fulfillment in heaven. The love of man and woman is made holy in the sacrament of marriage and becomes the mirror of your everlasting love."[143]

d) A SACRAMENTAL COUPLE

"Through the power of their mutual love, each spouse calls the other to be more fully the complete person God created. Rather than losing their individuality, each spouse becomes more clearly defined as a distinct person. Paradoxically, it is by dying to self that each finds himself or herself. The fear is that one will be absorbed into the other's personality and become totally dependent upon him or her. But in a properly balanced marriage, there is a wholesome interdependence that strengthens each person psychologically and spiritually.

"The personal dignity of each spouse is nurtured and honored as the couple judges actions in all parts of their lives according to what is best for their relationship. As a sacramental couple, they weigh these decisions in light of how they help build the Body of Christ, the Church. Just as they are to be one in flesh, they are to strive to be of one will and one spirit by developing a workable process for making couple-decisions, a process that considers the feelings and thoughts of each spouse and is immersed in prayer.

"In the sacrament of matrimony, husband and wife make a commitment to each other, which is permanent, total, exclusive, faithful, and unbreakable. They know the whole Church is supporting them in prayer and action. Bolstered by their awareness of the sincerity and solemnity of this mutual commitment, each partner has the courage to risk even greater intimacy. The experience of being so totally loved by another person is but a shadow of God's love for us.

"The best way for a man to be a good father is to truly love his wife. The best way to be a good mother is for a woman to truly love her husband. This rich conjugal love becomes a wholesome environment in which the children thrive. They feel secure, wanted, and joy-filled, as well as predisposed to learning how to grow up and become lovers too. When children see selfishness, discord, tension, and conflict between their parents, their whole world is threatened. Husbands and wives will, at times, fight and are called to forgive each other, reconcile, and seek healing. In doing this, they teach their children, the Church, and the world how to restore peace."

 Serving Life

The infinite love between members of the Holy Trinity does not stop there, but overflows in a generative way to create and sustain the universe and all living

---

137. Ibid., no. 18.
138. Ibid., no. 19.
139. Ibid., no. 20.
140. Eph 5:29-32.
141. Jn 14:11,1-17,20.
142. 1 Jn 14:9-10.
143. *Rite of Marriage*, Preface for Nuptial Mass, no. 117.

beings in this world of ours. In mysterious and wondrous fashion, God shares that generative, loving, and creative power with men and women.

As we discussed in the lengthy section on "Responsible Childbearing and Childrearing," every infant's conception and birth is a miracle—the product of a cooperative effort involving the divine Creator, the father, and the mother.

That miraculous event, however, is not an end, but a beginning—the start of a journey through life toward eternity. Like the God who not only creates, but sustains life, wives and husbands must not only be open to the transmission of life and responsibly bring forth new human life, but also responsibly bring up the children who are the Trinity's unique gift to them. No work of father or mother exceeds in importance the physical, intellectual, emotional, and spiritual formation of their daughters and sons.

Just as the Trinity's love reaches out in a creative manner, so, too, Christian parents and their children must extend loving arms to other persons—especially the young—who are in need. To adopt or to foster children, to serve as a "Big Brother" or "Big Sister" of those with special burdens is to make God's loving care present to them through us.

Infertile and elderly couples, while never or no longer serving life by the begetting of children, still contribute to that function by nurturing growth in each other and in others, through loving service, in a variety of ways.

a) OUR AUTHENTIC TRADITION

God calls a man and a woman "to a special sharing in his love and in his power as creator and Father through their free and responsible cooperation in transmitting the gift of human life....

"Thus, the fundamental task of the family is to serve life ... [through] transmitting by procreation the divine image from person to person.

"... The fruitfulness of conjugal love is not restricted solely to the procreation of children ...: It is enlarged and enriched by all those fruits of moral, spiritual and supernatural life which the father and the mother are called to hand on to their children, and through the children to the Church and to the world."[144]

"Since parents have conferred life on their children, they have a most solemn obligation to educate their offspring. Hence, parents must be acknowledged as the first and foremost educators of their children."[145]

"[T]he mentality which honors women more for their work outside the home than for their work within the family must be overcome."[146]

"[E]fforts must be made to restore socially the conviction that the place and task of the father in and for the family is of unique and irreplaceable importance."[147]

"Christian families, recognizing with faith all human beings as children of the same heavenly Father, will respond generously to the children of other families, giving them support and love not as outsiders but as members of the one family of God's children."[148]

b) GOD'S INSPIRED WORD

"God created man in his image; in the divine image he created him; male and female he created them.

"God blessed them, saying: 'Be fertile and multiply; fill the earth and subdue it. Have dominion over the fish of the sea, the birds of the air, and all the living things that move on the earth....' God looked at everything he had made, and he found it very good."[149]

"Notice the ravens: they do not sow or reap; they have neither storehouse nor barn, yet God feeds them. How much more important are you than birds!"[150]

144. *On the Family*, no. 28.
145. "Declaration on Christian Education," in *Vatican Council II*, no. 3.
146. *On the Family*, no. 23.
147. Ibid., no. 25.
148. Ibid., no. 41.
149. Gn 1:27-31.
150. Lk 12:24.

"But grace was given to each of us according to the measure of Christ's gift. . . .

"And he gave some of us as apostles . . . others as pastors and teachers, to equip the holy ones for the work of ministry, for building up the body of Christ, until we all attain to the the unity of faith and knowledge of the Son of God, to mature manhood, to the extent of the full stature of Christ, so that we may no longer be infants, tossed by waves and swept along by every wind of teaching arising from human trickery. . . . Rather, living the truth in love, we should grow in every way into him who is the head, Christ. . . ."[151]

"If a brother or sister has nothing to wear and has no food for the day, and one of you says to them, 'Go in peace, keep warm, and eat well,' but you do not give them the necessities of the body, what good is it? So also faith of itself, if it does not have works is dead."[152]

c) THE WEDDING LITURGY

"Will you accept children lovingly from God, and bring them up according to the law of Christ and his Church?"[153]

Lord, grant that as they begin to live this
    sacrament they may share with each other
    the gifts of your love
and become one in heart and mind
    as witnesses to your presence in their
    marriage.
Help them to create a home together
(and give them children to be formed by
    the gospel
to have a place in your family).

Give your blessing to N., your daughter,
so that she may be a good wife (and mother),
caring for the home,
faithful in love for her husband,
generous and kind.

Give your blessings to N., your son,
so that he may be a faithful husband
(and a good father).

Father, grant that as they come together to
    your table on earth,
so they may one day have the joy of sharing
    your feast in heaven.[154]

d) A SACRAMENTAL COUPLE

"Matrimonial spirituality is very sexual in its practice. One basic purpose for sexual intercourse in marriage is the procreation of children. By being open to God's plan, the couple can be full partners in enlarging and enriching the Body of Christ. When they are thus completely open to God's plan in this area of their relationship, that spills over into all other areas and greatly assists them in becoming one.

"Both the husband and the wife must accept and practice their responsibility in being procreators. They both have an obligation to be fully informed about the Church's teaching and then practice the necessary self-discipline. However, they must also be aware of their responsibility to use sexual intercourse as a means of building their oneness and thus bringing new life to their relationship. They will discover that, as their couple relationship grows, each of them will individually grow closer to God, which is their vocation in the sacrament of matrimony.

"Many couples who use Natural Family Planning have experienced periods of abstinence from sexual intercourse. They report how they added activities of a nongenital nature which brought them much romantic excitement and enthusiasm. It is important to realize that it is not uncommon in marriage, for reasons of health or extended separation, that couples must forego intercourse. During those times, they are called to develop acceptable alternatives to express their sexual love for each other. That is what the Church means by 'chastity' —the appropriate use of our sexuality. At such times, we use this form of spiritual energy to defend our love against the perils of selfishness and aggressiveness.

"Through the power of the sacrament of matrimony, married couples are able to lead lives of holiness. Their holiness evolves from the sanctifying of the ordinary daily events of their lives. Matrimonial spirituality is marked by the call to denial of self and acceptance of suffering as a normal part of living as a Catholic Christian. Suffering is a reality for all people. In matrimony, each spouse can be a compassionate, consoling listener, and thus make the response to the suffering become a way to grow closer together and closer to God."

3 Participating in Society's Development

The well-being of society depends upon the well-being of families, which make up this society, because the family is the fundamental unit or primary cell of every society. Obviously, new citizens come forth constantly from the home to keep that society alive and growing. But the family also serves as the initial training ground of future adult citizens in those human virtues or values essential for the survival and flourishing of any society.

The current deterioration of so many family rela-

---

151. Eph 4:7,11-16.
152. Jas 2:15-17.
153. *Rite of Marriage,* Questions before Consent, no. 24.
154. Ibid., Nuptial Blessing, no. 120.

tionships within the United States underscores, in negative fashion, the truth of these statements.

However, the family is also a "domestic," "small-scale," "little" or "miniature" church. As such, it does or should radiate not only human virtues, but likewise gospel values, including and particularly a preferential option for the poor or those in any need. That concern for the needy will express itself first of all in direct service efforts—of various types—to alleviate people's immediate burdens. Second, it will also manifest itself in astute social justice advocacy to bring about long-term solutions by eliminating the causes of poverty, through appropriate governmental legislation or institutional action.

In these as in other undertakings, Christian couples receive through the sacrament of matrimony sufficient divine grace, providing them with the wisdom and power necessary to fulfill all their responsibilities.

a) OUR AUTHENTIC TRADITION

"[T]he family is the first and vital cell of society. . . .

"It is from the family that citizens come to birth and it is within the family that they find the first school of the social virtues that are the animating principle of the existence and development of society itself."[155]

"Families therefore, either singly or in association, can and should devote themselves to manifold social service activities, especially in favor of the poor or at any rate for the benefit of all people and situations that cannot be reached by the public authorities' welfare organization."[156]

"The social role of families is called upon to find expression also in the form of political intervention: Families should be the first to take steps to see that the laws and institutions of the state not only do not offend, but support and positively defend the rights and duties of the family."[157]

"[T]he sacrament [of matrimony] gives to Christian couples and parents a power and a commitment to live their vocation as lay people and therefore to 'seek the kingdom of God by engaging in temporal affairs and by ordering them according to the plan of God.'"[158]

"The Christian family is thus called upon to offer everyone a witness of generous and disinterested dedication to social matters through a 'preferential option' for the poor and disadvantaged."[159]

b) GOD'S INSPIRED WORD

"'Come, you who are blessed by my Father. Inherit the kingdom prepared for you from the foundation of the world. For I was hungry and you gave me food, I was thirsty and you gave me drink, a stranger and you welcomed me, naked and you clothed me, ill and you cared for me, in prison and you visited me. . . .

[W]hatever you did for one of these least brothers of mine, you did for me.'"[160]

"They devoted themselves to the teaching of the apostles and to the communal life, to the breaking of the bread and to the prayers. Awe came upon everyone, and many wonders and signs were done through the apostles. All who believed were together and had all things in common; they would sell their property and possessions and divide them among all according to each one's need. Every day they devoted themselves to meeting together in the temple area and to breaking bread in their homes. They ate their meals with exultation and sincerity of heart, praising God and enjoying favor with all the people. And every day the Lord added to their number those who were being saved."[161]

"Let love be sincere; hate what is evil, hold on to what is good; love one another with mutual affection; anticipate one another in showing honor. . . . Contribute to the needs of the holy ones, exercise hospitality. Bless those who persecute you, bless and do not curse them. . . . Do not repay anyone evil for evil; be concerned for what is noble in the sight of all. If possible, on your part, live at peace with all."[162]

"'My grace is sufficient for you, for power is made perfect in weakness.'"[163]

c) THE WEDDING LITURGY

God the eternal Father keep you in love with
    each other,
so that the peace of Christ may stay with you
and be always in your home.

May (your children bless you,)
your friends console you
and all live in peace with you.

May you always bear witness to the love of
    God in this world
so that the afflicted and the needy
will find in you generous friends,
and welcome you into the joys of heaven.[164]

d) A SACRAMENTAL COUPLE

"Catholic couples living in the sacrament of matrimony are radical and countercultural. In a contemporary culture that puts a supreme value on 'expressive individualism,' the matrimonied couple is an anomaly. They are not self-centered. They are other-

155. *On the Family*, no. 42.
156. Ibid., no. 44.
157. Ibid.
158. Ibid., no. 47.
159. Ibid.
160. Mt 25:34-40.
161. Acts 2:42-47.
162. Rom 12:9-18.
163. 2 Cor 12:9.
164. *Rite of Marriage*, Blessing at the End of Mass, no. 125.

centered. Other-centeredness is a gospel value. The fundamental call to matrimonied couples is to die to self, to make one's spouse the first priority, and thus to risk rejection and move toward oneness in a truly intimate relationship.

"Married couples soon discover they have entered into a new world of total sharing, which ranges from their most interior personal knowledge to the mundane activities of each day. It might be that the wife is alarmed to have him walk into the bathroom while she is showering or he gets upset when she uses his razor to shave her legs. Or, suddenly, both their paychecks go into a common pot and the other spouse now has a voice in how 'my' money is spent. It is a powerful lesson of how rights must yield to responsibilities and duties.

"Having learned, as a married couple, the importance of sharing in their own home, they must now reach out to those outside the family. This is the next level of dying to self and demands that they make themselves more aware of the needs of others and then respond within their means. That could mean, financially, by sacrificial giving or tithing. It could mean by contributing used clothing or household appliances to a parish Human Development Committee instead of having a garage sale and keeping the money for their own purposes. It could mean being involved actively in the Pro-Life Movement.

"In a world marked by consumerism and greed, a married couple can choose voluntary poverty and remove themselves from an anxious preoccupation with job promotions and salary increases for the sake of acquiring more things. They can choose instead to emphasize family relationships and a simplified life style. The nonverbal witness of their actions will be a sign to others that it is possible to choose how we want to live."

 ## 4 Sharing in the Church's Life and Mission

By God's unique marriage with humanity—through Jesus' paschal or Easter mystery of coming into this world, suffering, and dying on it out of love for all, and rising to bring us divine life both here and hereafter—a new covenant between Creator and creature has been established. This heavenly covenant, made possible by Christ's saving action, is reflected in the human covenant between husband and wife.

In carrying out his work of salvation, Jesus Christ served and serves as a prophet, a priest, and a king. The married couple and the family that grows from their mutual love, in parallel fashion, are meant to fulfill prophetic, priestly, and kingly roles or functions while living out a Christian marriage.

As *prophets* who speak in the name of God and proclaim God's message, married couples, above all,

must have faith in the gospel and be eager to share that faith with others. They will be the first teachers of their children in the ways of faith and are urged to be also the best of teachers.[165] This requires ongoing efforts to renew and deepen themselves spiritually so that they may proclaim the good news to those within their home and beyond its walls.

These tasks will, likewise, demand generosity and courage—qualities always needed by prophets and evangelists in the Church's history. Only courageous and generous parents can maintain great interior serenity when their young children reject or do not practice the faith, or, on the other hand, decide to follow a temporary or permanent missionary career far away from home.

As *priests* who mediate between God and other human beings, married couples are called through this sacrament of matrimony to live holy lives that will radiate Christ's love to all those who come in contact with them.

Such marital holiness will center on the Eucharist, but it will also find expression and nourishment in the other sacraments, especially reconciliation and penance, as well as in private, family, and liturgical prayer.

As *kings*, spouses, with their families, have the task of building a better Church and world through their loving service of others. This, of course, includes members of our faith community but also embraces sisters and brothers outside our spiritual family since true love can discover the face of Christ in everyone, especially those who are poor or weak, who suffer or are unjustly treated.

a) OUR AUTHENTIC TRADITION

"It is thus in the love between husband and wife and between members of the family—a love lived out in all its extraordinary richness of values and demands: totality, oneness, fidelity and fruitfulness—that the Christian family's participation in the prophetic, priestly and kingly mission of Jesus Christ and his Church finds expression and realization."[166]

"[T]he Christian family fulfills its prophetic role by welcoming and announcing the Word of God: It thus becomes more and more each day a believing and evangelizing community. . . .

"Only in faith can they discover and admire with joyful gratitude the dignity to which God has deigned to raise marriage and the family, making them a sign and meeting place of the loving covenant between God and man, between Jesus Christ and his bride, the Church."[167]

"By means of the sacrament of marriage, in which

---

165. *Rite of Baptism for Children*, Final Blessing, no. 105.
166. *On the Family*, no. 50.
167. Ibid., no. 51. Sections 51-54 speak very concretely to the practical meaning of the prophetic role for married couples.

it is rooted and from which it draws its nourishment, the Christian family is continuously vivified by the Lord Jesus and called and engaged by him in a dialogue with God through the sacraments, through the offering of one's life and through prayer.

"This is the priestly role which the Christian family can and ought to exercise in intimate communion with the whole Church through the daily realities of married and family life."[168]

"[T]he Christian family is inspired and guided by the new law of the Spirit and, in intimate communion with the Church, the kingly people, it is called to exercise its 'service' of love toward God and toward its fellow human beings.

"Inspired and sustained by the new commandment of love, the Christian family welcomes, respects and serves every human being, considering each one in his or her dignity as a person and as a child of God."[169]

b) GOD'S INSPIRED WORD

"As the bow appears in the clouds, I will see it and recall the everlasting covenant that I have established between God and all living beings—all mortal creatures that are on earth."[170]

"Therefore, if you hearken to my voice and keep my covenant, you shall be my special possession, dearer to me than all other people, though all the earth is mine, You shall be to me a kingdom of priests, a holy nation."[171]

"For I will take you away from among the nations, gather you from all the foreign lands, and bring you back to your own land. . . . I will put my spirit within you and make you live by my statutes, careful to observe my decrees. You shall live in the land I gave your fathers; you shall be my people, and I will be your God."[172]

"Then he took a cup, gave thanks, and said: 'Take this and share it among yourselves; for I tell you that from this time on I shall not drink of the fruit of the vine until the kingdom of God comes.' Then he took the bread, said the blessing, broke it, and gave it to them, saying, 'This is my body, which will be given up for you; do this in memory of me.' And likewise the cup after they had eaten, saying, 'This is the new covenant in my blood, which will be shed for you.'"[173]

"But you are 'a chosen race, a royal priesthood, a holy nation, a people of his own, so that you may announce the praises' of him who called you out of darkness into his wonderful light. Once you were 'no people' but now you are God's people; you 'had not received mercy' but now you have received mercy."[174]

"Husbands, love your wives, even as Christ loved the church and handed himself over for her to sanctify her, cleansing her by the bath of water with the word, that he might present to himself the church in splendor, without spot or wrinkle or any such thing, that she might be holy and without blemish. . . .

"This is a great mystery, but I speak in reference to Christ and the church."[175]

"Go into the whole world and proclaim the gospel to every creature."[176]

"[Y]ou will receive power when the holy Spirit comes upon you, and you will be my witnesses . . . to the ends of the earth."[177]

"He began to speak boldly in the synagogue; but when Priscilla and Aquila heard him, they took him aside and explained to him the way of God more accurately."[178]

"Come to him, a living stone, rejected by human beings but chosen and precious in the sight of God, and, like living stones, let yourselves be built into a spiritual house to be a holy priesthood to offer spiritual sacrifices acceptable to God through Jesus Christ."[179]

"'Again, amen I say to you, if two of you agree on earth about anything for which they are to pray, it shall be granted to them by my heavenly Father. For where two or three are gathered together in my name, there am I in the midst of them.'"[180]

"'You say I am a king. For this I was born and for this I came into the world, to testify to the truth. Everyone who belongs to the truth listens to my voice. . . .

"'But, as it is, my kingdom is not here.'"[181]

"For the kingdom of God is not a matter of food and drink, but of righteousness, peace and joy in the holy Spirit; whoever serves Christ in this way is pleasing to God and approved by others."[182]

c) THE WEDDING LITURGY

Holy Father, Creator of the universe,
maker of man and woman in your own
    likeness,
source of blessing for married life,
we humbly pray to you for this woman
who today is united with her husband in this
    sacrament of marriage.
May your fullest blessing come upon her and
    her husband

---

168. Ibid., no. 55. Sections 55-62, likewise, treat specific details of the priestly function of married couples.
169. Ibid., nos. 63-64.
170. Gn 9:16.
171. Ex 19:5-6.
172. Ex 37:21-28.
173. Lk 22:17-20.
174. 1 Pt 2:9-10.
175. Eph 5:25-27,32.
176. Mk 16:15.
177. Acts 1:8.
178. Acts 18:26.
179. 1 Pt 2:4-5.
180. Mt 18:19-20.
181. Jn 18:37,36.
182. Rom 15:17-18.

so that they may together rejoice in your gift
    of married love
(and enrich your Church with their children).

Lord, may they both praise you when they are
    happy and turn to you in their sorrows.
May they be glad that you help them in their
    work
and know that you are with them in their
    need.
May they pray to you in the community of
    the Church,
and be your witnesses in the world.
May they reach old age in the company of
    their friends,
and come at last to the kingdom of heaven.[183]

d) A SACRAMENTAL COUPLE

"The fundamental responsibility of a husband is to reveal to his wife God's image and likeness within her. That is, not to solve her problems or offer good advice, but rather to listen in prayer and then tell her how she reveals the kingdom of God to him. She must do the same for him. It is so simple. When we do this, grace flows abundantly and we slip-slide into becoming one, which is our sacramental, gospel call. As St. Paul writes, in Ephesians 5:21:33, the world will see how much Jesus loves the Church by observing how this husband loves his wife.

"A common problem in marriages is that one spouse wants to grow spiritually and the other one is not at all interested. As sacramental couples, each of us is responsible for our own spiritual growth, and responsible to be supportive of our spouse's spiritual growth.

"Each married couple has a responsibility to help the Church come to a greater understanding of the meaning of the sacrament of matrimony as a vehicle for communicating what the Church is all about. This can be done by reflecting on the grace-filled experience of their own sacramental life and by the public sharing of their story in their parish. This will call for courage because usually there are suffering and mistakes to be shared. But through sharing, we grow as a Church.

"One direct way to be filled with Jesus Christ is to receive more frequently the Eucharist. A married couple will find the Eucharist to be an unequalled, rich source of nourishment for their marriage. Eucharist is the symbol of our oneness in the Body of Christ and thus is a parallel to the symbol of oneness expressed by a sacramental couple. Eucharist is also a powerful gift from God to help us become more one. There is a divine, transcendant analogy between this act of spiritual intercourse and a married couple's act of physical intercourse."

Part D
Liturgical Preparation and Celebration

Introduction

As the letter introducing this section of the manual indicated, the potential bride and groom may question the Church's competency in certain areas of married life and, perhaps, therefore resist elements of the preparation process. But ordinarily, they do consider the wedding ceremony or liturgy as the prerogative of the clergy and, in most cases, are anxious to tap the priest's or deacon's expertise in this field. Today, couples about to marry share at least one thing in common: they all want the liturgical celebration to be uniquely personal, beautiful in itself, and impressive to the guests present. The Church shares their hopes for the nuptial liturgy.

The *Rite of Marriage* recommends that the couple should be given a review of the fundamentals of Christian doctrine:

> This may include instruction on the teachings about marriage and the family, on the rites used in the celebration of the sacrament itself, and on the prayers and readings. In this way, the bridegroom and the bride will receive far greater benefit from the celebration.[184]

Pope John Paul II suggests that the nuptial liturgy be "valid, worthy, fruitful, simple and dignified."[185] He also stresses:

> Inasmuch as it is a sacramental action of the Church, the liturgical celebration of marriage should involve the Christian community, with the full, active and responsible participation of all those present, according to the place and task of each individual: the bride and bridegroom, the priest, the witnesses, the relatives, the friends, the other members of the faithful, all of them members of an assembly that manifests and lives the mystery of Christ and His Church.[186]

The *Code of Canon Law* urges a grace-filled and effective liturgical celebration of marriage that will clearly teach that "the spouses signify and share in that mystery of unity and of fruitful love that exists between Christ and the Church."[187]

---

183. *Rite of Marriage*, Nuptial Blessing, no. 121.
184. Ibid., Introduction, no. 5.
185. *On the Family*, no. 67.
186. Ibid.
187. *Code of Canon Law*, c. 1063.

In this part of the manual, we will treat, from a pastoral viewpoint, the preparations for the nuptial liturgy, wedding music, rehearsals, and the liturgical celebration itself.

Preparations for the Nuptial Liturgy

ENGAGEMENT

Most persons in pastoral ministry have found, through their past experiences, that very few couples ask for a formal betrothal or engagement ceremony. A greater number of couples may seek some simple blessing upon an engagement ring, but even then, the request is seldom for a solemn ritual service.

Persons in Hispanic pastoral ministry may find a variety of customs, depending on the origin of the couple. Generally, Hispanic couples have a traditional formal request for engagement. Usually, the prospective groom asks the bride's father for his daughter's hand; this is called *pedir la mano*. The prospective groom may request his father to do this for him, or else a more dignified person such as the priest may do the honors. This formal request sets the engagement time (*plazo*) and perhaps any conditions for the marriage. There is no exchange of rings. Once the formal aspects are mutually agreed upon, a celebration may follow.

There are good reasons for encouraging an integration of the couple's religious practices and their nuptial engagement. We promote bringing the Church's official blessing upon other significant occasions or everyday elements of human life (e.g., a vehicle or a home, religious article or lengthy journey). Since the bestowal of an engagement ring or a formal declaration of the intention to marry are major moments in our own culture, surrounding these activities with a simple prayer or solemn blessing could help bring an added spiritual dimension to those secular events.

The *Book of Blessings*, which was recently issued by the universal Church after many years of research—following the directives of the Second Vatican Council—and which was adapted further for use in the United States, provides a blessing for an engagement. It should be noted that this rite can be carried out by one (or both) of the parents, as well as by a priest or a deacon.

In the United States, the engagement is usually viewed as a more serious, but still tentative, declaration of one's intention to marry and as an extended period for testing the relationship. The freedom and even responsibility of either person or both to terminate the engagement and not proceed with the marriage must always be taught and fostered. Such a dissolution is never without pain, nor is it always

lucidly apparent that the pair should end their relationship and cancel the wedding plans.

Are our differences so deep-seated that a marriage joining us for life would be disastrous? Or, are our doubts and difficulties merely the natural anxieties of people taking a serious and permanent step into the future? Those are not easy questions to answer. While the engagement blessing rite offers many benefits for the woman and the man preparing to marry, that ritual should be accompanied by a delicate, but clear, explanation to the couple about its nonbinding force. An engagement ritual ought to enrich them, not burden or limit, albeit in an indirect way, their future ability to discern the correct response to those above questions and to act accordingly, despite the consequences.

Some have suggested that a blessing of this type be celebrated in a communal or even eucharistic context.[188] The *Book of Blessings* (no. 198), however, indicates that such a ritual should not be combined with Mass. Perhaps, the more realistic and wiser possibility is a cordial, but gentle, invitation—expressed generally or individually—to bless the engagement ring or the engagement itself in a less public setting. Couples often seek that in an informal manner following a Sunday eucharistic liturgy or on another occasion when they encounter the clergy. Moreover, this could be suggested during the initial interview or, for a group, during one of the marriage preparation sessions such as has been described at the end of an Engaged Encounter weekend.

For such quasi-private blessings of ring or engagement, it still is desirable that such a sacramental be done with the rites of the Church, including Scripture and prayer, not restricted to a mere mechanical gesture and a few words of benediction. The following biblical texts could be helpful in that regard, together with a blessing from the *Book of Blessings*, adjusted to the circumstances: Hosea 2:21-26; Philippians 2:1-5; 1 Corinthians 13:4-13; John 15:9-12; or Psalm 145:8-10,15,17-18.

SELECTING THE TEXTS

Prior to the Second Vatican Council, there were, practically speaking, no alternative texts for the nuptial liturgy. The priest employed the same biblical reading for every wedding Mass and followed an identical rite for each marriage. Given that long tradition, some judged that neither the clergy nor the couple about to marry would take advantage of the rich variety of optional readings, prayers, and blessings in the revised *Rite of Marriage*. Our nearly two decades of experience has shown that judgment to be in error. Most of the engaged are anxious to select the alter-

188. *To Love and to Honor*, pp. 1-5. See also, "Engagement Ceremony," Diocese of Albany.

natives that best fit their present situations and their future hopes; most of the clergy are both willing to provide them with a resource booklet of available texts and open to using those texts selected.

We strongly applaud that development, but would like to make two observations:

First, we encourage the clergy and parish to provide the engaged couple with an actual gift of the resource booklet rather than loan them a used copy. The available publications are relatively inexpensive, and the free offering of such a manual creates a positive attitude within the couple and counteracts any negative notions about commercialism that they may harbor toward the Church.

Second, we urge publishers to either print or, as a minimum, list all of the optional texts provided by the Church for the wedding celebration. To reduce the choices published out of economic expediency deprives the bride and groom of opportunities that rightfully belong to them.

As we mentioned earlier, distributing a copy or two of such a resource booklet during the initial interview both sets a positive climate through this free gift and starts them reading about the wedding liturgy before a later, hectic premarital pace enters their lives. Several of our clergy have devised methods for using these texts as stepping stones for more than mere liturgy planning.

One West Coast pastor, as described in the letter introducing this section of the manual, reads all of the texts to and with the couple. The very reading of that material, along with his personal comments, makes for an excellent instruction on marriage and assures him that all the major topics needing discussion prior to the wedding have been covered.

A second pastor—on the East Coast—employs the booklets with the available texts as a means of teaching the couple how to read Scripture in a listening, prayerful, and sharing way. Having presented each of the engaged pair with a copy, he establishes a meditative climate toward the end of the initial interview, then reads a biblical passage to them at a slow, reflective pace. Next, he asks the couple to pause in silence, to allow the words to penetrate their minds and hearts, and to decide what phrase or sentence most spoke to them about their lives here and now. Afterwards, he invites the bride and groom to share with each other—and with him, if they wish—their responses. As they prepare to leave on that occasion, the priest urges both to continue this process in the days ahead with all the other passages of the booklet. Out of those experiences, they will eventually select the excerpts that best fit their own tastes and insights.

A third pastor—also on the East Coast—uses the booklet as a tool for teaching the couple how to communicate with each other and how to pray together. He follows the same technique as the previous pastor in modeling a listening, prayerful, and

sharing approach to the Scriptures. However, he also suggests that they read through the biblical texts and commentaries one at a time. On those occasions, the priest recommends that the groom read aloud one scripture passage and that the bride read the connected commentary. Afterwards, they discuss their reactions and, perhaps, give the particular excerpt a rating. A day or so later, they move to another text and reverse the process. At the end of the procedure with all the readings, prayers, and blessings, the couple can review their reactions and make their selections.

The couple may, of course, choose scriptural passages other than the ones listed in the marriage ritual, provided they appear in an approved lectionary.[189] Most couples, it seems, confine themselves to those provided by the rite.

In the United States, this process of selecting the wedding texts has become a wonderful teachable moment and a superb pastoral technique for thousands of couples and clergy.

BOOKLETS FOR THE ASSEMBLED GUESTS

Many engaged couples have been preparing printed leaflets or booklets for distribution to guests assembled for the wedding. These vary in detail but contain at least the order of the service, together with the names of the wedding party and main liturgical ministers.

In some cases, they take the form of extensive booklets, including the people's responses in word and song for the appropriate parts of the Mass. When the music is printed in such leaflets, those entrusted with the pastoral care of each engaged couple should be careful to remind and guide them in securing the necessary copyright permissions. To facilitate this, diocesan directors of liturgy and music might prepare some simple guidelines and procedures to help parish personnel carry out, with relative ease, that important matter of social justice.

The question of printing or not printing the scripture texts in worship participation aids remains an ongoing discussion among biblical and liturgical scholars or leaders. However, the pastoral benefit from not including the passages of Scripture in wedding booklets seems to outweigh the advantages from doing so.

A personal message from the engaged couple to

---

189. "At the same time, the National Conference of Catholic Bishops employed the faculty of no. 325 (concerning further adaptations of readings) to authorize that the priest, when he is otherwise free to choose the readings of Mass in accord with no. 319 of the *Institutio Generalis,* may choose readings not found in the current week, provided they are within the approved lectionary, and appropriate to the particular celebration, and are not chosen to the disadvantage of the ordinary use of the weekday lectionary" (*Lectionary for Mass,* Foreword).

their invited guests can be an especially attractive and inspirational feature of these booklets.

The above suggestions presuppose couples in more affluent faith communities. We have many poor parishes—such as in inner-city and Hispanic areas—where these practices would become a burden, a financial impossibility, or a luxury. Nevertheless, many of these parishes are resourceful and creative with their liturgical celebrations, even where literacy is very low.

COOPERATION WITH OTHER CLERGY

Given the currently high percentage of interreligious marriages (about 40 percent) within the Catholic Church, we have frequent occasions in which the wedding celebration will include joint participation by the priest or deacon and a member of the clergy from another Christian tradition or other religion.[190]

Pope John Paul II has made explicit comments about a practice, which common courtesy would almost dictate in these circumstances. He remarks that, in order to highlight the ecumenical importance of interreligious marriages, "an effort should be made to establish cordial cooperation between the Catholic and non-Catholic ministers from the time that preparations begin for the marriage and the wedding ceremony. . . ."[191]

A few decades ago, the place and nature of the wedding celebration for an interreligious marriage were sources of real division and great pain for the bride and groom, as well as for their families. However, changes in church directives with regard to joint involvement in the worship service, and even dispensations from form, permitting Catholics to be married in other churches or locations, have almost totally eliminated that difficulty. Couples must still resolve the often thorny question of their spiritual differences and the religious upbringing of the children. But working out the actual wedding liturgy no longer appears to be such a serious problem or challenge.

When the marriage is to take place in a Catholic church, we hope the host priest or deacon would, when so requested, personally contact the other minister and warmly welcome him or her to participate. This invitation should be extended almost immediately after the initial interview. Later, as the actual wedding date draws near, they can discuss the specifics of this joint liturgical collaboration. Under the section treating "Interreligious Marriages," we outlined contemporary Catholic legislation about such mutual participation in the ceremony and offered some pastoral cautions.

When the marriage is to take place in the church of the one who is not Roman Catholic, the priest or deacon need not be present—although that is highly desirable and usually the wish of the Catholic party. When the priest or deacon does participate, he should

simply fulfill any role the minister suggests for him (e.g., read a scripture passage or pronounce a blessing). Again, current Catholic directives covering this situation can be found under the section on "Interreligious Marriages."

Interreligious marriages for Hispanics usually involve contact with members of storefront churches such as Evangelicals, or with Mormons and Jehovah's Witnesses, who are more inclined to proselytize and less concerned with sincere ecumenical efforts. By developing a sensitivity to the type of proselytizing to which Hispanics are subjected, the priest or deacon will become more prudential in his judgments and better suited to offer the proper advice to these couples.

THE PLACE FOR THE WEDDING

The *Code of Canon Law* indicates that marriages between Catholics or between a Catholic and a baptized non-Catholics should take place in the parish church. However, the local ordinary or parish priest can grant permission for the marriage to be celebrated in another church or oratory.[192] Moreover, the local ordinary can allow a marriage to be celebrated in another suitable place.[193] Finally, marriages between Catholics and unbaptized persons may be celebrated in a church or in another suitable place.[194]

Many dioceses have established policies that marriages, generally, should take place in a church to emphasize the spiritual and sacramental nature of the event. Regularly acceding to requests for weddings in other nonreligious locations (e.g., parks or wedding chapels) may undermine the notion that the nuptial ceremony is meant to be a prayerful celebration of a sacrament, in a worship context. Nevertheless, there are special occasions when the greater good of the couple and the families involved will warrant the celebration of marriage in a place other than a church. Even in such circumstances, however, care should be taken to preserve the sacred and religious dimension of the wedding ceremony.

THE WEDDING HOMILY

In its Introduction, the *Rite of Marriage* contains this very pastoral note:

> Priests should show special consideration to those who take part in liturgical celebrations or hear the gospel only on the occasion of a wedding, either because they are not Catholics, or because they are Catholics who rarely,

190. See "Religiously Mixed Marriages: A Challenge in the '80s," by Cecelia M. Bennett, in *Families in the '80s* (Washington, D.C.: USCC Office of Publishing and Promotion Services, 1980), pp. 39-41.
191. *On the Family*, no. 78.
192. *Code of Canon Law*, c. 1118:1.
193. Ibid., c. 1118:2.
194. Ibid., c. 1118:3.

if ever, take part in the eucharist or seem to have abandoned the practice of their faith. Priests are ministers of Christ's gospel to everyone.[195]

While the bride and groom may, because of their nervousness and preoccupation with all the day's events, hardly hear a word of the homily, the assembled guests, especially those who are married, appreciate a practical and encouraging message about matrimony.

The ritual gives clear, even if general, guidelines about the homily. It should be "drawn from the sacred text" and speak "about the mystery of Christian marriage, the dignity of wedded love, the grace of the sacrament, and the responsibilities of married people, keeping in mind the circumstances of this particular marriage."[196]

After the couple have made their selections of the readings or other texts and completed the marriage preparation process, the priest or deacon might visit with them about the reasons behind their choices. That information, plus the background details gathered through the initial interview and other encounters, will provide good resource material for the type of homily described by the ritual.

As noted in other liturgical books, the homily may be delivered from the lectern, presidential chair, altar, or whatever place the Word can best be proclaimed. The priest or deacon should, of course, make certain that his voice will be heard and that he can be seen fully by the entire assembly, not just by the bride and groom.

CULTURAL ADAPTATIONS

Both the revised marriage ritual and Pope John Paul II encourage the use of appropriate elements of local cultures in the wedding ceremony. Thus, the latter notes that church authorities may include in the liturgical celebration "such elements proper to each culture which serve to express more clearly the profound human and religious significance of the marriage contract, provided that such elements contain nothing that is not in harmony with Christian faith and morality."[197]

Here in the United States, several additions to or alterations of the basic nuptial liturgy have popularly developed over the past two decades—although they are not officially approved. In time, these will need to be evaluated in terms of their pastoral value, sustained popularity, liturgical appropriateness, and theological suitability. Moreover, in the future, we hope that our Bishops' Committee on the Liturgy, in concert with its various consultative bodies and other liturgical experts, will also examine carefully the texts in the current *Rite of Marriage*, for possible adaptation to the circumstances in this country. Among those spontaneous, unofficial additions or

alterations that have arisen during the last twenty years, we wish to mention the following:

Wedding candle. Perhaps the most popular of all these additions or alterations, it can be a single decorated candle held by the bride and groom together or an arrangement of three candles in a stand, with the center one the designated wedding taper. A simple lighting ritual usually takes place in silence after the exchange of vows or at the very conclusion of the nuptial liturgy, as part of the final blessing. Couples who do opt for this symbol might consider an added feature of decorating their own candle, after the procedure sometimes practiced for baptism, confirmation, or first Eucharist.

"Arras," "Lazo," Bouquet to the Blessed Virgin Mary. In many Hispanic weddings, these added elements are very common. *Arras* are the silver or gold coins offered by the groom to the bride as a sign of his responsibility for food, clothing, and shelter; the bride accepts them with the promise of good stewardship. *Lazo* is a figure-eight band (such as two rosaries put together) that signifies the sacramental union of husband and wife. The *Bouquet* is offered by the bride to the Blessed Virgin Mary as a personal surrender to the Virgin Mary and as a request for her protection during their entire married life.

Comments from parents or guests. The speaking of a few prepared remarks by the parents to the couple, after the postcommunion prayer or before the blessing in a ceremony outside of Mass—following the pattern observed at a funeral liturgy—has a precedent in certain cultures (e.g., among African and Vietnamese people). Spontaneous words of blessing or greeting, just prior to the dismissal, can find a similar tradition among Quakers. In Hispanic communities, parents often impart a blessing upon their children, especially at solemn occasions such as a trip, a voyage, a long absence, and, above all, at marriage. Sometimes, they prefer to do it at home or to do it in church.

Facing the assembly for the exchange of vows. Rather than face the clergy or each other, certain couples wish to turn toward the assembly for the exchange of consent. The priest or deacon in this arrangement ordinarily takes a position in the aisle among the assembled community where he can lead the bride and groom in the recitation of their vows to one another.

Procession. Instead of the bride processing down the aisle accompanied by her father, several variations have developed—for different reasons—in our country such as: bride accompanied by father and mother; or both bride and groom, accompanied by parents, processing down the aisle. The most cogent reason for these variations is the desire to express

195. *Rite of Marriage,* no. 9.
196. Ibid., no. 22.
197. *On the Family,* no. 67.

more clearly that the bride's family—both mother and father—has brought her to this point in life and, similarly, both sets of parents are the origin of this young couple.

Seating Arrangement. We usually expect the relatives of the bride to take their seating on the side of the bride, and the groom's relatives on his side. Normally, the parents and relatives are escorted and seated in their proper places. Afterwards, the white carpet is rolled down the aisle before the procession begins. For Hispanics, this custom does not always catch their attention. Seating takes place at random, without such an artificial separation, because the families have become much more intertwined and interrelated.

Secular readings. The desire to use readings from favorite secular authors is less popular today than a decade ago, but still persists. There are cautions to be noted here and reasons for discouraging the practice: first, secular readings may not replace the required two scripture passages; second, in our highly video-saturated society, verbal overkill through excessive readings, prayers, or blessings can weaken the effectiveness of the liturgical celebration.

Gift for the poor. A few couples have made an offering for the world's poor part of their celebration, sometimes dramatizing this by having a basket of food brought to the altar during the presentation of the gifts. That seeks to symbolize their desire to foster, in their marriage, an attitude of reaching out to the needy. Of those few, some have decided to tithe or take a percentage of the wedding's total cost and give that sum for the indigent.

While we praise that gesture, we also raise a more radical concern. In our pastoral letter *Economic Justice for All*, we stated, "All of us could well ask ourselves whether as a Christian prophetic witness we are not called to adopt a simpler life style, in the face of the excessive accumulation of material goods that characterizes an affluent society."[198]

The deeper question, then, is whether a couple about to marry in the Catholic Church should, in view of these words, not seek to simplify some of the events surrounding the nuptial celebration, notably the reception. Would that not offer an example of resistance to our growing materialism and the consumerism of our culture? Are there ways we can "Christianize" the reception? Given modern society's better approach to alcoholism—understanding its nature as a disease, recognizing its prevalence, promoting its prevention —should we not address that concern in connection with the gatherings before and the festivities after the liturgy? Deciding to tithe or to take a percentage of the total wedding costs as a gift for the poor, might be a step in this direction and help to raise everyone's sensitivity on the matter, leading eventually to that greater simplicity urged in our document.

Composing personal vows. Some couples wish to write their own vows, and some clergy, as part of the preparation process, encourage them to formulate the nuptial promises in their own words. In both situations, these modifications of the vows may only be made by adding to the text of the ritual rather than by substituting their own words for the official formula. The Second Vatican Council empowered episcopal conferences to draw up their own rite for marriage. However, it retained as essential the requirement that the priest, deacon, or person assisting at the marriage must ask for and receive the consent of the contracting parties.[199]

Both forms given in the new marriage ritual for expressing consent (by declaration at the invitation of the minister or by response to question) contain the elements of (1) acceptance of one another as husband and wife; (2) fidelity; and (3) permanence. These should not be omitted in any modification of the text submitted by the couple.[200] The ritual for the United States, of course, provides both an old and a new version for the exchange of vows.

Prayer of the couple. This petition, composed by the couple who seek God's blessing on their marriage, is read by them after the exchange of vows, following communion or before dismissal.

Some additional ethnic adaptations. With more and more ethnic groups residing in the United States, some of their unique wedding customs will inevitably begin to surface and become known in our society. The following are illustrative of a few adaptations or the absence of them in contemporary marriage ceremonies:

- *Hmong Catholics* tend not to incorporate their marriage customs into the Catholic wedding liturgy.

- *Cambodian Catholics*, similarly, do not integrate their ethnic rites into the Catholic celebration. They may, however, have their traditional ritual before going to the church for a Catholic celebration of marriage. Even so, it is not usual for the bride to take the hand of the bridegroom in public, and it is very much against Cambodian customs and feelings for the bride to kiss the bridegroom in public.

- *Filipino Catholics* have incorporated some of their customs into the Catholic marriage liturgy. These include secondary sponsors for the candle, veil, and cord; blessing and giving of the coins or *arrhae*; principal sponsors, usually older relatives or friends of the couple who act as witnesses of the marriage. Nevertheless, in the United States, the role of the principal sponsor is still desired, but in an honorary manner only, since the best man and maid of

---

198. *Economic Justice for All*, no. 334.
199. *The Constitution on the Sacred Liturgy*, no. 77.
200. "The Couples and the Wedding" (Chicago: Liturgy Training Program, 1977), p. 14.

honor are considered official witnesses of the marriage.

- *Laotian Catholics* do not incorporate their own customs into the liturgical rite, but in many instances observe certain rituals at the home prior to the church ceremony.

Any of these additions and variations must be options selected by the couple, not by the clergy. Their celebration should be a nuptial liturgy with which they are comfortable, not a ceremony made tense for them because of nonessential elements, however attractive, forced upon the bride and groom by well-meaning, but unwise, pastoral leaders.

Wedding Music

In 1972, the Bishops' Committee on the Liturgy issued a document *Music in Catholic Worship*, which was revised in 1983. That statement has become a basic text or reference guide for liturgical musicians throughout the Catholic Church in the United States. It addressed briefly the issue of music at weddings. After mentioning that the norms governing music during eucharistic liturgies should be observed when marriage is celebrated within a Mass, it went on more specifically to declare:

> Great care should be taken, especially at marriages, that all the people are involved at the important moments of the celebration, that the same general principles of planning worship and judging music are employed as at other liturgies, and, above all, that the liturgy is a prayer for all present, not a theatrical production.[201]

In 1982, the same committee published a second document *Liturgical Music Today*, which expanded slightly its recommendations for music during a nuptial liturgy:

> Weddings present particular challenges and opportunities to planners. It is helpful for a diocese or a parish to have a definite (but flexible) policy regarding wedding music. This policy should be communicated early to couples as a normal part of their preparation in order to avoid last minute crises and misunderstandings. Both musician and pastor should make every effort to assist couples to understand and share in the planning of their marriage liturgy. Sometimes the only music familiar to the couple is a song heard at a friend's ceremony and one not necessarily suitable to the sacrament. The pastoral musician will make an effort to demonstrate a wider range of possibilities to the couple, particularly in the choice of music to be sung by the entire assembly present for the liturgy.
>
> Particular decisions about choice and placement of wedding music should grow out of the three judgments proposed in *Music in*

Catholic Worship. The liturgical judgment: Is the music's text, form, placement and style congruent with the nature of liturgy? The musical judgment: Is the music technically, aesthetically and expressively good, irrespective of musical idiom or style? The pastoral judgment: Will it help this assembly to pray? Such a process of dialogue may not be as easy to apply as an absolute list of permitted or prohibited music, but in the long run it will be more effective pastorally.[202]

One midwestern archdiocese has issued a helpful booklet that spells out, in detail, the meaning of those general norms and also provides a list of suitable musical pieces, along with the names of the pertinent publishers.[203]

A southern diocese has prepared a flier—for distribution to engaged couples—that contains guidelines for the use of music in the celebration of the sacrament of matrimony.[204] The publication first explains that marriage is a sacrament, with its celebration consequently designed not just for the bride and groom, family, and friends, but also for the whole Christian community in which the wedding takes place. It then notes that, since marriage is meant to be a community celebration, the engaged couple are not planning merely their own prayer—and certainly not their own show; the focus, instead, is seeking to help those in attendance to pray. After reassuring the bride and groom that the wedding will, nevertheless, remain very much "their own," the guidelines offer

201. *Music in Catholic Worship*, no. 82.
202. *Liturgical Music Today*, (Washington, D.C.: USCC Office of Publishing and Promotion Services, 1982), nos. 28-29.
203. *Handbook of Church Music for Weddings*, compiled by Chicago Archdiocesan Office of Divine Worship's Music Staff; Mary Ann Simcoe, ed. (Chicago: Liturgy Training Publications, 1985).
204. *Guidelines for the Use of Music in the Celebration of the Sacrament of Matrimony*, Diocesan Commission on Sacred Liturgy, Art and Music (Baton Rouge: Diocese of Baton Rouge, 1985).

practical, but flexible, suggestions for selecting wedding music.

As an aid in this often delicate task for pastoral musicians and others involved with marriage preparation, we reproduce edited excerpts of that text below. It should always be kept in mind, however, that many Hispanic and other couples are too poor to afford this luxury and must rely on whatever musical enhancement the parish can provide.

Planning the Music for Your Wedding

Music will add much joy to the occasion of your wedding. Its primary purpose will be to help the people to pray. Congregational singing, therefore, is to be preferred, even though a vocal soloist or choir may be very appropriate at certain times before and during the liturgy.

Here are some guidelines to help you plan the music for your wedding Mass in such a way that it will not only recognize the presence of the community of faith, gathered to pray with and for you, but will also help them to pray.

Introductory Music

While the guests are assembling, appropriate music may be performed by instrumentalists, choir, or vocal soloists. The function of this preludial music is to gather up and unite the thoughts of all present and to prepare them for the celebration of the marriage.

The goal of the entrance music is to escort the wedding couple with honor to the altar and to gather the congregation into a worshiping community.

A congregational hymn may be sung during the procession or after the procession is completed and the presiding clergy has welcomed all and invited them to stand and sing together. Such singing makes the people participants rather than spectators. The selected song should express joy and be well known by all the congregation.

The Liturgy of the Word

The responsorial psalm should be sung and would be very appropriate for a soloist alternating with the congregation which sings a simple response.

The Gospel Acclamation or Alleluia is also to be sung, possibly by a soloist (cantor) and the congregation.

After the exchange of vows, a brief song which focuses on God's presence to individual love may be used, but is optional.

The Liturgy of the Eucharist

It is recommended that instrumental music accompany the preparation of the gifts of bread and wine. This rite is a brief part of the liturgy and should not be overly emphasized. A short choral or vocal solo may be used which brings out the message of the readings.

The Eucharistic Acclamations (the Holy, Holy, the Memorial Acclamation, and the Great Amen) are to be sung in the familiar musical settings known by the community. The soloist (cantor) or choir may lead the people in these sung acclamations.

If using musical settings would keep the majority of people from participating in the acclamations, it would be better not to sing them but to recite them together, as these acclamations, as well as the Lord's Prayer and the Lamb of God which follow, belong to all of the people and, as such, should properly be prayed by them.

The Song of Communion accompanies the communion procession and expresses our unity in the Body of Christ; therefore, this song should speak of a wider community love than do those sung during the wedding ceremony itself. Congregational singing, by its very nature, reflects the meaning of Communion.

If there is no Communion Song, a hymn of praise and thanksgiving may be sung after Communion by the congregation, choir, or soloist. Instrumental music is also appropriate at this time for creating a mood of silence, prayer, and reflection.

Concluding Rite

The dismissal is followed immediately by strong, joyous recessional music which may be a hymn sung by the assembly or choir, or an instrumental selection.

The Three Standards

The Committee on the Liturgy of the National Conference of Catholic Bishops has given us three standards to be used in choosing music for any celebration of liturgy:

1. ***The Musical Standard.*** Music used in liturgy must be technically correct and of good quality. That which is merely cheap, trite musical cliche should not even be considered. By consulting with the organist or musical director to plan the music for your wedding, you will avoid many mistakes and possibly embarrassing situations; this person has probably been involved in hundreds of weddings and can be most helpful to you.

2. ***The Liturgical Standard.*** The sacrament of matrimony is a public act, a sacred sign, an encounter with Christ. The music at weddings should

serve to emphasize the sacred event, not distract from it. It should assist all who are present to share the gift of faith and to join with the Church in prayer for the couple. For this reason, if you wish to use songs at your wedding, you should be aware that, while they ought to be as musically attractive as possible, it is the text (the words) that should be considered most important: each text sung at your wedding ought to be readily identifiable as prayer; if it cannot, then it is out of place in a liturgical context. It is clearly possible that musical selections designed for purposes other than liturgical worship (such as popular show tunes, love songs, and secular ballads) may also express some dimension of Christian faith and may, in some cases, help people pray. However, the practical fact remains that, in the vast majority of cases, compositions that are the most successful in fulfilling the purpose for which they were created will usually be only minimally successful when they are redirected toward a much different end. For this reason, it is recommended that music of this type is best left to the family reception, where another dimension of the celebration prevails.

*3. **The Pastoral Standard.*** Each wedding is unique; the music at a particular wedding must be judged on how well it will enable this particular group of people present at this particular wedding to express their faith. If it is meaningful for this type of experience, then it is appropriate. When choosing music, do not overlook religious songs of ethnic origin. These are very helpful in reflecting your background and in involving your friends, relatives, and family.

Since many or most couples have a limited awareness of attractive and appropriate sacred wedding music, a critical pastoral step is an early encounter between the parish musician and the engaged pair. At that time, they can have these basic principles explained and hear some of the perhaps unfamiliar, but beautiful, possibilities available for their wedding.

3 The Rehearsal

The wedding rehearsal presents the clergy or parish leaders who may conduct them with one of the greatest challenges in pastoral ministry. They meet for the first time ever—normally at the end of a long working day, with the depletion of energy that entails—an enormously complex mix of people. Some are known, others unknown; some are warm and cordial, others cold and distant; some are very familiar with Catholic practices, others totally ignorant of all religious traditions; some are comfortable and at ease about the rehearsal, others awkward and uncomfortable. In addition, the bride and groom are excited about all the events soon to happen but, often, also extremely anxious over the details of the rehearsal and the wedding itself.

The confluence of all these factors—a gathering of strangers; the complexity of their attitudes or feelings; and the couple's high level of nervous anxiety—tends to manifest itself in diverse ways. Sometimes, the assembled persons will be loud and unruly; at other times, the group may be silent and almost sullen.

The clergy or parish leader responsible has, in the presence of such a situation, the difficult task of bringing order out of chaos, assembling the people together; immediately relaxing the group and establishing a relationship with them; calming their fears; creating a serious prayerful atmosphere; deftly handling special requests; and working through the mechanics of the ceremony. That requires great tact and enormous patience, combined with gentle firmness and confident leadership. The stakes, however, are very high: people tend never to forget the clergy who have carried out rehearsals well; on the other hand, they tend never to forgive those who have carried them out poorly, offending those gathered in the process.

Some parishes have developed parish or volunteer coordinators who take charge of the details of the rehearsal. There is much to be said on behalf of this development, particularly in view of the increasing demands made upon a declining number of priests. However, with the personalized nature of each couple's nuptial ceremony today, there must be close communication between the coordinator and the clergy about details. Moreover, since the presiding liturgist will be relating to this wedding party in an important way the next day, some contact with them at the rehearsal itself is highly desirable. Perhaps, a way of blending these two tasks is for the clergy to assemble the group and lead them in prayer, then introduce the coordinator, who will conduct the rehearsing of the next day's movements.

A brief informal period of prayer can be very helpful in quickly creating that serious, reverent atmosphere. To accomplish this, there is a value in bringing them forward and seating them in the front pews. Then, the priest or deacon might offer a few words of warm welcome; a bit of light humor about the situation; a simple explanation of the church structure; and, then, an invitation to join for a short prayer on behalf of the bride and groom.

Here is a brief sample service of prayerful silence and scripture reading:

All of us are thankful to _____ and _____ for bringing us together tonight. We know how important this event is to them and to their future. We want them to know that, even through our joking, we feel this is an important occasion for us, too.

So, before we begin the wedding practice, I am asking all of us to spend a moment in prayer and listening to God's Word from the Scriptures. Our brief prayer will also be a way of preparing ourselves for tomorrow, when we gather to pray with the larger community of the Church. In your own way, because of your unique relationship to _____ and _____ I want you to join with me in praying for them tonight.

Think about your deepest ideals and hopes for them. Pray that these come to reality in them and in their married life together.

Think of their limitations and their needs and pray that they will always turn to God and to those who can help them.

Let us pray, first, for a moment in silence.

(A period of silence follows.)

We now hear God speak to us about love and marriage. (One of the texts from the *Rite of Marriage* could be used here, e.g., Mt 22:35-40; Jn 15:9-12; 1 Jn 4:7-12; 1 Cor 12:30—13:8.)

(A moment of silent reflection follows.)

Let us pray as Christ taught us: "Our Father. . . ." (Perhaps, use the longer ending.)

O Lord God of love and compassion, you have brought us together as family and friends. For this, we thank you. _____ and _____, and all of us, are preparing now for a new life together. Strengthen us with understanding and fill us with joy. Hear the prayers we ask of you, for you will guide and direct us always, as long as we turn to you in faith. We ask this in the name of Jesus Christ, our Lord. Amen.[205]

Providing an opportunity for penance or reconciliation after the actual rehearsal was formerly a standard procedure. Today, fewer priests offer and fewer penitents request an occasion for going to confession at that moment. Canon 1065:2 strongly recommends that couples receive the sacraments of penance and the Eucharist before marriage so that

their marriage may be fruitful. While both positive and negative issues could be raised about the time of the rehearsal being the appropriate moment for celebrating the sacrament of penance, nevertheless, entering marriage provides a touchable moment to invite the partners to celebrate conversion and spiritual renewal in the sacrament of penance.

However, for Hispanic couples and their retinue who come to the practice, it is a most important moment to provide the opportunity for penance or reconciliation as a standard procedure. It is expected. When the couple's friends and relatives were asked to take part in their wedding, they also knew they were committing themselves to penance and Eucharist. No one is forced to go to confession. This great teachable moment cannot be neglected or let go unnoticed.

Another approach might be to address the issue of reconciliation or penance directly with the engaged couple in an early interview. Then, as a further encouragement, the couple might be urged to have the wedding party receive communion—as a display of prayerful solidarity with them—on the three Sundays beforehand, when the parish bulletin may announce the approaching marriage. That would, likewise, prompt many to make an effort to seek reconciliation prior to rehearsal night.

Obtaining the civil license and securing the necessary signatures can sometimes cause a needless expenditure of time and energy. Normally, this can be avoided if the presiding clergy, at the last meeting with the engaged couple, strongly directs them to bring this document to the rehearsal. If they still forget the license, one can eliminate this problem by insisting that a free member of the party go after the document and return with it before the rehearsal has finished. In some cases, Hispanic couples and couples from other foreign countries may bring forth the civil marriage certificate; normally, in those situations, the clergy should simply proceed as if it were the license.

In a good liturgical celebration, the participants need to be relaxed, but reverent, and comfortable, but not casual. When the wedding party has been rehearsed properly and understand clearly their function, that spirit of a relaxed, comfortable, and reverent ceremony can predominate. Then, the lead participants will not be preoccupied with the external movements, but are better able to concentrate on the total event and the inner realities behind the celebration. Should the party be willing, a swift second run-through of the ritual—procession, vows, recession—can be an aid in achieving this comfortable assurance.

205. *Rites: The Engagement, the Rehearsal, the Anniversary*, adaptation of "Rehearsal Prayers," format I, pp. 7-8 (Chicago: Liturgy Training Program, 1977).

For Hispanic couples, the above observations also stand. The participants are to be both familial and formal. The minister needs to recognize that he wields great authority; hence, he needs to be extremely gentle.

4 The Liturgical Celebration

Since the celebration of marriage is a sacramental action of sanctification, it should be inserted into the liturgy, which is the summit of the Church's action and the source of her sanctifying power.[206]

In our time, the question across the United States is whether matrimony should be celebrated within or outside of Mass. Church directives urge that, ordinarily, marriage be celebrated within Mass. The bishops at the Second Vatican Council said that "matrimony is normally to be celebrated within the Mass."[207] The marriage ritual speaks about the celebration of marriage "which normally should be within the Mass." It also underscores the importance of "the reception of holy communion by the groom and the bride, and by all present, by which their love is nourished and all are lifted up into communion with our Lord and one another."[208] Pope John Paul II, in drawing out the connection between the Eucharist and marriage repeats the teaching of the Second Vatican Council about matrimony within Mass. He says that "by partaking in the eucharistic bread, the different members of the Christian family become one body, which reveals and shares in the wider unity of the Church."[209]

This ideal of marriage within Mass has become more and more of a pastoral difficulty in our country for the following reasons:

- The decline in the number of priests has compelled many of them to offer multiple Masses each weekend. The further addition of a nuptial Mass or two on Saturday, plus the always present possibility of a funeral for that day, imposes a nearly too heavy burden upon some presiding priests.

- Deacons, obviously, cannot preside at Mass, but they—especially permanent ones—are with increasing frequency celebrating marriage.

- Engaged couples of a marginal nature (i.e., those who rarely participate at Sunday Mass) may have sufficient faith for reception of matrimony, but seemingly inadequate faith for reception of the Eucharist. Many of the clergy are more comfortable with and judge it pastorally wiser to celebrate the marriage of such couples outside of Mass.

- As we have mentioned earlier, there are several reasons in support of the position that it is better to celebrate interreligious marriages outside of rather than within Mass.

- If the episcopal conference and the Holy See approve, the diocesan bishop can delegate lay persons to assist at marriages where priests or deacons are lacking.[210]

In such circumstances, the Church does provide the option of distributing communion at the end of the rite.[211] However welcome this is in the context, frequent use of communion services can undercut the notion of the eucharistic sacrifice in the minds of people.

The significant number of divorces and church annulments in our day means that convalidations and weddings involving persons who have been married before are more common occurences. Great pastoral sensitivity and wisdom are needed here. The appropriate solemnity for such a situation, the tensions caused by the blending or merging of families now taking place, the location of guests, the participation of children, the thrust of the homily are some of the areas to be discussed by the clergy and those about to marry.

To foster active participation in the wedding, the bride and groom may enlist the services of relatives and friends as musicians, leaders of song, readers, gift bearers, greeters, eucharistic ministers, and the like. In such circumstances, the pastor may appoint, on a temporary basis, the bride and groom or others as ministers of communion. Nevertheless, they should be trained adequately beforehand.

When selecting these persons, the bride and groom should seek to blend two elements: process and product. By *process*, we mean the enlisting, training, and assigning of relatives or friends for specific tasks in the wedding liturgy. By *product*, we mean that those selected be capable of carrying out satisfactorily the particular function. For example, the mere fact that a brother or sister will proclaim the Scriptures is a positive development; but the fact that neither one can read well in public would be a negative factor. There is an almost inevitable tension in reconciling those two ingredients.

Christ is present, in a unique way during the liturgy, in the people gathered for worship, in the Scriptures proclaimed, in the Eucharist offered and received, and in the sacrament of matrimony that bride and groom minister to one another.[212] However, this "gift of Jesus Christ is not exhausted in the actual celebration of the sacrament of marriage, but rather accompanies the married couple throughout their lives."[213]

---

206. *On the Family*, no. 67.
207. *The Constitution on the Sacred Liturgy*, no. 78.
208. *Rite of Marriage*, no. 6.
209. *On the Family*, no. 57.
210. *Code of Canon Law*, c. 1112.
211. *Rite of Marriage*, no. 54.
212. *The Constitution on the Sacred Liturgy*, no. 7.
213. *On the Family*, no. 56.

Section IV: Pastoral Care after Marriage

"Married couples have influenced me through their struggle to open themselves to growth with one another. Their ability to express where they are and how they are without fear of rejection by their spouses calls me to be more open and honest with myself and with the many people I relate with each day.

"I am drawn to appreciate and cherish my own response to fidelity as a Religious woman. I need what happens to me when I see a family struggling to improve communication, to pay bills, or to carpool children. Discipline takes on new meaning time after time following an evening or a few hours with a family. Poverty is a lived experience in many families.

"All in all, I give thanks for the couples I know through Engaged Encounter, Natural Family Planning, and countless other groups. Three out of four of my own siblings have experienced divorce and its pain. I pray daily for the grace to be open to all that will continue to nourish me as a Religious woman."

(Mississippi)

Definition of Pastoral Care after Marriage

Marriage preparation, as we have seen, begins in reality from the first moment of conception. It also, in effect, continues on after the marriage takes place and, ideally, should be sustained until death separates the two who become one. As the testimony of the religious sister exemplifies, the direct and indirect support of others is equally as necessary in married life, as the intense marital preparation efforts may have proved beneficial just prior to the wedding celebration. Moreover, a cycle of life immediately begins again since the new husband and wife usually will become parents and thus embark upon the process of remote preparation.

Pope John Paul II places the duty of this aftercare help upon "all members of the local ecclesial community" who are entrusted with the task of "helping the couple to discover and live their new vocation and mission." The bride and groom should be aided "and trained in their responsibilities as they face the new problems that arise."[1]

The Holy Father envisions a mutual exchange between young married couples and those with experience in marital life:

Young married couples should learn to accept willingly and make good use of the discreet, tactful and generous help offered by other couples that already have more experience of married and family life.[2]

Such a family-to-family ministry becomes, in Pope John Paul II's mind, a model of collaboration and mutual concern:

---

1. *On the Family*, no. 69.
2. Ibid.

127

Thus within the ecclesial community—the great family made up of Christian families—there will take place a mutual exchange of presence and help among all the families, each one putting at the service of the others its own experience of life, as well as the gifts of faith and grace. Animated by a true apostolic spirit, this assistance from family to family will constitute one of the simplest, most effective and most accessible means for transmitting from one to another those Christian values which are both the starting point and goal of all.[3]

The aftercare of married couples, therefore, is extensive in time and diverse in approach.

Challenges during Certain Periods or Passages of Married Life

There are particular challenges that married couples must face at certain developmental periods or passages of their marital lives. For the sake of simplicity, we have categorized those phases into the initial years of marriage, the in-between years, and the years after the children have left home as adults.

THE EARLY YEARS

Pope John Paul II recognized the challenges of early marital living. He observed that young families particularly need assistance because, finding themselves in a context of new values and responsibilities, they "are more vulnerable, especially in the first years of marriage, to possible difficulties such as those created by adaptation to life together or by the birth of children."[4]

His theoretical observation about the struggles of early married life finds support in empirical data. Some 50 percent of all divorces occur during the first five years, and 33 percent of all separations happen within two years.[5]

Four New England dioceses and one archdiocese addressed this problem by combined research efforts to determine what are the most significant areas of conflict or difficulty for couples married less than three years. They mailed a survey to young spouses who had participated in marriage preparation programs and enclosed a prepaid envelope to facilitate the response.[6]

Totals from the combined answers of husbands and wives revealed that the first twenty areas of conflict or difficulty listed in the order of importance or weight were the following:

1. finances
2. moodiness
3. division of household responsibilities
4. communication
5. expectations of each other
6. in-laws
7. personal habits
8. listening
9. decision making
10. criticism
11. body clocks (wake/sleep patterns)
12. how to spend leisure time
13. sex
14. showing affection
15. my spouse's career
16. my career
17. television
18. family celebrations
19. marital expectations
20. friends

The summary of female responses listed these twenty:

1. finances
2. listening
3. communication
4. division of household responsibilities
5. moodiness
6. in-laws
7. expectations of each other
8. personal habits
9. priorities/values
10. body clocks (wake/sleep patterns)
11. how to spend leisure time
12. decision making
13. showing affection
14. sex
15. criticism
16. my spouse's career
17. my career
18. television
19. marital expectations
20. family celebrations

The summary of male responses listed these twenty:

1. finances
2. moodiness
3. division of household responsibilities
4. communication
5. criticism
6. decision making
7. sex, expectations of each other
8. priorities/values
9. how to spend leisure time
10. in-laws

3. Ibid.
4. Ibid.
5. *Family Communication*, p. 190.
6. 1985 survey conducted by the Family Life Offices for the Archdiocese of Hartford (Connecticut); the Dioceses of Fall River, Springfield, and Worcester (Massachusetts); and the Diocese of Providence (Rhode Island).

11. listening
12. body clocks (wake/sleep patterns)
13. personal habits
14. showing affection
15. my career
16. television
17. my spouse's career
18. health
19. family celebrations
20. jealousy

The Family Life Office in the Archdiocese of Hartford is trying to help with those particular challenges by a pilot counseling referral project. During the marriage preparation program, the engaged couple are introduced to and speak with a professional counselor on the diocesan staff. They are then encouraged, when significant difficulties or challenges arise in those first years of married life, to make contact with this counselor, who can facilitate their talking things through and resolving the conflict in constructive fashion.

Cultural imperatives would demand more attention to areas such as in-laws and family relationships among Hispanics. Obviously, we need to make similar surveys among our Hispanic brothers and sisters and, thus, surface a list of priorities.

THE IN-BETWEEN YEARS

Throughout those early and no-children years, as well as in between them, certain common challenges do tend to occur.

The Diocese of Cleveland conducted an extensive research project from 1982 to 1985, to determine what type of problems present themselves in marriage counseling. They took a list of marital difficulties from an annual national survey of Marriage and Family Therapists, rearranged the ten topics, and then asked the following groups to rate the issues: college professors, clergy, attorneys, physicians, and professional marriage counselors.

The original list of problems contained these items:

1. communication
2. unrealistic expectations of marriage/spouse
3. power struggles
4. serious individual problems
5. role conflict
6. lack of loving feelings
7. demonstration of affection
8. alcoholism
9. extramarital affairs
10. sex

Nearly all the Cleveland groups ranked "communication" and "unrealistic expectations of marriage/spouse" as the first two problems, with "extramarital affairs" as number ten.[7]

THE NO-CHILDREN YEARS

Demographic studies of the past and projections for the future show a radical shift in the marital pattern, a change that we would all sense from everyday experience.

Declining fertility and rising life-expectancy rates mean a new phenomenon for married couples.

Persons born in 1960 have a life expectancy of 69.7 years, while those born in 1982 have an expectancy of 74.5 years. The male life expectancy is 70.8 years; the female life expectancy is 78.2 years. Since most people marry before the age of thirty, a continuous marriage may last forty to fifty years.[8]

A century ago, a wife and husband had only about a year and half together before they became parents. Couples marrying today, on the other hand, are likely to spend nearly twenty-two years, about half of their married life, alone together with no children in the house—mostly after the children are grown. Moreover, during a substantial part of that time, neither partner will be in the full-time labor force. This will result in a decade or so of "young old age," a period between retirement from the labor force and the onset of physical disability.[9]

Such a development raises questions, challenges, and difficulties. What do women do instead of raising children? What do spouses do instead of working for money? How much satisfaction can husbands and wives get from each other alone, after two decades of a marital relationship that has been children centered?

This points out that, if a marriage is overfocused on job, children, financial security, and so forth, a time will come when the couple will drift apart. Marriage needs, from the very beginning, a focus on each other.

Surveys reveal, nevertheless, that marital satisfaction seems to be the greatest during those periods before and after the birth of children. Divorce rates decrease with age; the highest rates occur among the twenty to twenty-four year-olds.[10] Consequently, the marital disruptions among older couples are not proportionately as numerous as we might judge from common observation.

Learning how to manage those conflicts that occur between spouses seems to be the best method for ensuring the highest degree of marital satisfaction. Conversely, unresolved conflicts lead to divorce.[11] These facts buttress our previous recommendation for constant teaching and deepening of communication skills, including problem solving and conflict management.

7. Cleveland Diocesan Department of Marriage and Family Concerns, *Covenant* 4:4 (October 1985).
8. *Family Communication*, p. 7.
9. *Here to Stay*, pp. 24-25.
10. Ibid., pp. 25-26.
11. *Family Communication*, p. 190.

The following story puts all of this into perspective:

When I asked my wife what she wanted for our 25th wedding anniversary, she said, "Marriage counseling. The next twenty-five years have to be better than the first." I knew we had many fights, but I never knew she was that unhappy. I agreed to the counseling, and we really worked on our differences and ways of resolving them. After a few months, we were able to talk rationally about things we always fought over—money, my schedule, our youngest son. Next month, we will celebrate our 28th anniversary, and I can say, "The last three years were a lot better than the first twenty-five."[12]

While we rejoice over the newly founded and experienced growth and happiness of that couple—or any couple—in the later years, we feel sad that those first twenty-five were so unfulfilling, at least for the one spouse. Perhaps, good marriage aftercare might have prevented such unhappiness. We pray that increased efforts of this sort in the future may help all married couples deal better with the seasons and passages of their lives.

 Faithful Forever

Married persons and those who promote the dignity of matrimony can be disheartened by the apparently increasing incidence of infidelity in American society. Personal conversations, the popular media, and sociological studies point to a large percentage of extramarital sexual affairs or encounters among today's couples.[13] Catholic spouses may find that such a surrounding environment causes their own commitments to waver or weaken.

In the face of such a deterioration in fidelity to the married bond, we would like to underscore Pope John Paul II's comments:

Just as the Lord Jesus is the "faithful witness" ... and the supreme realization of the unconditional faithfulness with which God loves his people, so Christian couples are called to participate truly in the irrevocable indissolubility that binds Christ to the Church, his bride, loved by him to the end.

The gift of the sacrament is at the same time a vocation and commandment for the Christian spouses, that they may remain faithful to each other forever, beyond every trial and difficulty, in generous obedience to the holy will of the Lord: "What therefore God has joined together, let not man put asunder."

To bear witness to the inestimable value of the indissolubility and fidelity of marriage is one of the most precious and most urgent tasks of Christian couples in our time. . . . Thus in a humble and courageous manner they perform the role committed to them of being in the world a "sign"—a small and precious sign, sometimes also subject to temptation, but always renewed—of the unfailing fidelity with which God and Jesus Christ love each and every human being.[14]

A current author gives secular support for these theological truths and translates those theoretical statements into practical realities. Noting that the fear of AIDS has suddenly sent millions of Americans back into monogamy or the type of relationships that their parents, or possibly grandparents, had years before, he explains that trend in this way:

A monogamous relationship—one based on perfect fidelity and complete trust between partners—is now the only safe relationship. The suspicion that your partner may be playing around is no longer just a question of throwing a tantrum, breaking the dishes, going home to mother or writing him/her off as one of life's bad choices—it can be a death sentence.[15]

But monogamy is not easy, and the writer contends that "what truly binds people together on a permanent basis is romance, curiosity, shared interests, affection, caring about each other."
He goes on to say:

Romance remains the most powerful bond between people. If there's a strong romantic bond plus sex, everything else in the relationship can be negotiated. People stay together because each makes the other feel special, and stay together over the long haul because they never stop trying to make the other feel special. And feeling special is what romance is about.

Our lives are so busy that it's hard today for people to devote much time to making each other feel special. Between the scramble to earn more, become successful and save up for the future, there may be time for sex, if we're lucky, but there's never enough time for making each other feel good in any other area.

---

12. Ibid.
13. "Back Off, Buddy," *Time* Magazine (October 12, 1987): 68-73. This issue's cover story analyzed the controverted "Hite Report," which cites these results of its survey: 70% of women married five years or more said that they are having extramarital affairs, and 76% responded that they do not feel guilty about their infidelity.
14. *On the Family,* no. 20.
15. "Romancing Monogamy," by Michael Korda, in *Self* (September 1987): 126-127. The passages below are all from this article.

And yet, that's what monogamy is about. We have to learn to make time, to slow down the clock. We have to invest something in simply learning to enjoy each other in small, simple, everyday ways. My grandfather and grandmother were married for at least 50 years; I have no idea what their sex life was like (nor would I really care to speculate), but every day he brought my grandmother her breakfast on a tray. Admittedly, it was prepared in the kitchen by a maid, but still he insisted on taking it up to her, and sat for a few minutes while she drank her tea, before he went to work. She shopped every day for the flower he invariably wore in his buttonhole, and there was clearly some complicated and secret code between them that had to do with the color and species of the flower, a kind of secret language that made them smile and was never explained.

The author cites both the challenge and the benefits of a long-term faithful relationship:

One of the charms of monogamy over quick affairs lies precisely in the continuous process of discovery and change. It is only by living with someone for a long time, and sharing the various crises of their life, that we discover their strengths, their hidden courage, their weaknesses—the real person, as opposed to the surface.

Admittedly, not all of these are pleasant discoveries, but that is simply part of the undeniable fact that all life is a gamble, with no sure things. A short affair with someone can be exciting, but it's only in long-term

monogamy that we're going to discover whether he or she is supportive when we're ill, caring when we're in trouble, generous when generosity matters, tough-minded in a crisis, understanding of our needs. . . . These are things that can only be revealed gradually, which is one of the reasons why any successful monogamous relationship requires a considerable degree of patience.

His conclusion is devoid of a religious content, but it does supply added motivation for being faithful forever:

What we have to find are those things that make living together not just a refuge from the dangers of the single life, or a substitute for something else, but the central life experience that puts everything else in context. We have to reinvent romance, not in the old sense of sexual longing, which in most modern relationships makes no sense (the unattainable having already been attained), but in the sense of deep caring about the other person, making ourselves interesting to him or her, believing always that in the end nothing is more romantic than two people choosing, voluntarily, to spend their lives together.

Living monogamously because it's safer isn't enough to hold two people together. The truth is that living monogamously is the most daring and romantic of adventures, the only way to truly know another person—and ourselves.

 Some Delicate Areas of Concern

ABORTION

The teachings of the Second Vatican Council are often cited in a general, nonspecific way to support certain theological attitudes or pastoral practices at variance with official statements of the Church. Passages that clearly uphold the Church's position may then be ignored or omitted. The evil of abortion is one of those issues.

In the *Pastoral Constitution on the Church in the Modern World,* the bishops taught that God, the Lord of life, has entrusted to human beings the noble mission of safeguarding life, and they must carry it out in a manner worthy of themselves. The authors of that document go on to establish a succinct and now well-known moral principle: "Life must be protected with the utmost care from the moment of conception: abortion and infanticide are abominable crimes."[16]

---

16. *Pastoral Constitution on the Church in the Modern World,* no. 51.

Pope John Paul II reinforces this norm and speaks about the "scourge of abortion."[17]

Despite these and other often-reiterated church statements on the sanctity of a person, the consistent ethic of life philosophy with its reverence for life from conception to death, and the need to protect the defenseless unborn, many Catholics fail to accept that teaching and/or yield to abortion as a solution to a difficult pregnancy.[18]

The pastoral task here is probably not so much to repeat the fairly well-known Catholic teaching on abortion as to provide motivation for resisting abortion, alternatives for a difficult pregnancy, and compassionate forgiveness for repentent persons who have undergone or abetted abortions.

The published testimony of an obstetrician and gynecologist, who at one time was the most prominent doctor in the fight to liberalize abortion laws, and who directed a major clinic performing these operations, could be helpful in providing motivation to resist abortion.

After considerable scientific study and personal reflection, he came to this radical conclusion and took this major step as a result:

> Some time ago—after a tenure of a year and a half—I resigned as director of the Center for Reproductive and Sexual Health. The Center had performed 60,000 abortions with no maternal deaths—an outstanding record of which we are proud. However, I am deeply troubled by my own increasing certainty that I had in fact presided over 60,000 deaths.
>
> There is no longer serious doubt in my mind that human life exists within the womb from the very onset of pregnancy, despite the fact that the nature of the intrauterine life has been the subject of considerable dispute in the past.[19]

A periodical, espousing social justice causes from a biblical perspective, some years ago published an issue on abortion. Many of its contributors admitted that to be anti-war and pro-abortion was inconsistent.[20] Subsequent letters to the editor contained tragic, yet touching, accounts of women's experiences with abortion. The one that follows argues powerfully in behalf of our position that the Church needs to provide viable alternatives for difficult pregnancies:

> I was very moved by your issue on abortion, but I think that it was lacking one important voice—that of someone who has had an abortion.
>
> Five years ago I had an abortion, so it is from experience that I would like to reinforce certain points you made. At the time, I had been recently engaged. My fiance felt that choosing for or against abortion was a decision I should make. I think that in part he

was really trying not to interfere with my rights as a woman, but in part he was unwilling to take the responsibility himself. He didn't want to talk about it.

> At Planned Parenthood, they asked me how I planned to handle my pregnancy. I said I wanted an abortion. They offered no alternatives. Outside the women's health clinic, the right-to-lifers shoved pictures of dead babies in my face. It made me hate them. Even now I don't like to think of myself as one of them.
>
> There didn't seem to be any choice for me then. The thought of killing my baby was frightening and horrible, but the thought of having it was also frightening. I had help and approval for the abortion; I would have been alone had I chosen to have the child.
>
> I am not excusing my actions. I murdered (it is difficult to say that), and though I have grown in awareness over the last five years, I think that even then I knew that what I was doing was wrong. All that I am saying is that our response to the abortion issue should not just be saying that it is wrong, especially saying so constitutionally, but in being the support behind the right answer. It is difficult to do anything alone.[21]

Another respondent to those articles made a different choice, but only after an intense inner struggle and with the invaluable help of a close friend:

> Having just come through a pregnancy alone, I am moved to respond to your abortion/life issue, particularly to the section "Alternatives of Hope." Last February, I came to terms with abortion as a woman and a Christian.
>
> Besieged with disbelief, doubt, fear, resentment, anger, and physical stress I turned in confidence to a close friend. She told me

17. *On the Family*, no. 6.
18. *Time* Magazine (September 7, 1987), with its cover story on Pope John Paul II's 1987 visit to the United States, contains (p. 48) the results of its current survey, which cites the following: only 14% of Catholics agree that abortion should be illegal in all circumstances; 57% would allow abortion under certain circumstances; 27% agree that abortion should be available on demand. Their opinions do not differ substantially from Protestants. A poll of New York State youth, reported in the Syracuse *Herald Journal* (June 17, 1986): C1, revealed that 56.2% of Catholic young people believe that abortion should remain legal, and 72.9% judged that having sex before marriage is okay. Pastors and confessors know, from their counseling and sacramental ministries, that pregnant Catholic women, sometimes at the strong insistence of parents or spouses, reluctantly or otherwise do, with some frequency, undergo abortions. Their pastoral experience is confirmed by abortion statistics.
19. *Aborting America*, by Bernard N. Nathanson, M.D., with Richard N. Ostling (Garden City: Doubleday and Company, Inc., 1979), p. 164. Details in that book describe his journey and current position that, while not identical with Catholic teaching, greatly approximates our principles.
20. *Sojourners* (November 1980).
21. Ibid. (January 1981): 38.

to momentarily forget the million and one worries going through my mind all at once, the concerns of finances, support, medical care, my future life, and my unreadiness for a child. Instead, she asked me to try to direct my thoughts to the real issue: the life of the unborn child. What did I believe life meant, the life inside me? Focusing on the center of my problem, rather than on the comparably unimportant details surrounding it, made all the difference in helping me realize my responsibility to the life growing inside me. Realizing that a new life—not just a group of cells—was within me completely ruled out abortion.

Instead, I was filled with hope through the Hosea passage, "Come back to me with all your heart; don't let fear keep us apart." I was given the promise that if I acted responsibly and in obedience to God, God would give me the strength each day to endure the trials and would work out the details of my unknown journey to ensure that a new, healthy life would be born, despite my detached feelings. Scripturally, I knew this life inside me was a gift from God—God's child, not mine. I was told that this child would be a blessing upon my own life and others.

As the months passed, the details worked out as I relinquished control over my life to God. I lived one day at a time and was given strength enough for only that day's trials. As the memory of early physical and emotional stress faded, my feelings of detachment and fear turned to acceptance and love for the child inside me. I prepared for natural childbirth with a midwife and support group (in which I was the only single woman). Then, finally, I gave birth on All Saint's Day, confirmation that this new life was a child of God, a blessing, a light of new hope, a miracle indeed.

My journey was not yet over; I had also been preparing to have my child adopted. I did not realize until after he was born that I would be giving him up not because I didn't want him, but because I loved him so very much. I gave him up with my hands, but not with my heart.

Although the emotional aspect is difficult, I am at peace, knowing that his reception into a childless family carried with it as much love as I had had for him in the giving. Praise God for the blessing of a child, the seed of hope, love, and a new life.[22]

In our preaching and teaching, we must not only uphold the principle about abortion, show its reason-

ableness, provide motivation, and offer alternative assistance. We also need regularly to reach out with gentle compassion to those who, for whatever reason or under whatever circumstances, have undergone or assisted anyone in procuring an abortion.

In this context, we need to know our Hispanic community among us and recognize the effects of poverty. Hispanic parishioners are often subjected to intimidation, lack of information, and forced sterilization. Local pastoral leaders must recognize that pressure and investigate local hospitals and clinics to ascertain these facts.

Persons under such unique pressures, and others as well, do not always emerge victorious in the struggle, as the woman above did. The burden of guilt for such people, like the other woman we cited, can be overwhelming. We must proclaim that our God is always "rich in mercy" with a heart open to anyone who repents and wishes to move forward.[23] Despite the fact that abortion truly is a scourge, an abominable crime, it can still be forgiven. Whenever a homily or instruction addresses the evil of abortion, the possibility of forgiveness for the repentent should be included, lest those crushed by their failure give up hope.

STERILIZATION

The Vatican Council bishops, likewise, mentioned this concern, although a bit more indirectly. They taught that our sexuality and the faculty of reproduction wondrously surpass the endowments of lower forms of life; therefore, the "acts proper to married life are to be ordered according to authentic human dignity and must be honored with the greatest reverence."[24]

Pope John Paul II is more specific. He sees a disturbing degradation of some fundamental values in our day and cites as examples "the ever more frequent recourse to sterilization" and the "appearance of a truly contraceptive mentality."[25]

Those in the pastoral ministry can testify to the frequency of that situation, especially among married couples.

Our earlier remarks about "Responsible Childbearing and Childrearing" are pertinent to this issue. Here, too, we need to deal compassionately with after-the-fact repentance and to be conscious, as noted, of the social and medical pressure upon many Hispanics, even to the point of forced sterilizations.

PASTORAL CARE OF INFERTILE COUPLES

An agonizing problem will present itself to some couples, namely, the inability to conceive a child of

22. Ibid., p. 39.
23. Eph 2:4.
24. *Pastoral Constitution on the Church in the Modern World*, no. 51.
25. *On the Family*, no. 6.

their own. Current 1988 estimates indicate that about 14 to 16 percent of couples will be clinically diagnosed as sterile (i.e., after one year of unprotected intercourse, the couple will not be successful in achieving a pregnancy).

When this happens to a couple, they may often be devastated, perhaps even blaming themselves for being inadequate. This can introduce a new and threatening dynamic within the relationship. From the data, it appears that in about 40 percent of the instances, the source of infertility is from the male; in about 40 to 45 percent, it is from the female. The rest are either of unknown causes or from the particular chemistry brought about by the marriage of these two persons.

Once this infertility is determined by competent medical experts, the couple always has the highly recommended option of adoption. While, sadly, given the high number of abortions, there is a shortage of newborn babies available for adoption, there are still many older children seeking stable homes.

Should the couple wish to have a child of their own, certain moral considerations present themselves. Many recently well-publicized solutions are today offered to married couples to secure a pregnancy when sterility, in one way or another, has been diagnosed. These include, among others, artificial insemination, in vitro fertilization, surrogate parenthood, and tubal ovum transfer.

In 1971, we addressed, in a general way, those issues through our document on the *Ethical and Religious Directives for Catholic Health Facilities* (no. 21), where we noted: "Because the ultimate expression of conjugal love in the marital act is viewed as the only fitting context for the human sharing of the divine act of creation, donor insemination and insemination that is totally artificial are morally objectionable."

More recently, the Congregation for the Doctrine of the Faith issued a comprehensive statement *Instruction on Respect for Human Life in Its Origins and on the Dignity of Procreation*, which provides authoritative moral guidance for dealing with biomedical and legal developments in the field of human infertility.[26]

Because of the rapid scientific advances in this field, the technical nature of procedures involved, the complexity of the moral issues connected with such processes, the publication of official church documents on the subject, and the teachings of moral theologians about artificial procreation and reproduction, we encourage couples and the clergy to consult competent persons, within the diocese or surrounding dioceses, who can assist them in evaluating a proposed course of action.

DIVORCE AND REMARRIAGE

The statistics about divorce that we have cited at the beginning and throughout this manual indicate that many Catholics, in fact, do divorce. Those people deserve our best pastoral attention. We wish to mention several matters that affect them.

The divorced individual. No marital disruption, either through separation or divorce, happens without enormous pain for all concerned. It represents a real type of death experience, with all the denial, anger, bargaining, and sadness that accompany a dying event. Regrettably, too many Catholics judge for some reason that the mere marital breakup, legal separation, or final divorce, by itself, excludes or excommunicates them from the Church. Many older generations of Hispanic parents sometimes believe that they are excluded from the Eucharist and feel culpable because their daughter or son has divorced. We need to correct those false views and to reassure them that God and the Church are never closer to us than during such a painful time. Moreover, they need the Lord's grace and the Church's help more than ever throughout those dark moments.

Pope John Paul II offers some practical words in this regard:

> Loneliness and other difficulties are often the lot of separated spouses, especially when they are the innocent parties. The ecclesial community must support such people more than ever. It must give them much respect, solidarity, understanding and practical help, so that they can preserve their fidelity even in their difficult situation; and it must help them to cultivate the need to forgive which is inherent in Christian love and to be ready perhaps to return to their former married life.[27]

He also goes on to offer words of support for those who are divorced, have entered into a second union, and find themselves in perplexing spiritual circumstances:

> I earnestly call upon pastors and the whole community of the faithful to help the divorced and with solicitous care to make sure that they do not consider themselves as separated from the Church, for as baptized persons they can and indeed must share in her life. They should be encouraged to listen to the Word of God, to attend the sacrifice of the Mass, to persevere in prayer, to contribute to works of charity and to community efforts in favor of justice, to bring up their children in the Christian faith, to cultivate the spirit and practice of penance and thus implore, day by day, God's grace. Let the Church pray for

---

26. *Instruction on Respect for Human Life in Its Origins and on the Dignity of Procreation: Replies to Certain Questions of the Day*, Congregation for the Doctrine of the Faith (Washington, D.C.: USCC Office of Publishing and Promotion Services, 1987).
27. *On the Family*, no. 6.

them, encourage them and show herself a merciful mother and thus sustain them in faith and hope.[28]

We here praise those parish, regional, and diocesan groups that seek to provide guidance and support for the many divorced in our country. We also urge pastoral leaders to make efforts to see that divorced persons, including single parents, are most welcomed in the faith community and are encouraged to become as actively involved as their situation permits.

Annulment procedures. Given all the negative influences that are attacking marriage, which we sketched at the beginning of this manual, it should be no surprise that many Catholics experience divorce and wish to remarry. In our society, remarriage rates are high, and most divorced individuals will form a new partnership. After a divorce, five out of six men and three out of four women remarry.[29]

Catholics are not free to remarry after a civil divorce unless the previous spouse(s) is deceased or the previous marriage(s) has been declared null by a Tribunal. An annulment is a declaration that the first marriage suffered from a canonically recognized and proven defect that prevented a sacramental marriage bond from coming into existence.

There are a number of grounds on which a marriage may be annulled. Lack of canonical form, impotence, lack of due competence, simulation, conditions, error, lack of due discretion, and force or fear are the categories wherein evidence may show that the marriage was invalid. As in any judicial proceeding, the subtleties and nuances of canonical jurisprudence require expert advice and counsel. For this reason, referral should be made to the professional staff of the diocesan Tribunal.

Contrary to many civil procedures, the annulment process is not aimed at determining a "winner" and a "loser." The procedure seeks, above all, to come to the truth of the situation while protecting the legitimate rights of the concerned parties. In fact, the Tribunal process for a marriage annulment frequently becomes a moment for healing the pain and hurt of the breakdown of the relationship between the spouses. The insight gained during the process often serves to strengthen the quality of the relationships that may come into existence in any subsequent marriage.

Finally, an annulment does not in any way denigrate the positive aspects of the relationship that the spouses once had, nor does it illegitimize any children born of the union. It is the recognition that factors that precluded a valid sacramental bond from coming into existence—for which the spouses often bear no personal responsibility—were at play at the time they entered marriage.

It is in the interest of justice, therefore, that we have for the investigation of those broken marriages

procedures that are thorough, but reasonable in cost, time, and mechanics. This means adequate and suitably trained staff. We praise those who have worked long and hard in this crucial pastoral ministry to people who are deeply wounded. We also hope that, eventually, all our dioceses will be able to offer annulment processes that fit those goals, mentioned above, and that throughout the United States the annulment approaches and results will be very similar and nearly identical.

Remarriage. In this country, about half of those who remarry do so within three years after the divorce.[30] While that is understandable, such a rapid remarriage raises concerns. As we observed, divorce is something of a death experience. It takes time to sift through and properly accept all the thoughts and feelings that accompany such a dying event. Too swift an entrance into a new relationship can cause another future disaster.

We encourage those groups, movements, and agencies that offer unique assistance to the divorced, to widows, and to widowers, helping them to understand their grief and to prepare them better for possible future remarriages.

 Help from the Church

We note here some programs or approaches of the Church to assist in the aftercare of marriages.

MARRIAGE ENRICHMENT PROGRAMS

There are a number of religion-based marriage enrichment programs basically designed to nurture good marriages. For example, "Marriage Enrichment," sponsored by the United Methodist Church is a small-group experience conducted by a leader or leader-couple who works with four other couples through a structured weekend.[31] Another is the "Marriage Communication Lab" of the United Methodist Church, which consists of a different couple-led small-group weekend experience.[32] A third illustration is "Marriage Encounter," which began in the Catholic Church, but has grown now to include Jewish and Protestant Marriage Encounters.

The National Leadership Team for Marriage Encounter in the United States offers this current description of that experience:

Marriage Encounter is a weekend program conducted by three couples and a priest. The

---

28. Ibid., no. 84.
29. *Family Communication*, p. 6.
30. Ibid.
31. *Celebrating Marriage: Growing in Love Training Manual*, by Bennie E. Heacock (Nashville: United Methodist Church, 1987). Write: United Methodist Church, Section on Ministry of the Laity, P.O. Box 840, Nashville TN 37202.
32. *Family Communication*, p. 296.

format follows a simple pattern. Each husband and wife "give" each other the Encounter, with the team members merely providing the information and modeling through their personal lived experiences to help facilitate each couple's private reflection and dialogue. Through a series of eleven talks, team members reveal personal and intimate information to encourage participants to do the same when alone. After each talk, each husband and wife separate and write individual responses to the issues raised in each talk. Specific questions are provided to stimulate discussion, and individuals are asked to identify and describe the feelings that they are experiencing. The couple then come together for private dialogue, using each other's written responses as a starting point. The Marriage Encounter process involves exposition, reflection, encounter, and mutual understanding. Dialogue topics include understanding of the self; the often negative impact of the modern world or society's values on marriage; learning how to be open and communicate with their spouse in difficult areas such as sex, death, and finances; understanding God's dream for them as a couple and their relationship with God, their children, and the world; a deeper exploration of the sacrament of Matrimony as a living sacrament and how they are called to bring their sacrament outward to the Church and to the world by being an open and apostolic couple.[33]

Two secular university family life scholars provide this critique of Marriage Encounter:

In their admittedly critical appraisal of the Marriage Encounter, Doherty et al. (1978) suggest that the program can create illusions through emotional "highs," deny the importance of differences between people, lead to a kind of ritual dependency and guilt if the couple does not engage in the follow-up, and other possible difficulties. Yet, these authors also point out the strengths of such a program. In her follow-up study of Marriage Enrichment couples, Ellis (1982) reported that participants talk more freely about their feelings to spouses and to other persons than they had before their involvement. Former participants are able to express negative feelings more constructively. Yet, some participants reported that although they were emotionally expressive during the weekend, they could not sustain this later (205-206). Additional critiques of programs note positive and negative effects (L'Abate, 1981; De Young, 1979; Wampler and Sprenkle, 1979).

Even the structure of the program may affect the outcome. In a study comparing psychological changes in couples who attended a weekend program with couples who were involved in a five-week program, the latter group gained more improvement in their marital adjustment scores. In both groups, wives changed in more positive ways than did their husbands (Davis et al., 89).

Research on the long-term effectiveness of marital enrichment programs is too limited to draw conclusions.[34]

While Marriage Encounter is not as strong and flourishing as it was a decade ago, it still grows internationally, and the weekend experience is currently being presented in sixty-seven countries and in four languages in the United States: English, Spanish, Korean, and Portuguese, with the addition of Vietnamese and Philippine in the near future. It also continues to provide an invaluable enrichment experience for those who wish to make the weekend. Moreover, it does offer helpful dialogue techniques for couples who carry the instruction of the weekend over into their subsequent marrried life. Finally, the many who have experienced Marriage Encounters in the past are now some of the more active members of our parishes. We wish to commend and encourage those clergy and couples who have given and are continuing to contribute so much time and energy to this form of the marriage ministry.

NEWLY MARRIED MINISTRY

A small but growing number of dioceses, through their appropriate agencies, are offering programs for newly married couples and assistance to parishes seeking to provide support and enrichment groups for young marrieds. We wish to praise the Ad Hoc Committee for Newly Married Ministry of the National Association of Catholic Diocesan Family Life Ministers for developing their booklet containing a statement of principles and guidelines, together with a sketch of such existing diocesan programs and an extensive list of resources for this newly married ministry.[35]

Marriage Encounter is now in the process of formulating an experience for couples in their early years of marriage that is based on the concepts from the Marriage Encounter weekend, but geared to the needs of the young married couple.

The need is certainly there. We hope these pioneering steps will multiply.

33. For information contact: National Office, Marriage Encounter, 1908 East Highland Avenue, Suite A, San Bernardino CA 92404.
34. *Family Communication*, p. 296.
35. *Newly Married Ministry: A Statement of Principles and Guidelines*, Ad Hoc Committee for Newly Married, National Association of Catholic Diocesan Family Life Ministers (St. Meinrad, Ind.: Abbey Press, 1984).

serve as resources for couple and group sessions. Occasional liturgical celebrations for these groups can be a source of sacramental and pastoral support and encouragement.

Marriage preparation involvement. Pastors and parish leaders should be constantly observing couples of the parish who would be suitable for the marriage preparation ministry. Distinct from the sponsor couples, these married people are more teachers, models, and facilitators—whether it be in a one-to-one or couple-to-couple arrangement, an Engaged Encounter, or a regional or diocesan pre-Cana conference. As with the sponsor couples, there is a twofold, positive impact from such involvement. They make an invaluable contribution to the engaged, but they find their own relationship and vision of matrimony enriched in the process. Also, as with sponsor couples, they require renewal sessions from time to time to gain fresh insights and sustain their enthusiasm.

Clergy follow-up. A few clergy have tried to develop a system of sending appropriate cards on the couples' anniversaries, sometimes with inspirational literature enclosed. That always has been a beautiful ideal, but usually difficult to realize, and even more so in our highly mobile society. Early and frequent changes of address on the part of married couples make maintenance of any mailing list a monumental task. However, parishes with computer access and sponsor couples may find this practice more feasible. The encouragement it offers the married justifies that expenditure of time, energy, and money. One pastor in the Midwest, at his last meeting with the couple, schedules them for a "6,000-mile checkup" and reports that most of them come back—some out of friendship and others to talk over issues and concerns.

Anniversaries. Parish, regional, or diocesan liturgical celebrations of anniversaries—silver or golden jubilees, for example—ritualize a major event in people's lives, dramatize the importance of marriage, and create opportunities to speak on issues of concern for married couples.

Homilies. Sunday Mass and the weekly homily remain the single most important time and situation in which our faith communities assemble together and hear God's word. When the scriptural readings, the feast, the season, or the circumstances are opportune, we encourage homilies that treat some aspect of married life.

Couples need to hear words from the altar about taking time for each other, understanding the true meaning of love, keeping a certain romance in their relationship, seeking to give one another specific daily compliments, and developing a spirit of mutual for-

PASTORAL OR PARISH SUPPORT

A Vision and a Strategy. In 1978, we issued the document *A Vision and a Strategy,* which contained our "Plan of Pastoral Action for Family Ministry."[36] Among other things, it outlined a series of ministries for parish implementation. While many of these projects have been at least initiated, their continuation and strengthening, as well as the introduction of the additional efforts mentioned in that text, will provide great aftercare for married couples and their families.

Sponsor couple. We described the function of a sponsor couple earlier in the manual, under the section "A Variety of Preparation Programs." However, some parishes use or plan to use them further to follow up, in a more personal way, the newly marrieds. This has a double benefit: it provides support for those recently married, while the very discharge of that reaching out ministry inspires and strengthens the sponsor couple. Both parish and diocesan leaders need to provide occasional, but ongoing, gatherings of these sponsor couples for their enrichment and renewal.

Married couple support/enrichment groups. Small groups of married couples who gather in one another's homes to conduct sharing and discussion group sessions have developed in some parishes throughout the United States. Such groups serve couples by providing a means of peer support in living out their "countercultural" marriage commitment in a nonsupportive society. Published marriage enrichment group manuals, books, and videos can

---

36. *A Vision and a Strategy.*

giveness. They also should receive from the Church warnings, skills, motivations, and insights about the asceticism required to cope with the routine of married life.

When preachers prepare these homilies, we strongly suggest that they seek input from people in the parish, especially married couples, families, and single parents. Their insights and practical illustrations will give an authentic ring to the message. Celibate priests or deacons, in particular, should find this of great assistance as they seek to collate and reflect the married experiences of others to the parish community. Such an involvement of lay persons in preparation of the homily can be carried out very simply or in more structured fashion. We discussed this concept and suggested a format in our document on the homily, *Fulfilled in Your Hearing.*[37]

This manual contains a wealth of material for potential use in Sunday or special-occasion homilies. It would be a service for our clergy if someone would prepare a set of several homilies, spread throughout the year, that take a few of these concepts and integrate them with certain Sundays in which the biblical readings of the day or feast are appropriate. Such a set, continued for a number of years, could assist the clergy in presenting many valuable comments on relationships, marriage, and the family without jeopardizing the integrity of the church year.

Materials. The weekly bulletin, a parish newsletter, take-home materials, and fliers mailed at intervals (as in baptismal follow-up programs) are communication vehicles with a track record of proven success. We judge that many of the concepts in this manual could easily be adapted for use in those various vehicles. We urge authors and publishers to develop them, including and especially materials for home distribution and implementation.

Parenting skills. Our "Plan of Pastoral Action" includes ministry for parents. This is spreading rapidly across the country.[38] We praise that growth and encourage it.

Teachable moments. Those major moments of people's lives—birth and baptism, first penance and Eucharist, confirmation and marriage—are teachable and touchable events for them. They are more open than usual to hearing about and experiencing God's presence in their lives. Since, for many, the marital and family relationship is central to them, injecting relevant ideas from this manual into those preparation programs and momentous events would be welcome. We made that recommendation earlier with regard to communication skills.

These suggestions do not exhaust the possibilities for pastoral or parish support of marriage aftercare, but they should stimulate discussion and planning among parish or diocesan leaders.

5 Conclusion

The future of humanity passes by way of marriage and the family.[39] But today, those who prepare for or are living out the sacrament of matrimony can often be tempted to discouragement because of the difficulties that the marital state encounters in our society.[40] They need hope and confidence. The Church wishes to give them both, and we pray that this handbook will be an instrument in doing so. The ultimate answer is for all—those about to marry, those already married, and those who help prepare couples for marriage—to follow Christ.[41] If, in their lives and ministries, they look and cling to Jesus, then we can be certain that Christian spouses, despite any trials or troubles, will remain "faithful to each other forever."[42]

37. *Fulfilled in Your Hearing: The Homily in the Sunday Assembly*, NCCB Committee on Priestly Life and Ministry (Washington, D.C.: USCC Office of Publishing and Promotion Services, 1982).
38. For example: St. Benedict's Church in the Bronx has developed a successful, substantial program on parenting with a director trained at parish expense; the Family Life Education Office for the Diocese of Syracuse has published a workbook by Carol A. Marshall (affiliated with that staff), on *Parenting Today* (Syracuse: Family Life Education, 1986), Family Life Education, 1342 Lancaster Avenue, Syracuse, NY 13210.
39. *On the Family*, no. 86.
40. Ibid.
41. Ibid.
42. Ibid., no. 20.

Appendices

Process and Acknowledgments

In compiling this handbook, we have attempted to follow an approach similar to the one used to develop our recent pastoral letters. We have gathered the material for this work from the input of as many experts and concerned people in the marriage preparation field as possible.

The list of committees, groups, and persons below follows a generally chronological order, beginning with the project's practical initiation in December 1985.

A number of bishops at our general meetings have raised the question of a uniform program for premarital preparation, in light of canon 1067. The NCCB Committee on Canonical Affairs, after several discussions on the matter, agreed that the only possible and satisfactory way to respond to this issue was in an interdisciplinary fashion. The committee recommended that the following National Conference of Catholic Bishops entities be directly involved: Doctrine, Liturgy, Family Life, Canonical Affairs, Ecumenical and Interreligious Affairs, Pro-Life. The NCCB Administrative Committee, informed of this suggestion, gave general endorsement to have the matter studied in this manner.

Since the NCCB Committee for Pastoral Research and Practices represents most of these disciplines, it was judged that this committee and its secretariat act as lead agent in coordinating the project.

Under the chairmanship of Bernard Cardinal Law, and staffed by the executive director Rev. Msgr. Richard Malone, the NCCB Committee for Pastoral Research and Practices met in Boston, December 18-19, 1985, to discuss at length the desired handbook. Members of the committee present were Most Rev. Anthony J. Bevilacqua; Most Rev. Edward D. Head; Most Rev. William Levada; Most Rev. Michael J. Murphy; Most Rev. Stanley J. Ott; and Most Rev. John F. Whealon. Bishop William Levada agreed to serve as the project's coordinator, working with the handbook's editor.

The following committees, groups, and people offered helpful ideas with regard to a timetable, resource persons and materials, general and specific content ideas, as well as the design of the actual outline: Rev. Msgr. Daniel Hoye; Rev. Thomas Lynch; Rev. Ronald Krisman; Rev. John Hotchkin; Mr. Neil Parent; Rev. Philip Murnion; Sr. Barbara Markey, ND; Mr. George Spielman; Mrs. Mary Helen Leal; National Pastoral Life Center; Mrs. Patricia Livingston; Rev. David K. O'Rourke, OP; Rev. Peter Casey; United States Catholic Conference, Commission on

Marriage and Family Life, chaired by Most Rev. Howard Hubbard; Board of Directors, National Association of Catholic Diocesan Family Life Ministers; Most Rev. Kenneth Povish and Most Rev. James Sullivan, with the Liturgical Commission for the Diocese of Lansing; Rev. Msgr. James McHugh; Rev. John R. Connery, SJ.

The NCCB Committee for Pastoral Research and Practices examined, emended, and approved the detailed outline on June 14, 1986, during its meeting at St. John's in Collegeville. Bernard Cardinal Law presented the entire revised outline to the NCCB Administrative Committee at the September 1986 meeting, in Washington, D.C.

With the recomposition of a new NCCB Committee for Pastoral Research and Practices, Most. Rev. John R. Quinn assumed the position of chairman and appointed, in February 1987, the following members to the committee: Most Rev. Robert J. Carlson; Most Rev. Eugene J. Gerber; Most Rev. John J. McRaith; Most Rev. Donald Pelotte, SSS; and Most Rev. Phillip F. Straling. Rev. Michael J. Buckley, SJ, replaced Msgr. Malone as executive director. At its first meeting, Bishop Straling agreed to serve as the new coordinator of the project, working with the handbook's editor.

The following made valuable, specific, and general contributions during the actual composition of the handbook: Most Rev. John Keating; Rev. Patrick O'Leary; Rev. Michael Donovan; Rev. John Roark; Mr. and Mrs. George and Nancy Spielman; Sr. Barbara Markey, ND; Most Rev. Anthony Bevilacqua; Mr. and Mrs. Michael and Pamela Panebianco; Mr. Donald Paglia.

Most Rev. James McHugh; Rev. Peter Worn; Most Rev. Matthew Clark; Mr. and Mrs. Charles and Elizabeth Balsam; Mr. and Mrs. Sam and Nancy Galizia; Mr. and Mrs. Robert and Dorothy Thompson; Mr. and Mrs. Tom and Patricia Okoniewski; Rev. Thomas Lynch; Mr. Robert Pawlewicz and Miss Lisa Khammar; Mr. and Mrs. William and Ann Tully and Family; Mr. and Mrs. Robert Offerman and Family; Rev. Anthony LaFache; Sr. Charla Commins, CSJ; Rev. Neal Quartier; Mr. and Mrs. John and Carol Lawyer; Rev. James Hayes; Rev. William Regan; Rev. Lawrence A. DiNardo; Rev. Paul J. Bradley; Most Rev. Thomas J. Costello.

Mr. and Mrs. Kathleen and Jerry Watson; Mr. Wayne Smith, assistant director of the Religious Education Department, National Catholic Education Association; Ms. Lois Bowman, acting assistant secretary, United States Department of Education; Ms. Nancy Fix; Hanna Klaus, M.D. (Sr. Miriam Paul); Bro. John McGovern, FSC; Sr. Eloise Emm, OSF; Mr. Charles D. Champlin; Bro. Martin Helldorfer, FSC.

Rev. Joseph M. Melito; Sr. Mary Ellen Hughes, MSW; Mr. Dennis A. Bagarozzi; Ms. M. Jane Lucid; Rev. Jeffrey Keefe, OFM Conv., Ph.D.; Ms. Mary Jane Saia; Mrs. Maureen Falge; Mr. and Mrs. Robert and

Judith Daino; Most Rev. William H. Keeler, chairman, NCCB Committee for Ecumenical and Interreligious Affairs; Rev. Gene Hemrick, NCCB/USCC Office of Research; Rev. John F. Hotchkin, executive director, NCCB Committee for Ecumenical and Interreligious Affairs; Mr. Gene Fisher, NCCB Secretariat for Catholic-Jewish Relations; Mr. James Murphy.

Rev. David Barry; Rev. Thomas Kramer; Ms. Kay Shaunessy; Most Rev. Adam J. Maida, chairman, NCCB Committee on Canonical Affairs; Ms. Kathy Carr; Mrs. Peg Dupee; Mr. Thomas Brody; Mr. and Mrs. Joseph and Linda Sorbello; Most Rev. George H. Speltz, bishop of St. Cloud; Rev. Joseph Witmer, Secretariat, NCCB Commitee for Ecumenical and Interreligious Affairs; Mrs. Beth Fitzgerald.

Rev. Robert Chryst; Mr. and Mrs. Dan and Vicky Ryan; Rev. Gene Contadino; Sr. Mary Kateri Battaglia; Sr. Magdalen McNemar, SSND; Ms. Joan M. Wagner; Ms. Nancy Fisher; Mr. Dennis B. Keenan; Mr. and Mrs. John and Kathy Colligan; Mrs. Benni E. Heacock; Mrs. Patricia Gale; Mrs. Carol Sheldon; Rev. Tom Ranzino; Most Rev. Stanley J. Ott, bishop of Baton Rouge; Rev. Donald Krebs.

The NCCB Committee on Canonical Affairs approved the proposed Prenuptial Investigation Form, with two minor suggestions, at its July 2, 1987, meeting in Pittsburgh, under the chairmanship of Most Rev. Adam J. Maida.

The first draft of the completed manuscript was presented to the NCCB Committee for Pastoral Research and Practices on September 24, 1987, at its meeting in Washington, D.C. That initial version contained a section on "Responsible Childbearing and Childrearing," which had already been through several drafts and had received approval, with minor recommendations from the previous committee at its September 1986 meeting in Pittsburgh. Those revisions were subsequently incorporated into the draft included within the completed manuscript. In addition, that initial version contained a section on "The Prenuptial Investigation" which, likewise, had been through several drafts and was approved as noted above by the NCCB Committee on Canonical Affairs. Their minor suggestions also were incorporated into the complete manuscript proposed at the September 1987 meeting.

The NCCB Committee for Pastoral Research and Practices reviewed the text at its September session. At that time, Archbishop Quinn appointed a subcommittee to work with the editor in reviewing the comments and recommendations of consultants. Bishop Straling and Bishop Carlson agreed to serve on this group, with Bishop Straling acting as its director. Most Rev. James P. Lyke, OFM, Ph.D., and Most Rev. Plàcido Rodriguez, CMF, were asked and accepted the invitation to join the subcommittee, bringing to the document, in particular, the perspective of the black and Hispanic communities.

Extra copies of this first draft were distributed to all members of the Committee for Pastoral Research and Practices, to Bishop Lyke and Bishop Rodriguez, and to a few other selected consultants, with directions to submit comments directly to the editor.

The subcommittee met at Niles College of Loyola, in Chicago, on November 5, 1987, for an all-day session to review observations received up to that time. Bishop Straling subsequently updated the full Committee for Pastoral Research and Practices a few weeks later at the November 17 meeting in Washington, D.C.

The editor then prepared a second draft, based on the considerable input gained through this consultation process and the suggestions of the subcommittee.

The following persons, in addition to members of the committee and subcommittee, were of special assistance in this stage of the development process: Very Rev. Robert McLaughlin; Mrs. Pamela Panebianco; Sr. Charla Commins, CSJ; Ms. Patricia Livingston; Mrs. Margaret Champlin; two dozen Roman Catholic Air Force chaplains, assembled for a week-long workshop in Scottsdale, Arizona, and a different, but same size, group gathered for a similar purpose in Menlo Park, California; Rev. John Roark; Rev. Patrick O'Leary; Rev. William Spencer, OFM; Rev. Peter J. Casey; Mr. and Mrs. Mike and Therese Wescott; Rev. Robert Hemberger; Anthony J. Iezzi, Ph.D.; Rev. Charles Froehle; Mr. Jack Quesnell; Mr. and Mrs. Art and Patricia Gale; Rev. Arturo J. Pérez; Alicia Rivera.

Copies of the second draft were distributed at the end of December 1987 to over fifty persons, with members of the current NCCB Committee for Pastoral Research and Practices also receiving multiple copies for additional consultation with their various advisors. These fifty consultants included: NCCB Committee for Pastoral Research and Practices (all members of the present and immediately past committees); NCCB Committee on the Liturgy; Seven liturgists and sacramentologists; Chairman, NCCB Committee on Marriage and Family Life; NCCB Committee on Canonical Affairs; Chairman, NCCB Committee on the Women's Pastoral; President, National Association of Catholic Diocesan Family Life Ministers; Diocesan Development Office for Natural Family Planning; NCCB Secretariat for Black Catholics; NCCB Secretariat for Laity and Family Life; a dozen individual experts in marriage, family, and pastoral life.

Nearly 100 copies of this draft were sent out for examination, with a request for responses to be submitted directly to the editor by February 1, 1988. We received 260 pages of comments from 18 persons. The subcommittee on evaluation met at Niles College of Loyola, in Chicago, on March 17, 1988, to review these observations. The members—Bishop Straling as chairman of this task force on the handbook, Bishop Carlson, and Bishop Rodriguez—were joined by the manuscript's editor and Rev. Michael J. Walsh. Father Walsh had been appointed in January 1988 as associate director of the NCCB Committee for Pastoral Research and Practices and was subsequently assigned to assist with the work of the marriage preparation handbook project.

While the volume of comments received was massive, the subcommittee judged that the relatively few number of persons responding, as well as the very nature of their suggestions, indicated that the second draft enjoyed good overall approbation. The criticisms or proposed changes were, for the most part, concerned with minor textual modifications. There were not many major objections or suggestions. The subcommittee accepted almost all of them; those few they rejected came from only one or two sources. Nevertheless, the subcommittee spent the entire day carefully examining each comment and making specific judgments about the inclusion or exclusion of every proposal from the final draft of the document.

Bishop Straling submitted a progress report to the full NCCB Committee for Pastoral Research and Practices, in Washington, D.C., at its regular meeting on March 22, 1988.

The editor then reworked the manuscript by incorporating over 450 changes—mostly small word or phrase alterations, but also several major additions or revisions.

The committee wishes to extend here its appreciation to the following persons for their assistance in the consultation process connected with the second draft and the development of the final version: Joseph Cardinal Bernardin; Most Rev. James P. Lyke, OFM, Ph.D.; Ms. Marlene Skavnak, SFO; Most Rev. Eugene J. Gerber; Most Rev. Howard J. Hubbard; Ms. Jerrie Goewey; Deacon Len Soper; Mr. Anthony Iezzi, Ph.D.; Most Rev. William J. Levada; Mr. and Mrs. John and Barbara Bertrand, U.S. national coordinators, Marriage Encounter; Ms. Dawne Mumford; Rev. Vern Arseneau; Ms. Juanita Allen; Ms. Valerie R. Dillon, president, National Association of Catholic Diocesan Family Life Ministers; Most Rev. Anthony J. Bevilacqua; Rev. Michael J. Walsh; Rev. Michael T. Buckley, SJ; Most Rev. Adam Maida; Most Rev. John R. Keating; Rev. Robert E. Lawrence, JCL; Rev. David N. Power, OMI; Most Rev. Robert J. Carlson; Sr. Barbara Markey, ND; Sr. Charla Commins, CSJ; Mr. Jack Quesnell; Rev. Fran Gillespie, SJ, president, Center for Applied Research in the Apostolate; Rev. Donald Conroy, National Institute for the Family; Rev. Msgr. Alan F. Detscher and Rev. John Guerrieri, Secretariat, NCCB Committee on the Liturgy; Ms. Alicia Rivera; Most Rev. Plàcido Rodriguez, CMF; Mr. and Mrs. Art and Patricia Gale; Mr. Arturo J. Pérez; Mr. Rick McCord, Secretariat, NCCB Committee on Laity and Family Life; Ms. Beverly Carroll, Secretariat, NCCB Committee for Black Catholics; Rev. Louis Leduc, MEP; Most Rev. Joseph T. O'Keefe; Mrs. Winifred Honeywell; Rev. Daniel E. Taillez, OMI, director, Hmong Catholic Center; Rev. John Hotchkin, Secretariat, NCCB Committee for Ecumenical and Interreligious Affairs; Rev. Erno Diaz, director, San Lorenzo Ruiz Association of America; Rev. Rogatien Rondineau, MEP, Bishop Salas Cambodian Catholic Center; Most Rev. Wilton D. Gregory; Rev. Thomas O'Hagan; two dozen Air Force chaplains, assembled for a week-long study institute at North Palm Beach, Florida; clergy of the dioceses of Bismarck (North Dakota), Jackson (Mississippi), Portland (Maine), and Spokane (Washington); participants at the 1988 Los Angeles Archdiocesan Religious Education Congress in Anaheim, California.

In May 1988, the third and final draft was sent to members of the present and immediately past NCCB Committee for Pastoral Research and Practices for examination at their meeting in St. Paul, Minnesota, on June 27-28, 1988. At that meeting, on June 27, the committee unanimously approved the document, as submitted, and also proposed that a plan be drawn up for the proper publication of the document itself and a popular promotion of its contents. The NCCB Administrative Committee approved the publication of the handbook as a document of the NCCB Committee for Pastoral Research and Practices, as well as a plan for its implementation, at its meeting of September 15, 1988.

Index of Pastoral Topics

Freedom and/or Baptismal Affidavit

Prenuptial Inquiry

FOR MARRIAGE OF

_____ and _____
Groom (print full name)   Bride (print full name)

_____
(Parish of Marriage and Address)

Affidavit of Witness for _____
Bride or Groom

Two witnesses must be interviewed on this form

1. To assist in proving baptism, when certificate is unavailable.

2. To establish freedom to marry when party has lived outside the diocese for more than six months after puberty, or when some doubt exists in the mind of the priest concerning freedom to marry.

3. To investigate the attitude of BOTH parents, when the party is under twenty-one years of age.

4. To investigate the stability of the marriage when the party is under eighteen years of age.

Parental testimony is always preferred and should be neglected for grave reasons only.

---

1. Do you solemnly swear to tell the whole truth and nothing but the truth in answering the following questions? _____

2. Name? _____ Address? _____

3. What is your relationship to the person whose name appears above? _____

4. How long have you known this person? _____ How well? _____

5. Has the above mentioned person ever gone through any type of marriage ceremony? _____

   How many times? _____ With whom? _____

   Do these marriages still exist? _____

6. Is the above mentioned person related to the other party to this intended marriage? _____

   In what way? _____

7. To your knowledge, is the above mentioned person entering this marriage freely? _____

   To your knowledge, does the above mentioned person intend to enter a lifelong union? _____

   To your knowledge, does the above mentioned person intend to be faithful for life to the partner in this marriage? _____ If "no" to any part of q.7, explain _____

8. Do you know of any reason why this person should not be married? _____

   If "yes," explain _____

TO ESTABLISH BAPTISM OR NON-BAPTISM:

9. Was the above mentioned person ever baptized? _____ In what religion? _____

   When? _____ In what church and place? _____

   By whom? _____ Who were the sponsors? _____

   _____ Were you present? _____ If not, how do you know of the baptism?

   _____

10. If the above person was not baptized, how do you know of the non-baptism?

   _____

IF PARTY IS UNDER 21 YEARS OF AGE:

11. Have the parents of this person been consulted about this marriage? _____

   Have they given their consent? _____ If not, why not? _____

IF THE PARTY IS UNDER 18 YEARS OF AGE: (A letter of recommendation is required from the priest. The following questions should be answered.)

12. How long have these parties known one another? _____

13. How long have they been dating with a view to marriage? _____

14. When did you become aware of their intention to marry? _____

15. Have you tried to discourage them from entering this marriage? _____ Why? _____

   _____

16. Is there any reason why this person feels obliged to marry at this time? _____

   What is the reason? _____

17. How does the groom intend to meet his financial responsibilities to his wife and family? _____

   _____

_____
Signature-witness

PARISH SEAL

_____
Signature-interviewing priest

_____
Date   Place

Prenuptial Inquiry
AND
Necessary Documentation

Groom: _____ Bride: _____

Date/time of the nuptial celebration: _____ at _____

Location: _____

☐ Celebration with Mass   ☐ Celebration outside of Mass

Presider of the Liturgy: _____

Rehearsal on: _____ at _____

Best man: _____

Maid/matron of honor: _____

Entered in marriage register: Volume _____ page _____

Church and date of groom's baptism: _____

_____

Notification of Marriage: Sent _____ or Entered in baptismal register: Volume _____ page _____

Church and date of bride's baptism: _____

_____

Notification of Marriage: Sent _____ or Entered in baptismal register: Volume _____ page _____

Required notification sent to appropriate state agency: _____

Pastor or delegate: _____

(Each party must be interviewed alone. The pastor or his delegate will propose the questions and write the given answers.)

GROOM

The pastor or his delegate, having reminded the groom of the sacred character and binding force of an oath, will ask: Do you solemnly swear to tell the truth and nothing but the truth in answering the questions that shall be submitted to you, so help you God and these holy scriptures which you touch with your hand? _____

1. Your full name? _____
   (print)

   Address? _____
   (print)

   How long have you lived at this address? _____ Home: _____

   Phone

   Occupation: _____ Work: _____

2. Your religion? _____ To what parish and rite do you belong? _____

   _____ In what diocese do you live? _____

3. Date and place of your birth? _____

Father's	Mother's
Name: _____ (print)	Maiden name: _____ (print)
Address: _____ (print)	Address: _____ (print)
Religion: _____	Religion: _____

4. Were you ever baptized? _____ In what religion? _____

   Date? _____ Church? _____ Place? _____

QUESTIONS 5, 6 AND 7 ARE TO BE ASKED OF CATHOLICS ONLY

5. First Holy Communion   Yes? _____   No? _____

6. Confirmation?   Yes? _____   No? _____   Date? _____

   Church? _____ Place? _____

7. How would you describe your practice of your religion? _____

   When did you last approach the sacrament of Penance? _____

   When did you last receive Holy Communion? _____

---

8. Give the names and addresses of two persons (preferably parents or relatives) who could testify to your freedom to marry: _____

   _____

9. Have you ever previously been married or attempted marriage, even a civil marriage, or lived in

   a common law union? _____ If so, how many times? _____

   Name of former spouse(s) and her (their) religion? _____

Was it dissolved by (a) Death? (give date) _____

(b) Ecclesiastical Decree? (date and Tribunal) _____

10. Has your intended bride ever been married or attempted marriage, even in a civil marriage?

    If so, how many times? _____

    Give the name(s) of her former spouse(s) _____

11. Are you related to your intended bride by blood (kinship), or by a legal relationship (in-laws), or by adoption? _____

12. Have you or your intended spouse any physical, emotional, or psychological situations which may seriously affect your marriage? _____ Explain _____

    _____

13. Is any person or circumstance forcing you to enter this marriage against your will? _____

    Is any person or circumstance forcing the bride to marry against her will? _____

14. Are you attaching any conditions, restrictions, or reservations of any kind to your consent to this marriage? _____

15. Do you intend to enter a permanent marriage that can be dissolved only by death? _____

16. Do you intend to be faithful to your wife always? _____

17. Do you understand that one of the purposes of marriage is the begetting and rearing of children, God willing? _____

    Do you accept and intend to fulfill this aspect of marriage? _____

    Does your intended bride accept and intend to fulfill this aspect of marriage? _____

18. How long have you known your intended bride? _____

    How long have you been engaged? _____

19. Have either your or her parents any objections to this marriage? _____

20. Is there any major fact about you, either in the present or the past, which you have not made known to your proposed spouse and which might affect her willingness to marry you? _____

Date: _____ Groom: _____

Church: _____ Place: _____

Pastor or his delegate: _____

Church Seal

(Each party must be interviewed alone. The pastor or his delegate will propose the questions and write the given answers.)

BRIDE

The pastor or his delegate, having reminded the bride of the sacred character and binding force of an oath, will ask: Do you solemnly swear to tell the truth and nothing but the truth in answering the questions that shall be submitted to you, so help you God and these holy scriptures which you touch with your hand? _____

1. Your full name? _____
   (print)

   Address? _____
   (print)

   How long have you lived at this address? _____ Home: _____
   Phone

   Occupation: _____ Work: _____

2. Your religion? _____ To what parish and rite do you belong? _____
   _____ In what diocese do you live? _____

3. Date and place of your birth? _____

Father's	Mother's
Name: _____ (print)	Maiden name: _____ (print)
Address: _____ (print)	Address: _____ (print)
Religion: _____	Religion: _____

4. Were you ever baptized? _____ In what religion? _____

   Date? _____ Church? _____ Place? _____

QUESTIONS 5, 6 AND 7 ARE TO BE ASKED OF CATHOLICS ONLY

5. First Holy Communion Yes? _____ No? _____

6. Confirmation? Yes? _____ No? _____ Date? _____

   Church? _____ Place? _____

7. How would you describe your practice of your religion? _____

   When did you last approach the sacrament of Penance? _____

   When did you last receive Holy Communion? _____

---

8. Give the names and addresses of two persons (preferably parents or relatives) who could testify to your freedom to marry: _____

   _____

9. Have you ever previously been married or attempted marriage, even a civil marriage, or lived in

   a common law union? _____ If so, how many times? _____

   Name of former spouse(s) and his (their) religion? _____

   _____

Was it dissolved by (a) Death? (give date) _____

(b) Ecclesiastical Decree? (date and Tribunal) _____

10. Has your intended groom ever been married or attempted marriage, even in a civil marriage?

    If so, how many times? _____

    Give the name(s) of his former spouse(s) _____

11. Are you related to your intended bride by blood (kinship), or

    by a legal relationship (in-laws), or by adoption? _____

12. Have you or your intended spouse any physical, emotional, or psychological situations which

    may seriously affect your marriage? _____ Explain _____

    _____

13. Is any person or circumstance forcing you to enter this marriage against your will? _____

    Is any person or circumstance forcing the groom to marry against his will? _____

14. Are you attaching any conditions, restrictions, or reservations of any kind to your consent to

    this marriage? _____

15. Do you intend to enter a permanent marriage that can be dissolved only by death? _____

16. Do you intend to be faithful to your husband always? _____

17. Do you understand that one of the purposes of marriage is the begetting and rearing of children,

    God willing? _____

    Do you accept and intend to fulfill this aspect of marriage? _____

    Does your intended groom accept and intend to fulfill this aspect of marriage? _____

18. How long have you known your intended groom? _____

    How long have you been engaged? _____

19. Have either your or his parents any objections to this marriage? _____

20. Is there any major fact about you, either in the present or the past, which you have not made
    known to your proposed spouse and which might affect his willingness to marry you? _____

Date: _____ Bride: _____

Church: _____ Place: _____

Pastor or his delegate: _____

When the marriage is to be witnessed by a priest who is not a parochial vicar in the parish, the pastor will sign this form:

I hereby delegate Rev. _____ to assist in this marriage within my parish.

Date _____ Pastor's Signature _____

Church Seal

A Handy Checklist for the Pastor or Delegate

☐ Marriage date, time, and banns reserved in *Mass Book*.

☐ Marriage date noted in personal *appointment book*.

☐ Marriage preparation programs *information given*.

☐ Wedding details explained.

    * Church documents required

    * Special permission if needed

    * Organist/music director

    * Servers

    * Banns of marriage

    * Liturgy booklet

    * Offerings

    * Other local concerns

    * Any comments or questions about:

    License _____ flowers _____ runner _____ photographer _____

    reception _____ invitations _____ newspapers _____ rings _____

☐ Next Appointment(s): Date _____ Time _____ Date _____ Time _____

☐ Premarital inventory instrument

☐ Copy of records (baptism, death certificate, annulment decree, special permission if needed)

☐ Prenuptial Inquiry Form

☐ Dispensations

☐ Rehearsal date and time